Extreme Punishment

Palgrave Studies in Prisons and Penology

This is a unique and innovative series, the first of its kind dedicated entirely to prison scholarship. At a historical point in which the prison population has reached an all-time high, the series seeks to analyse the form, nature and consequences of incarceration and related forms of punishment. *Palgrave Studies in Prisons and Penology* provides an important forum for burgeoning prison research across the world.

Series editors:

Dr. Ben Crewe
Institute of Criminology, University of Cambridge, UK

Professor Yvonne Jewkes
Department of Criminology, Leicester University, UK

Dr. Thomas Ugelvik
Department of Criminology, University of Oslo, Norway

Series advisory board:

Anna Eriksson, Monash University, Australia
Andrew M. Jefferson, DIGNITY - Danish Institute Against Torture
Shadd Maruna, Queen's University Belfast, UK
Jonathon Simon, University of California, Berkeley, USA
Michael Welch, Rutgers University, USA

Titles include:
Deborah H. Drake, Rod Earle and Jennifer Sloan (eds)
PALGRAVE HANDBOOK OF PRISON ETHNOGRAPHY

Mark Halsey and Simon Deegan
YOUNG OFFENDERS
Crime, Prison and Struggles for Desistance

Andrew M. Jefferson and Liv S. Gaborit
HUMAN RIGHTS IN PRISONS
Comparing Institutional Encounters in Kosovo, Sierra Leone and the Philippines

Keramet Reiter and Alexa Koenig (eds)
EXTREME PUNISHMENT
Comparative Studies in Detention, Incarceration and Solitary Confinement

Vincenzo Ruggiero and Mick Ryan (eds)
PUNISHMENT IN EUROPE
A Critical Anatomy of Penal Systems

Peter Scharff Smith
WHEN THE INNOCENT ARE PUNISHED
The Children of Imprisoned Parents

Marguerite Schinkel
BEING IMPRISONED
Punishment, Adaptation and Desistance

Phil Scraton and Linda Moore
THE INCARCERATION OF WOMEN
Punishing Bodies, Breaking Spirits

Thomas Ugelvik
POWER AND RESISTANCE IN PRISON
Doing Time, Doing Freedom

Palgrave Studies in Prisons and Penology
Series Standing Order ISBN 978–1–13727090–0 hardback
(*outside North America only*)

You can receive future titles in this series as they are published by placing a standing order. Please contact your bookseller or, in case of difficulty, write to us at the address below with your name and address, the title of the series and the ISBNs quoted above.

Customer Services Department, Macmillan Distribution Ltd, Houndmills, Basingstoke, Hampshire RG21 6XS, England

Extreme Punishment

Comparative Studies in Detention, Incarceration and Solitary Confinement

Edited by

Keramet Reiter
University of California, Irvine, USA
and
Alexa Koenig
University of California, Berkeley, USA

First published 2015 by
PALGRAVE MACMILLAN

Palgrave Macmillan in the UK is an imprint of Macmillan Publishers Limited, registered in England, company number 785998, of Houndmills, Basingstoke, Hampshire RG21 6XS.

Palgrave Macmillan in the US is a division of St Martin's Press LLC, 175 Fifth Avenue, New York, NY 10010.

Palgrave is the global academic imprint of the above companies and has companies and representatives throughout the world.

Palgrave® and Macmillan® are registered trademarks in the United States, the United Kingdom, Europe and other countries.

ISBN: 978–1–137–44114–0

This book is printed on paper suitable for recycling and made from fully managed and sustained forest sources. Logging, pulping and manufacturing processes are expected to conform to the environmental regulations of the country of origin.

A catalogue record for this book is available from the British Library.

A catalog record for this book is available from the Library of Congress.

Contents

List of Illustrations

Foreword

The 2014 release of the Senate Intelligence Committee's report on the CIA's interrogation program developed out of the 'war on terror' provided shocking evidence of just how depraved the imposition of punishment could become in a democratic nation. In the name of national security and anti-terrorism, leaders at the highest levels of government developed, implemented, and lied about a worldwide underground network of sites of systemic torture. How such an operation could come about in political systems of checks and balances, with strong constitutional safeguards, and with international treaty obligations through the Convention against Torture, is a complicated question, and one that is central to the contributors to this volume.

This collection brings together the disturbing issues that confront industrialized societies in the 21st century around the concept of 'extreme punishment'. The punishments under examination here are the increasing use of administrative detention and solitary confinement within domestic prison systems, the growing use of immigration detention, and the use of military and 'black hole' detention sites as part of an anti-terrorist strategy. The contributors to this anthology also recognize that the meaning of 'punishment' has been considerably expanded in recent years to now include a variety of administrative sanctions imposed outside of the formal systems of punishment.

At first glance it may seem odd to link these forms of punishment across three distinct nations and three types of imprisonment systems. Although the contributors focus on three (primarily English-speaking) industrialized nations—Canada, the United States, and the United Kingdom—their respective punishment policies are arguably distinct in many ways.

In the realm of domestic incarceration and the related use of solitary confinement, for example, the US clearly stands alone in the magnitude of its commitment to such policies. The unprecedented rise in incarceration over the past 40 years has made the US the world leader in this regard, with a rate of incarceration more than five times that of other industrialized nations.

Along with these developments has come the vast expansion of 'supermax' prisons and forms of sensory deprivation, including solitary confinement and isolation units. Remarkably, no tracking system exists to determine how many individuals are housed in such environments in the US, although estimates are in the range of 80,000. To place some perspective on this figure, it represents about twice as many people in such units as the total population of the Canadian prison system. Similarly, the scale of immigration detention and extreme forms of military detention employed by the US is far more expansive than in the other nations under consideration.

While the scale of incarceration in Canada and the UK is but a fraction of that in the US, political dynamics in both these nations suggest the increasing influence of 'tough on crime' policies largely developed in the US. In recent decades we have seen calls in both nations for adopting mandatory sentencing penalties, restricting judicial discretion, and imposing greater restrictions on immigration.

Such transmission of ideas and policies suggests linkages across these nations and across the various sites of extreme punishment. And, in fact, as we examine these cross-national systems of punishment, three themes emerge in each nation and at each site. These themes are the ascendancy of punishment as the guiding strategy of public policy in both domestic and international conflict; the impact of globalization and the transfer of ideas, technologies, and profit-making interests across national boundaries; and the declining transparency in the functioning of these institutions as they are increasingly transformed to 'invisible' punishments. Let me describe how these developments have played out.

The historic buildup of the US prison population beginning in the 1970s exemplifies the evolving rationale for the use of incarceration. Much was changing in American society during those decades. The rise of the 'baby boom' generation led to a bulge of young males in the population, along with an increase in urbanization, factors which are both associated with greater engagement in crime. But most significantly, the economic disruptions of that period would create the context for the choice to embark upon mass incarceration, facilitating its chilling effects.

The early 1970s witnessed the 'oil shock' of OPEC asserting its economic power, which came at the same time as the accelerating decline of the US manufacturing economy. Prior to this, for a generation, the auto and steel plants of the upper Midwest and other parts of the country provided solid union-wage jobs for working-class whites, many of whom had migrated from Appalachia, and working-class blacks, many of whom had come up from the South. Thus, an auto-worker without an advanced education could buy a home in Detroit or Akron and support a family.

But the manufacturing sector of the economy steadily declined as employers shipped jobs overseas to low-wage nations. As a result, the sons and daughters of those workers became much more likely to be employed in minimum-wage jobs in the service sector. By the early 1980s, that decline in the legitimate economy led growing numbers of people in disadvantaged communities to engage in an underground economy, often related to drug markets.

American policymakers then faced the challenge of crafting a response to the decline in economic opportunity. But with little forethought or engagement with the affected communities, the primary response was a purely reactive one: 'getting tough' on crime problems in disadvantaged communities through punishment, thereby attacking the symptoms rather than the cause of the problems. This response took the form of federal and state initiatives across the country to wage a 'war on drugs' and to adopt a new generation of harsh sentencing policies designed to send more people to prison and to keep them there for longer periods of time. Indeed, an analysis conducted for the National Research Council finds that the *entire* increase in the prison population from 1980 to 2010 resulted from these changes in sentencing policy and practice, and not rising rates of crime (Travis, Western & Redburn 2014).

This punitive environment set the stage for the enhanced use of new and expanded forms of punishment as well, such as control units, solitary confinement, and other means of segregation. This was an almost inevitable development as the stated function of incarceration shifted from rehabilitation (no matter how poorly implemented) to warehousing and punishment. The ensuing and costly prison expansion only exacerbated this dynamic. Legislators were generally quite willing to expend funds on prison construction, no matter how unwise an investment that proved to be, but they rarely provided the support necessary to maintain even a modest level of educational programming or mental health services in the rapidly growing prison system.

On top of this came a predictable rise in the number of prisoners with histories of mental illness. The advent of deinstitutionalization policies for persons confined in mental hospitals beginning in the 1960s was premised on a substantial expansion of community-based mental health facilities. But those services were never supported sufficiently, and instead prisons became the 'new mental hospitals' in many states. Thus, rapid prison expansion, limited programming, and high rates of prisoners with mental health problems magnified the degree and breadth of the inherently tension-filled environment of prisons. Rather than explore and respond to these underlying drivers of mass incarceration, policymakers instead increasingly adopted managerial approaches of containment premised on isolation and deprivation of human contact.

Parallel developments are seen in the other extreme punishments covered in this volume. The vast expansion of immigrant detention, not only in the three nations examined here but worldwide, points to the adoption of punishment in the face of dramatic failures to address the effects of globalization and its impact on both developed and developing nations. As traditional economies have been uprooted in developing nations, affecting tens of millions of destitute people, emigration in search of economic opportunity has surged. Few industrialized nations have developed a comprehensive response to these developments, and so the leading policy question on the globalization agenda has narrowed to one of calculating law enforcement responses and determining the degree of punishment for immigrants.

The second theme linking together these extreme punishments is the global transmission of ideas, policies, and economic interests. Just as a rapidly interconnected world economy has enhanced the transmission of culture to a world stage, so that the music and art of many nations can now build on other traditions, so too are the punitive and oppressive ideas of public policy speedily connected. As has been true for many decades, ideas and imagery from the US play an outsized role in serving as models to be emulated.

One of my earliest encounters with this dissemination of ideas occurred in the mid-1990s when I participated at an international convening on incarceration issues in Europe. Striking up a conversation with a policymaker from the Czech Republic, I learned that his parliament was considering 'three strikes and you're out' legislation, similar to the policy that had recently been adopted in California. I was surprised, to say the least, that a sentencing policy based on the rules of baseball would resonate in a nation with little interest in that sport, so I asked him how that had come about. 'From CNN, of course,' he replied.

Direct economic interests are even more influential in advancing and diffusing these forms of punishment. Most prominent among these is the private prison industry, originating in the 1980s with proposals to state and federal governments in the US to lock people up safely and at less cost than public institutions. In practice, private prisons have been plagued by managerial problems, cost savings have been largely illusory, and there is emerging evidence suggesting that prisoners in such facilities are confined for longer periods of time than in public institutions. Nevertheless, the industry has achieved substantial growth, currently with contracts for housing about 130,000 prisoners in the US.

From these beginnings, the industry has worked to expand its 'market' share. A key goal has been international growth, with at least 11 nations now contracting for these services from both American and British companies. Among them, 19 percent of Australian prisoners are now incarcerated in private facilities, as are 17 percent in Scotland (Mason 2013).

As the industry became concerned about slowing rates of growth in domestic prisons in the US in the early 21st century, it shifted much of its attention to promoting and expanding contracts for immigrant detention. Most notable in this regard was the role of private prison industry operators in drafting the legislation that would eventually be adopted as SB 1070 in Arizona in 2010, the notorious bill that would have granted law enforcement officers broad latitude in stopping individuals when officers believed there was reasonable suspicion that they had an illegal status. In 2012, the US Supreme Court struck down certain provisions of the law but let others stand (*Arizona et al. v. United States*).

We have witnessed the role of private contracting in military detention locations as well. The shocking imagery emanating out of the torture at Abu Ghraib prison was in part a story of military contracting with private companies to supply personnel subject to little oversight or regard for human rights standards.

The third linkage among these various forms of extreme punishments comes about through the increasingly 'invisible' nature of state action and policy in these realms. That is, while states ostensibly employ detention on behalf of their citizens, the role of public scrutiny and oversight of these operations is increasingly limited. This is most obvious, of course, in relation to anti-terrorist black site detention. US policy, aided by Britain and other nations, was designed to not even acknowledge the existence of these facilities. Only through the dogged efforts of a handful of journalists did these operations originally come to light. We now know that soon after 9/11 the CIA secured the cooperation of Poland, Romania, Thailand, and other nations to establish these detention facilities in large part so that 'enhanced interrogation techniques' could be applied to persons captured in the war on terror. By definition, there were no due process safeguards built into these operations, nor any rationale presented as to why traditional interrogation and court procedures could not produce useful information. Even leaving aside the immorality of the policy, torture has failed to even produce useful information, as the Senate Intelligence Committee has reported in mind-numbing detail.

Similar trends toward invisibility can be seen in other areas of extreme punishment. In the area of solitary confinement in the US, for example, there are not even any national data on the number of people incarcerated under such conditions. And aside from occasional interventions by human rights groups or political leaders, there is little public discussion of the day-to-day operations of such punishments or their overall impact, either on individuals or on safety within the prison system.

This lack of transparency has effectively decreased oversight over prison and detention operations generally, sometimes through conscious action by prison officials and at other times as an outgrowth of other societal trends. One of the many outcomes of the 'death of journalism' through traditional media has been the rapid decline of serious investigative journalism. Reporting on prison conditions and operations was never an area of great attention for very many publications, but with only a handful of major newspapers and magazines now willing or able to devote the resources necessary to take on such projects, such scrutiny is even more rare. And, of course, in an era of mass imprisonment, the sheer number of penal institutions in a given state creates a virtually impossible task for public oversight even if additional resources were available.

In other instances, declining oversight has been a function of more direct policy initiatives by state officials. In California, for example, the corrections system has imposed a series of restrictions on journalists' ability to assess prison conditions. Face-to-face interviews with prisoners are only permitted if approved by the prison administration. During prison tours, journalists may only speak with inmates who have been handpicked and vetted by prison officials. Further, judicial oversight of prison conditions has been diminished as well, in large part due to Congressional adoption in 1996 of the Prison Litigation Reform Act. The statute, described by its sponsors as a way to cut back on 'frivolous' litigation around prison conditions, has made filing even legitimate challenges considerably more onerous.

Given these developments, is there any reason for optimism about the prospects for reform—and resistance from those detained in extreme conditions? From the vantage point of an observer in the US, one can argue that there are at least some openings in the political climate that create opportunities for challenging extreme punishments. To start, the zealousness with which mass incarceration has been produced has diminished, with calls for reductions in prison populations now being heard across the political spectrum. Liberal and conservative members of Congress, along with their colleagues at the state and local level, now propose getting 'smart on crime' rather than 'tough on crime'. This has led to the establishment of a range of programs that provide alternatives to incarceration, reentry programming, and restorative justice initiatives. To date, though, the scale of any impact is still quite modest.

This changing political environment is now reverberating to issues of solitary confinement as well. A high-profile hearing in the US Senate in 2013, accompanied by substantial media attention, marked the first such event devoted specifically to this issue. Corrections officials in a number of states are now making the case that extended and widespread use of solitary confinement increasingly conflicts with professional standards and operations, and some are beginning to explore initiatives to reduce the use of such measures. The former corrections commissioner in conservative Mississippi, faced with litigation regarding solitary confinement, reduced the number of prisoners in such facilities by 70 percent. Similarly, the executive director of the Colorado Department of Corrections has called for a far more limited use of confinement, while enhancing services for the mentally ill inmates who are disproportionately represented in these populations.

Executive actions by President Obama in his second term, while not without substantial political opposition, have also made strides toward shifting the national conversation on immigration detention and deportation. By creating a pathway to citizenship for some undocumented immigrants, and promising reduced deportations of others, there is now a possibility that the millions of individuals and families hiding in the shadows of America can begin to lead a more public life that is free of the daily terror of apprehension.

None of these initiatives in themselves shift the fundamental balance of power in the globalized world of the 21st century, and we should not lose sight of that sobering perspective. But one can hope that even within such a political environment, incremental shifts in policy and practice can contribute to a growing public demand for change. Just as US policies have been influential in contributing to the punishment environment in other nations, so too might the growing reform movement influence other nations to reconsider the breadth and wisdom of an expanded commitment to punishment. The challenge before us now is to promote a broad-ranging discussion that at the very least explores the consequences of a system of extreme punishments in today's world and considers what alternative perspectives for a healthy society might look like.

Marc Mauer
Executive Director of the Sentencing Project

References

Arizona et al. v. United States. 567 U. S. ___ (2012)

Mason, C 2013, *International growth trends in prison privatization*, The Sentencing Project, Washington, DC.

Travis, J, Western, B & Redburn, S 2014, *The growth of incarceration in the United States: exploring causes and consequences*, National Research Council, Washington, DC.

Acknowledgments

The idea for this book was born at a series of panels at the Association for the Study of Law, Culture, and Humanities conference hosted at Birkbeck College in London in the spring of 2013. We are grateful to the conference association and the college for creating a space in which scholars from both sides of the Atlantic could meet and start the conversations that inspired this book. This project has been especially inspiring to work on because of the patient, engaged contributors who wrote each chapter. They have worked with us through multiple rounds of edits and worked together to engage with each other's work.

In addition to each of our contributors, we would like to thank the following people, without whom this project would have never come to fruition. Yvonne Jewkes, as one of the editors of the Palgrave series in which this anthology appears, encouraged this project from its inception, providing guidance and inspiration. Hadar Aviram provided such helpful feedback on early drafts of these papers that we asked her to write the afterword. Mona Lynch and Susan Coutin both served as unofficial advisers, helping us to identify and recruit additional scholar-contributors to this collection. Stephen Cody and Mona Lynch provided critical feedback on framing our introduction. Melissa Barragan magically transformed a disorganized jumble of documents into a single, carefully edited manuscript.

Alexa would like to thank the staff of the Human Rights Center at the University of California, Berkeley School of Law for their collective insights and support; Peter Jan Honigsberg at the University of San Francisco School of Law, and Laurel Fletcher and Eric Stover at the University of California, Berkeley School of Law, for providing access to the interviews in her chapter; and Sophie, Don, and Zander Mercer for their patience during the long hours required to bring this project to fruition. Keramet would like to thank her colleagues at the University of California, Berkeley and the University of California, Irvine for providing multiple forms of support that made this project possible, and Thomas Blair for critical feedback and encouragement at multiple phases.

Our contributors also have specific funders and supporters they would like to acknowledge. Efrat Arbel is grateful to the Harvard Immigration and Refugee Law Clinical Program for supporting the Bordering on

Failure research, to the men and women who participated in the study, and to everyone who contributed to the final report. She also thanks the Social Sciences and Humanities Research Council of Canada for funding portions of this research through a Metropolis British Columbia grant, held with Professor Catherine Dauvergne. Finally, she would like to thank Catherine Dauvergne for very helpful comments on earlier drafts of this chapter. The views presented in her chapter are hers alone and do not necessarily reflect the views of her previous co-author in this research or of the Harvard Immigration and Refugee Law Clinical Program.

Mary Bosworth and Sarah Turnbull would like to thank the women and men who participated in the study and the center managers and Home Office for allowing research access. They are grateful to the European Research Council whose generous funding for Mary Bosworth's Starting Grant 313362, 'Subjectivity, Identity and Penal Power,' has made part of their research possible. Mary's fieldwork was also supported by the British Academy, the Nuffield Foundation, and the John Fell OUP Fund at the University of Oxford. Finally, she would like to thank Blerina Kellezi and Gavin Slade for conducting some of the interviews.

Emma Kaufman and Sam Weiss would like to thank The Marshall and Clarendon Funds and New College, Oxford, who made the British research in their chapter possible. Harvard Law School supported work in the United States. They are also grateful to Eric Gardiner for thoughtful edits, and to the many clients and prisoners who shared their experiences.

Stuart J. Murray and Dave Holmes would like to thank the Canadian Institutes of Health Research (CIHR) for funding support.

Finally, we extend our collective gratitude to the hundreds of men and women who shared their stories—the stories that comprise the heart and spirit of this anthology—so that the world might learn from their experiences, and in learning, fight for change.

Notes on Contributors

Efrat Arbel is an assistant professor at the University of British Columbia Faculty of Law. She completed her doctorate at Harvard Law School, where she was a Canada Research Fellow with the Weatherhead Center for International Affairs. Efrat researches and publishes in the areas of constitutional law, refugee law, Aboriginal law, and prison law, in Canada and the United States. She is co-author (with Alletta Brenner) of *Bordering on Failure: Canada-US Border Policy and the Politics of Refugee Exclusion* (2013). Combining her academic work with legal practice, she is also engaged in advocacy and litigation involving refugee and prisoner rights.

Hadar Aviram is a professor at University of California, Hastings College of Law and author of *Cheap on Crime: Recession-Era Politics and the Transformation of American Punishment.*

Thomas Blair, MD, MS is a resident physician in the Department of Psychiatry and the Semel Institute for Neuroscience and Human Behavior at the University of California, Los Angeles. His research concerns health services, medical education, and the history and philosophy of medicine. Current projects include a historical study of mental health professionals' response to HIV/AIDS at the beginning of the epidemic and a mixed-methods study of Laura's Law, California's statute for involuntary outpatient psychiatric treatment.

Mary Bosworth is Professor of Criminology and Fellow of St Cross College at the University of Oxford and, concurrently, Professor of Criminology at Monash University, Australia. Mary has published extensively on issues of race, gender, citizenship, and incarceration. Her most recent book, *Inside Immigration Detention* (Oxford University Press 2014) is the first national study of life in immigration detention centres in Britain. Mary is the UK editor-in-chief of *Theoretical Criminology.*

Kelly Hannah-Moffat is Professor of Sociology/Criminology and Vice Dean of Undergraduate Education at the University of Toronto, Mississauga and the Director of the Centre of Criminology and Sociolegal Studies. She has published several articles and books on risk, punishment, parole, gender and diversity, specialized courts, and criminal justice decision-making, including 'Actuarial Sentencing: An Unsettled Proposition' in *Justice Quarterly*, and 'Shifting and Targeted Forms of Penal Governance: Bail, Punishment, and Specialized Courts' in *Theoretical Criminology* with Paula Maurutto.

Dave Holmes is Professor and University Research Chair in Forensic Nursing at the University of Ottawa. To date, Professor Holmes has received funding, as principal investigator, from CIHR and SSHRC, to conduct his research program on risk management in the fields of public health and forensic nursing. Most of his work, comments, essays, analyses, and research are based on the poststructuralist works of Deleuze and Guattari and Foucault. His works have been published in top-tier journals in nursing, criminology, sociology, and medicine. Professor Holmes has published over 110 articles in peer-reviewed journals and 32 book chapters. He is co-editor of *Critical Interventions in the Ethics of Health Care* (2009), *Abjectly Boundless: Boundaries, Bodies and Health Care* (2010), *(Re)Thinking Violence in Health Care Settings: A Critical Approach* (2011), and finally, *Power and the Psychiatric Apparatus* (2014). He was appointed as Honorary Visiting Professor in Australia, the United States, and the United Kingdom.

Yvonne Jewkes is Professor of Criminology at University of Leicester. She has published many books on prisons and imprisonment and is co-editor (with Jamie Bennett and Ben Crewe) of the forthcoming *Handbook on Prisons*, Second Edition. Her main current research interest is prison architecture, and she is principal investigator on an ESRC-funded project investigating prison design in the United Kingdom and Scandinavia.

Emma Kaufman received her BA in philosophy from Columbia and her D.Phil. in law from Oxford, where she studied as a Marshall Scholar, and her JD from Yale Law School. Emma's doctoral dissertation, *Punish and Expel: Border Control, Nationalism, and the New Purpose of the Prison*, was published by Oxford University Press (2015). Her research focuses on American immigration policy, British prisons, and the links between race, gender, and punishment.

Amy Klassen is a PhD candidate in the Department of Sociology at the University of Toronto, Mississauga. Her research interests focus on the role of agency, resistance, and mental health in prison management. Her dissertation focuses on the challenges faced by correctional officers when they are confronted with difficult inmates through conducting an embedded ethnographic study of correctional officer training and qualitative interviews of officers working in Canadian provincial jails.

Alexa Koenig, JD, PhD, is Executive Director of the Human Rights Center and a lecturer in law and legal studies at the University of California, Berkeley Her research and commentary have appeared in such diverse outlets as the *Annual Review of Law and Social Science* and *US News and World Reports*. She is the author, with Eric Stover and Victor Peskin, of the forthcoming *Hiding in Plain Sight: The Pursuit of War Criminals from Nuremberg to the "War on Terror"* (UC Press). An expert in domestic human rights, she is often called upon to speak about US detention and drone policies as well as technology and human rights.

Alison Liebling is Professor of Criminology and Criminal Justice at the University of Cambridge and the Director of the Institute of Criminology's Prisons Research Centre, and is simultaneously Adjunct Professor at Griffith University's Key Centre for Ethics, Law, Justice and Governance. She has carried out research on measuring the moral quality of prison life, the effectiveness of suicide prevention strategies in prison, managing difficult prisoners, incentives and earned privileges, the work of prison officers, and values, practices, and outcomes in public- and private-sector corrections. Her most recent research is on staff-prisoner/prisoner-prisoner relationships in high-security prisons. She has recently been awarded an ESRC 'Transforming Social Science' research contract to explore the building of trust in high-security settings. Her books include *Prisons and Their Moral Performance: A Study of Values, Quality and Prison Life* (2004), *The Effects of Imprisonment* (with Shadd Maruna, 2005), *The Prison Officer* (2001; 2nd edition 2010), and an edited collection on prison officers and prison culture in the *European Journal of Criminology* (2011).

Mona Lynch is Professor in Criminology, Law and Society and, by courtesy, the School of Law at the University of California, Irvine. Trained as a social psychologist, she researches criminal sentencing and punishment, with a particular interest on how race intersects with criminal justice processes. Her current project uses mixed methods to examine the micro-mechanics of the deployment of criminal law and procedure in federal court, focusing on the adjudication of drug cases during a period of major policy flux. Her research has been published in a wide range of journals, law reviews, and edited volumes, and she is author of *Sunbelt Justice: Arizona and the Transformation of American Punishment* (Stanford University Press 2009).

Marc Mauer is Executive Director of The Sentencing Project, a US organization engaged in research and advocacy on criminal justice reform. His book, *Race to Incarcerate*, was a semifinalist for the Robert F. Kennedy Book Award, and the graphic novel version of the book was selected as one of the "Great Graphic Novels" of the year by the American Library Association. He is also the co-editor of *Invisible Punishment: The Collateral Consequences of Mass Imprisonment*. Mr. Mauer frequently testifies before Congress and state legislative bodies on criminal justice reform and is actively engaged on issues of sentencing policy, racial disparity, and the collateral consequences of mass incarceration.

Stuart J. Murray is Canada Research Chair in Rhetoric and Ethics in the Department of English Language and Literature at Carleton University in Ottawa, Canada. He is currently working on a book-length project on the rhetorical dimensions of biopolitics and bioethics after Foucault, tentatively titled *The Living from the Dead: Disaffirming Biopolitics*.

Nadya Pittendrigh is a visiting lecturer at the University of Illinois at Chicago. She is finalizing her dissertation, rooted in qualitative investigation of the political rhetoric of Tamms, the Illinois supermax prison, and the activism that mobilized against it. Her dissertation emerges from her involvement with Tamms Year Ten, a group that worked to reform, and eventually close, the prison.

Keramet Reiter, JD, PhD, is an assistant professor in the Department of Criminology, Law and Society at the School of Law at the University of California, Irvine. She has published articles in *Punishment & Society*, the *California Law Review*, the *South Atlantic Quarterly*, and *Qualitative Inquiry* about prisoners' rights and the impact of prison and punishment policy on individuals, communities, and legal systems. She is currently completing a book on the history and uses of long-term solitary confinement in the United States (forthcoming in 2016, Yale University Press).

Sarah Turnbull is a postdoctoral research fellow with the Centre for Criminology, University of Oxford. Her current research examines immigration detention and deportation with a specific focus on issues of identity, home, and belonging in the context of multicultural, post-colonial Britain.

Sam Weiss is a graduate of the University of Michigan and Harvard Law School. He has written about various aspects of the American criminal justice system. He is currently a Ford Foundation Fellow at the American Civil Liberties Union's Center for Justice.

Introduction

Alexa Koenig, University of California, Berkeley
Keramet Reiter, University of California, Irvine

Extreme Punishment examines the erosion of the legal boundaries traditionally dividing civil and military detention from criminal punishment. Together, the 11 chapters in this collection reveal how, in nominally distinct institutions, the mentally ill, non-citizen immigrants, and enemy combatants are treated like criminals, and how they experience their confinement as punitive. In the late 20th century, Foucault examined the pathologies common to a range of social institutions, including hospitals, schools, and prisons (1963, 1964, 1966, 1975). He suggested that each of these institutions exerts social control by disciplining individuals. Today, prisons represent the dominant institutional paradigm through which individuals experience this disciplining process. Increasingly, discipline has become synonymous with punishment.

The chapters in this anthology explore how punishers consolidate and exert control and how punished prisoners experience life in these new, hybrid civil-criminal institutions. For instance, in Canada in 2007, a 19-year-old mentally ill woman was locked in a prison isolation cell because she had repeatedly engaged in acts of self-harm. On 19 October, she fashioned a rope-like noose, wrapped it around her neck, and hung herself. Guards refused to enter the cell to release her from the ligature. She died soon after (Hannah-Moffat & Klassen in this volume). Anthony Gay, by contrast, survived his attempts at self-mutilation in Tamms, a US supermaximum-security prison in Illinois. In 2010, Gay cut his own testicle off. No psychologist evaluated him. Instead, guards charged him with malingering, extending his years-long term in solitary confinement (Pittendrigh in this volume). But at least Gay had some idea of when he might be released from solitary and where he would go, unlike immigrants detained in foreign nations. A Nigerian, housed in a secure detention center in the United Kingdom in 2009, described his experience of confinement as a non-citizen facing possible deportation: '[I]t's even more torturing than a prison', because 'you don't know' how your case will be decided (deported or not), when you will be released (there

1

are no legal limits on immigration detention in the United Kingdom), or where you will be released to (the United Kingdom, Nigeria, elsewhere) (Bosworth & Turnbull in this volume). A European detainee released from US military detention in Guantánamo Bay, Cuba, noted that the torture did not end for him, even after he was released from detention: 'I was living in hell in Guantánamo, and when I returned home, it was another hell' (Koenig in this volume). These individuals and their struggles inspired this anthology, which documents the lived experience of indefinite incarceration and permanent exclusion.

Ashley Smith, Anthony Gay, the Nigerian immigrant in the United Kingdom, and the man formerly detained in Guantánamo all experienced punishment in institutional contexts explicitly labeled as non-punitive—'administrative', 'detention', and 'civil' rather than 'disciplinary', 'prison', and 'criminal'. This dissonance between legal labels and lived realities is exactly what makes these punishments extreme.

Extreme Punishment comprises the first cross-national, empirical investigation into the relationship between the physical architecture, the legal administration, and the lived experience of 21st-century prisoners in multiple secure institutional contexts. We explore both the punishers and the punished in three of the world's oldest and wealthiest democracies: Canada, the United Kingdom, and the United States. Although we focus on democracies, many of the policies and practices detailed in subsequent chapters are fundamentally undemocratic: hidden, exclusionary, and oppressive. By juxtaposing multiple institutional contexts across three countries, the chapters collectively reveal an interrelated, increasingly global network of military, immigration, and penal policies.

Each of the authors contributing to this volume has gained unprecedented access to the administrative black holes that increasingly characterize punishment in these modern democracies. Across 11 chapters, each contributor asks: How do the punishers exert power, and how do the punished experience that power? The authors examine a variety of sources including legal and administrative documents, interviews with institutional staff and with currently and formerly incarcerated detainees, and ethnographic observations. The scholars deploy a range of qualitative empirical methods—from rhetorical analysis to coding of interviews to analytic interpretations of ethnographic data—and draw on a variety of disciplinary contexts, including law, criminology, history, philosophy, psychology, and sociology. This mixed-method and interdisciplinary approach represents the kind of creative scholarship required to begin to make sense of administrative black holes.

The richly detailed qualitative work at the core of these studies integrates and complicates two related conceptual frameworks: crimmigration and risk management. 'Crimmigration' refers to the blurring of criminal laws, which impose punishments, with immigration laws, which historically impose only civil sanctions (see Stumpf 2011; Legomsky 2007; Chacón 2009). Crimmigration scholars seek to understand the legal underpinnings of the increasingly harsh sanctions imposed on non-citizens for various civil infractions in the United States in the 21st century. For instance, between 2000 and 2010, the number of non-citizens deported from the United States doubled, yet the majority of these deportees had broken no criminal laws (Lopez & Gonzales-Barrera 2013; see also Kanstroom 2007). Unlike a criminal defendant, a non-citizen in a US deportation hearing does not have a right to a lawyer. Indeed, few legal rights and protections attach to civil sanctions like deportation. Coutin has argued that this blurring of criminal and immigration laws obscures 'distinctions between legality and illegality' (2005, p. 6). Such criminalization of status characteristics has not been limited to non-citizen immigrants either. Scholars have also noted the increasing criminalization of the mentally ill in the United States in the 21st century (Gilligan 2001; Harcourt 2011). Each of the chapters in this anthology pulls back the veil of administrative, civil labels to examine how and why a given status, like mental illness or non-citizenship, becomes criminalized and punished. As these chapters demonstrate, this phenomenon transcends national boundaries, taking place in Canada and the United Kingdom, as well as in the United States.

Administrators and government officials often justify crimmigration, and the associated criminalization of other statuses, as necessary to maintain institutional and national safety and security. Criminal punishments and civil sanctions alike once prioritized rehabilitation: individually oriented interventions designed to reform deviants. But now, both punishments and sanctions prioritize risk management: 'warehousing' entire categories of deviants labeled as dangerous (Feeley & Simon 1992; Coutin 2005). Ashworth and Zedner (2014) label this new focus on risk management *preventive justice*; they contextualize crimmigration and the warehousing of dangerous classes of people as two of many examples of a range of nominally civil laws deployed as preventive measures in liberal democracies across the globe. They explain how democratic states in the 21st century have increasingly imposed civil laws, justified as necessary to prevent wrongdoing, to control 'dangerous' people: 'depriving them of their liberty before they can do harm' (2014, p. 10). The punitive experiences detailed in this anthology involve exactly these kinds of preventive measures: attempts to control the mentally ill before they act out or hurt themselves; attempts to control non-citizens before they burden or corrupt host governments; attempts to control alleged terrorists before they commit acts of terror. The crimmigration scholars, along with Ashworth and Zedner, have developed a 'conceptual framework' for understanding the interrelationship among 'preventive endeavors' (2014, p. 10). This anthology presents complementary empirical work which examines the mechanisms by which such civil and preventive laws become the building blocks of punitive institutions and translate into punitive experiences.

The empirical work documented herein exposes a key output of this administrative control: new administrative laws, nominally focused on managing risk and preventing harm, ultimately *produce* both new criminal categories and newly criminalized individuals, despite purporting to operate outside the criminal legal framework (see also Dayan 2011 for an argument about the production of criminalized categories). Preventive laws offer many benefits for law enforcement administrators, broadly defined. Such laws allow for punishment without the (expensive, inefficient, and inconvenient) due process constraints that serve as a check in the criminal legal framework. And they concentrate discretionary power in the hands of prison administrators, detention facility operators, and border patrol agents, who assign individuals to marginal status categories, subject to restrictive sanctions like detention or isolation. Individuals who experience civil constraints as punitive provide the most vivid argument for how these preventive laws have exceeded their civil scope and perverted their protective mandate.

Together, the 11 chapters in this volume reveal three important steps in this process of producing 'criminals' through the application of civil, preventive laws. First, laws label entire categories of people as the 'worst of the worst'. As Coutin (2005) has argued in immigration contexts and Cohen (1988) has argued in criminal contexts, societal labeling processes define new criminal categories. The chapters in this volume reveal not just the creation of new categories, but the use of these categories to justify harsh conditions of confinement for both citizens and non-citizens. Once labeled as dangerous, entire classes of 'dangerous' people are othered, locked up, and socially erased. Historically, racial minorities, non-citizen immigrants, madmen, and now, increasingly, terrorists, constitute archetypes of dangerous outsiders. Once an institution or government labels an individual as a potentially dangerous outsider, that individual is absorbed into an architectural setting that feels like a traditional prison, with razor wire, locked doors, and severe restrictions on movement—despite the façade that the detention environment is legally and technically non-punitive. In such settings, an individual in need of assistance (such as an asylum seeker or someone with mental illness) becomes a wrongdoer in need of punishment. Officially, institutions like detention centers manage risk and prevent harm; individually, the institutionalized experience criminalization and punishment, reinforced by physical architecture, rights restrictions, persistent distrust, and the discounting of words and narratives.

Second, punishment increasingly involves the administrative—and, therefore, the largely invisible—policing of porous borders, within prison security levels and between countries. This administrative policing results in uncertainty for the people experiencing the sanctions. And this lack of predictability, in turn, exaggerates the punitive experience. One of the hardest things individuals described experiencing is the ambiguity of their confinement. How long will they stay? Will asylum seekers and individuals facing deportation be allowed to remain in the country or receive assistance to go to a safe place? Will military detainees be released, especially if captured in a war without end, such as a war on terrorism? Where will they end up—in their home country or a third country, or yet another detention facility? Will the mentally ill be confined to isolation permanently? Will they be treated or punished?

Third, administrative practices reshape identities. The individuals described in the subsequent chapters struggle with their newly imposed identities as purported wrongdoers, trying to understand who they are when their broader social context has been stripped away and an institutional one imposed. In particular, when these individuals have committed no crime—or at the very most a crime that is wildly disproportionate to the indefiniteness of their "sentence"—they experience a dissonance and illogic to their confinement. In this context, prisoners, detainees, and their advocates develop new, if limited, ways to exercise agency by resisting administrative policing paradigms. Coutin, too, has suggested that 'the logic of social exclusion suggests strategies for redefining the boundaries of illegality', including challenging the illegality of acts, challenging the policies that exclude offenders from a given society, and challenging the distinction between law and illegality (2005, pp. 15, 23). While the individual stories in this anthology reveal these kinds of attempts at redefining boundaries and legality, they also reveal how resistance can incur further preventive control and criminalization.

Exclusionary labeling, administrative policing, and resistance span the various contexts described in this collection: isolation of mentally ill prisoners, detention and deportation of immigrants, and military confinement of alleged terrorists. The constitutive aspects of such administrative detention are not well understood, but the empirical investigations featured in this anthology take us one step closer to comprehending how these attempts at totalizing control transform both the individual and the broader society in which each institution is embedded.

Many of the chapters that follow also document how preventive administrative measures became more 'extreme' after 11 September 2001. The terrorist attacks that took place in the United States; similar terrorist attacks in the United Kingdom; and the legal, cultural, and geographic proximity of Canada and the United Kingdom to the United States led to a diffusion of crackdowns on 'outsiders' and other undesirables. The three countries share a history of complex relationships with the 'other' and who gets citizenship, including colonialism, slavery, and the suppression of indigenous populations. All of this is operationalized through overlapping legal systems and languages. Because the three countries featured here are among the oldest and wealthiest democracies in the world, they provide a lens for investigating how democratic practices trickle down to protect (or not) the least privileged in the most privileged of environments.

Chapter overview

The anthology opens with Yvonne Jewkes' 'Fear-Suffused Hell-Holes: The Architecture of Extreme Punishment', which explores how physical structures influence confinement experiences. This chapter provides a framework for understanding how architecture produces criminals. Drawing on her extensive empirical research into prisons, Jewkes argues that modern prison structures in both the United States and United Kingdom impose a divine and Foucauldian justice: permanently othering criminal offenders by containing them in 'exaggerated and superfluous security conditions', which enhance political power. Jewkes notes how crime and security are political tools being used to create an industry of control, sweeping up thousands of American and British residents into long and harsh periods of imprisonment. The symbolism of the prison as an institution of othering reinforces the incarceration industry. Jewkes draws on case studies of architectural design in the United Kingdom and the United States and contrasts these with architectural design in Scandinavia to examine and explain how physical contexts influence fear and violence within and around high-security prisons. Her chapter explores the proposition that the unnecessary infliction of harm in contemporary punishment is not simply a *lack* of morality, humanity, or regard for human rights; rather, it might be regarded as a *force* of moral charge and positive intent to administer more than a 'just' measure of pain.

Emma Kaufman and Sam Weiss then discuss one aspect of this phenomenon in 'The Limits of Punishment', investigating the influence of non-criminal detention in the United States and United Kingdom. Drawing on their complementary fields of criminology and immigration, their chapter considers the expansion of immigration detention within prisons and penal contexts. Bringing together analyses of fieldwork in two contexts: 1) ethnographic observations of prisons in the United Kingdom and 2) clinical legal work with migrants in the United States, the chapter examines how prisons have been transformed into sites for migration control over the past several decades. Their empirical analysis suggests that some of the more pernicious—and punitive—effects of the criminal justice system lie beyond the parameters of punishment, in the realm of civil and administrative law. On both sides of the Atlantic, penal institutions increasingly serve technically non-punitive ends, expanding the gap between lived and legal notions of punishment. Ultimately, they examine the practical and ethical consequences of a justice system in which the concept of punishment remains stable, while the purpose of the prison expands, suggesting the collusion of crime and border control reveals the need for a new approach to state power.

In 'Immigration Detention and the Expansion of Penal Power in the United Kingdom', Mary Bosworth and Sarah Turnbull focus on the lived experience of immigration, drawing on detainee testimonies to identify the conditions that create an experience of punishment for those who are held in administrative detention. In the United Kingdom, as in the other two countries featured in this anthology, immigration detention is not legally categorized as punishment. Rather, detention is administrative and geared toward the removal of unwanted non-citizens. Yet, for those who are detained for immigration purposes and confined in one of the UK's 12 immigration removal centers (IRCs), the common experience is that of punishment. As detainees repeatedly note, IRCs both feel and look like penal institutions. Physically, UK immigration centers resemble prisons; procedurally, such facilities define detainees as excludable strangers, exaggerating detainees' punitive experiences and raising critical issues of identity and belonging, especially among those in the process of being ejected from the United Kingdom after residing there for years. Drawing on fieldwork from across several British IRCs, this chapter highlights how immigration detention is reflective of the broadening reach of penal power in the service of border control, and of race, gender, and postcolonial relations in an increasingly 'global' world. Mona Lynch then dives into a case study that provides a micro-level analysis of the diffusion of penal power in the post-9/11 era: '(Im) migrating Penal Excess: Sheriff Joe Arpaio and the Case of Maricopa County, Arizona'. Lynch illustrates the structural forces that shape experiences of punitive immigration enforcement at the local level. One of the theoretically under-explored mechanisms responsible for the criminalization and penalization of immigration is the delegation of immigration enforcement to local agencies whose core goal is traditionally criminal law enforcement. Lynch examines an extreme version of this process—the case of Maricopa County Sheriff Joe Arpaio's 'seizure' of immigration responsibilities—to illustrate the rhetorical and material techniques in play as the hegemonic logics of crime and punishment drive immigration enforcement practices. Lynch uses the context of immigration enforcement policies in Maricopa County as a lens to explore the mechanisms through which federal power, delegated to local law enforcement agencies, becomes a tool for expanding control over non-citizens and enforcing boundaries, both through a revision of institutional relationships and treatment of the individual. As the Maricopa County case illustrates, the risks posed by immigration delegation policies are multiple; once legal power is bestowed, it becomes difficult to govern, contain, and rescind.

In 'A New "Ecology of Cruelty"? The Changing Shape of Maximum-Security Custody in England and Wales', Alison Liebling provides another example of delegations of discretionary power being used to construct risk, this time drawn from the individualized perspective of ethnographic observations conducted in a high-security prison in the United Kingdom. Liebling contextualizes these observations within the political history of UK imprisonment over the last 50 years. Craig Haney's concept of the 'ecology of cruelty' provides a helpful paradigm for understanding the cycle of public fear—of terrorism and escapes—which produces further fear and violence within prisons and between prisoners. Liebling applies Haney's analysis to a form of long-term, high-security imprisonment emerging in England and Wales in response to a series of major escapes, a rising fear of terrorism, and the imposition of increasing and indeterminate sentence lengths. Drawing on a recent ethnographic study in a high-security prison, Liebling finds that an absence of trust, hope, and meaning has produced increased fear and violence, as well as new and complex uses of faith identities by prisoners. Ultimately, Liebling concludes, the changing shape of maximum-security prisons in

England and Wales is a dangerous and politically driven phenomenon that departs from 50 years of policy, ideology, and practice.

The anthology then shifts from exploring the exercise of power within existing institutional structures to exploring the construction and policing of boundaries—between the criminal and non-criminal, between the citizen and non-citizen, and between national borders. First, in 'Seclusive Space: Crisis Confinement and Behavior Modification in Canadian Forensic Psychiatric Settings', Stuart J. Murray and Dave Holmes explore the boundary between the psychiatric and the correctional. They develop a recurring theme in the anthology: how institutional practices and objectives are played out on prisoners' bodies, perverting the treatment of prisoners deemed problematic, often 'disappearing' them in the process. Drawing on observations in forensic psychiatry settings, this chapter argues that the distinction between rewards and punishments—while intended to soften punitive experiences—is largely spurious in the context of secure treatment units. Operant conditioning, whether it is construed as 'positive' or 'negative' reinforcement, relies on a token economy deeply informed by neoliberal values, whether these incentivizing 'tokens' are material benefits or 'life rewards'. Not only are psychiatric inmates rewarded for adopting a competitive stance toward their peers, their relationships with forensic nurses and health-care providers become 'correctional' and antagonistic, rather than caring and therapeutic. In spite of reforms, patients still experience behavioral modification plans (BMPs) as highly punitive.

In 'Normalizing Exceptions: Solitary Confinement and the Micro-Politics of Risk/Need in Canada', Kelly Hannah-Moffat and Amy Klassen focus on the specific case of Ashley Smith as a magnifying lens for further examining the problems with mental health treatment in prison, as theorized by Murray and Holmes. Drawing on data from recent prison inquiries and special investigations into deaths in custody, Hannah-Moffat and Klassen examine the use of extreme forms of punishment for women in Canadian prisons and how these sanctions coexist with narratives of treatment, mental health, and gender responsiveness. They detail how the extreme practices used against female inmates with mental health issues threaten to become a normalized part of institutional regimes. Institutional cultures, in turn, securitize and perpetuate inhumane practices. In the end, these cultures produce and reproduce the risky or difficult-to-manage prisoner, using the symptoms of mental illness to reaffirm the status of criminal.

Whereas Hannah-Moffat and Klassen's chapter examines the narratives produced by prisons about *prisoners*, the next chapter, by Nadya

Pittendrigh, considers the rhetoric of prisoners about *prisons*. In 'Making Visible Invisible Suffering: Non-Deliberative Agency and the Bodily Rhetoric of Supermax Prisoners', Pittendrigh focuses in on a single supermax prison in the United States—Tamms in Illinois—to explore the relationship between socio-political context and lived experience. Specifically, Pittendrigh asks: How does the rhetoric of supermax prisoners do political work (when it works), and what work does it do? Because what prisoners say is frequently regarded as suspect, and because the psychological harm that supermax prisoners experience is largely invisible, prisoners' most impactful expression of suffering often arises not from spoken text but from physical affects. Thus prisoners' most impactful 'voice' may ironically be one that is most outside of their control. Using methods from rhetorical ethnography, this inquiry considers the impact of an unlooked-for, unwilled rhetoric that does not pivot centrally on traditional conceptions of agency, arguing that such bodily rhetoric may best translate the 'unspeakable' for audiences outside the prison.

In 'Punishing Mental Illness: Trans-institutionalization and Solitary Confinement in the United States', Keramet Reiter and Thomas Blair continue the discussion of agency, exploring the ways in which prisons both produce and attempt to manage mental illness. They trace the historical connection between the deinstitutionalization of the mentally ill from hospitals and their reinstitutionalization in prisons within prisons, under conditions of long-term solitary confinement. They survey what is known about the mental health impacts of solitary confinement on both the apparently healthy prisoner and the known mentally ill prisoner. They then analyze how courts have dealt with this empirical evidence about the dangerous mental health effects of long-term solitary confinement. Finally, they present a close analysis of in-depth interviews with staff psychologists working in solitary confinement units in California prisons. As correctional psychologists categorize various degrees of severity of mental illness, and organize the mentally ill along spectrums of possible in-prison privileges, the most severely ill prisoners, who earn the fewest privileges, become 'illustrations' of why solitary confinement continues to be necessary and useful despite its documented harms. While existing research and litigation has suggested that the status of mental illness is being wrongly criminalized and punished within US prisons, this chapter argues that the criminalization of mental illness perversely works to reinforce correctional justifications for the necessity of solitary confinement.

In 'Between Protection and Punishment: The Irregular Arrival Regime in Canadian Refugee Law', Efrat Arbel describes a similar phenomenon in a different geographic and punitive context. While Reiter and Blair note the ways in which the mentally ill are transformed from patients in need of care into threats who must be managed, Arbel analyzes the transformation of refugees from individuals in need of protection into criminals who must be punished. While the Canadian refugee regime is technically administrative, Arbel documents the ways in which it is experienced as predominately punitive. This sense of punitiveness comes from the architecture used to confine refugees (razor wire and high fences, confinement alongside general criminal populations), as well as the 'mark' experienced by refugee populations even after they achieve refugee status (being deemed 'irregular' for five years). She also documents the ways in which such punitiveness occurs without due process and thus circumvents the basic constitutional protections that would typically be available to convicted criminals, who arguably have committed much more egregious wrongs. Finally, her chapter illustrates the powerful expansion of Western countries' territorial reach into other countries through legal and theoretical expansions of borders.

The final substantive chapter considers yet another site of extreme punishment and its effects. In 'From Man to Beast: Social Death at Guantánamo', Alexa Koenig explores the constitutive impact of detention on those who are held in extreme settings and the work that institutionalization does for societies more generally. Koenig considers the ways in which the United States has imported domestic prison practices into military detention, both to contain a perceived internal threat, but also as a means to police populations outside US borders. Relying on 78 semistructured interviews with men who were formerly detained at Guantánamo (and before that at Bagram and Kandahar military bases), this chapter posits that extreme detention contexts—such as Guantánamo—are often experienced as egregious because of the extent to which they threaten not just a literal but a social death—an erasure of identity that parallels that noted by Pittendrigh and Murray and Holmes earlier in the anthology. Ultimately, the perceived punitiveness does not end with the conclusion of the detainees' confinement; instead, detainees find themselves 'marked' by their institutionalization in a manner that impacts their social identities long after their release.

Conclusion

The chapters in this anthology reveal that today's 'prisons' are used for increasingly disparate purposes, many of which are administrative. Regardless of the administrative purposes, we also find—as Goffman did years ago in his analysis of total institutions (1961)—that there are similarities across these hidden, liminal spaces in terms of the ways they are run, the ways in which they are experienced, and the work they do for society in labeling and disappearing 'abnormal' outsiders. Cumulatively, this anthology illustrates the ways in which the law and institutions inadvertently *produce* criminals as they purport to be managing risk.

In all three countries examined here, the predominate model for dealing with threats and danger has been application of a criminal-legal framework. Societies flag unconvicted individuals as wrongdoers by confining them in conditions that reflect the most extreme prison environments, absent any adjudicated wrong. Who becomes confined in these extreme contexts, in turn, defines who is considered dangerous in the aggregate, absent an individualized conviction for any crime. Collective experiences of the physical architecture of the spaces in which they are held, of never-ending administrative discretion over experiences and durations of confinement, and of physical and social exclusion resulting from punitive labels and public distrust dissolves individuals into dismissible and excludable groups.

Ultimately, this anthology demonstrates the various mechanisms at play when societies attempt to control perceived risks through the delegation of power to administrative officials, labeling, and social exclusion. Civil institutions and administrative procedures are deployed to punish all 'dangerous' people who do not fit into traditional systems of crime control—those who by national origin, race, mental challenge, or immigrant status are perceived as threatening key ways of life in three of the most powerful liberal democracies in the world. Such experiments permit the expansion of penal power into new legal, social, and geographic spaces. Once power expands into those spaces, controlling it, or retracting it, is nearly impossible.

References

Ashworth, A & Zedner, L 2014, *Preventive justice*, Oxford University Press, Oxford.

Chacón, JM 2009, 'Sidebar: managing migration through crime', *Columbia Law Review*, vol. 109, pp. 135–48.

Cohen, S 1988, *Against Criminology*, Transaction Books, New Brunswick, NJ, pp. 235–76.

Coutin, S 2005, 'Contesting criminality: illegal migration and spacialization of illegality', *Theoretical Criminology*, vol. 9, no. 1, pp. 5–33.

Dayan, C 2011, *The Law Is a White Dog*, Princeton University Press, New Jersey.

Feeley, M & Simon, J 1992, 'The new penology: notes on the emerging strategy of corrections and its implications', *Criminology*, vol. 30, no. 4, pp. 449–74.

Foucault, M 1963, 1994, *The birth of the clinic: an archeology of medical perception*, trans. AM Sheridan, Vintage Books, New York.

Foucault, M 1964, 1988, *Madness and civilization: a history of insanity in the Age of Reason*, trans. AM Sheridan, Vintage Books, New York.

Foucault, M 1966, 1994, *The order of things: an archeology of the human sciences*, Vintage Books New York.

Foucault, M1975, 1995, *Discipline and punish*, trans. AM Sheridan, Vintage Books, New York.

Gilligan, J 2001, 'The last mental hospital', *Psychiatric Quarterly*, vol. 72, no. 1, pp. 45–61.

Goffman, E 1961, *Asylums: essays on the social situation of mental patients and other inmates*, Random House, Inc., New York.

Harcourt, BE 2011, 'Reducing mass incarceration: lessons from the deinstitutionalization of mental hospitals in the 1960s', *Ohio State Journal of Criminal Law*, vol. 9, pp. 53–88.

Kanstroom, D 2007, *Deportation nation: outsiders in American history*, Harvard University Press, Boston, MA.

Legomsky, SH 2007, 'The new path of immigration law: asymmetric incorporation of criminal justice norms', *Washington & Lee Law Review*, vol. 6, pp. 469–528.

Lopez, MH & Gonzalez-Barrera, A 2013, 'High rate of deportations continue under Obama despite Latino disapproval', *Pew Research Center*, 19 September. Available from: <http://www.pewresearch.org/fact-tank/2013/09/19/high-rate-of-deportations-continue-under-obama-despite-latino-disapproval/>. [29 January 2015].

Stumpf, J 2011, 'Doing time: crimmigration law & the perils of haste', *UCLA Law Review*, vol. 58, pp. 1705–48.

1

Fear Suffused Hell-holes: The Architecture of Extreme Punishment

Yvonne Jewkes, University of Leicester

Is Hook at last heading for Hell? Abu Hamza to be moved to top security jail.... 'Hell' is what they call the fearsome jail where the soul-destroying isolation has driven some of America's toughest prisoners to suicide (Leonard 2012).

Prisons tend to reflect the society that oversees them; they are physical manifestations of a state's aims and approaches for dealing with offenders (Johnston 2000; Wener 2012). In recent years, the prison has been analogously compared to transportation and slavery (Davis 2000; Alexander 2010) and the urban ghetto (Wacquant 2002) and used as a means of understanding state power and security apparatuses in post-9/11 societies (Drake 2012). In these analyses, imprisonment is explicitly linked to wider processes of racial discrimination, criminalization, and extreme punishment. A further analogous framework by which prisons might be viewed and understood, both structurally and experientially, is that of Hell.[1] This chapter draws on images of Hell from Dante's *Inferno*, the cultural purchase of which, it is suggested, remains undiminished 700 years after it was written.

Informed by the early findings of a comparative study of prison architecture, design, and technology,[2] together with the published findings of fellow prison ethnographers, the chapter focuses principally on case studies of architectural design in the UK and US and briefly contrasts these with penal design elsewhere in order to examine and explain how physical contexts influence fear and violence within and around high-security prisons. The chapter argues that the 'fear-suffused' environments (Hassine 2011) of contemporary high- and maximum-security prisons resonate with Medieval imaginings of eternal damnation and represent a form of barbarity that is out of place in 21st century civilized societies.

In making this claim, the chapter is premised on two related propositions. The first is that both the US and UK imprison many thousands of people unnecessarily, and many thousands more for dramatically overextended periods of time under exaggerated and superfluous security conditions. The second proposition is that over the last two decades, crime and security have become the major battlegrounds on which political entrepreneurs have staked their hegemonic power, and prisoners have become expedient tools for politicians wishing to look more tough on crime than their opponents. Of course, some crimes challenge the beliefs of even the most fervent abolitionists. Nonetheless, the actions of an individual (whether a particularly horrible or newsworthy offense or a security breach, for example an abscondment from prison) can be a fortuitous catalyst for those who seek political gain by introducing more oppressive security and control measures across the prison estate, catching *all* inmates in a tightening carceral net (Drake 2012).

The result of these interlinked processes is that we appear to have returned to pre-Enlightenment, expressive forms of punishment, where penal strategies of excessive and unprecedented punitiveness are implemented and enacted in the pages of the popular press, for an audience perceived to be hungry for excessive displays of retribution (Loader 2009). Politically advantageous discourses of crime and incarceration have thus become culturally embedded, recasting offending 'folk devils' as 'evil monsters' and generating widespread tolerance for subterranean, infernal hell-holes as the most fitting repositories for the permanently excluded prisoner (Dolovich 2011).

The contemporary relevance of Dante's vision of Hell

Now moans, loud howls and lamentations echoed through the starless air, so that I also began to cry. Many languages, strange accents, words of pain, cries of rage, voices loud and faint, the sound of slapping hands—all these whirled together in that black and timeless air, as sand is swirled in a tornado (Alighieri & Kirkpatrick 2006, 3: 22–30).[3]

Dante's *Inferno* frames this analysis because it contains themes and motifs of a subterranean, multi-layered vision of Hell that lends itself particularly well to contemporary cultural ideas about the prison or penitentiary. Underpinning the collective imagination via novels, computer games, art, television, and film, Dante's imagining of Hell has become part of the common stock of knowledge, informing ideas about justice and punishment, about what places of punishment should look and feel like, even among those who have not actually read *Inferno*. Dante thus offers an enduring analogy of perpetual suffering for the increasing numbers of individuals regarded as deserving extreme punishment.

Widely regarded as being as important as Homer and Shakespeare in literary history, Dante Alighieri (c. 1265–1321) wrote *Inferno* as a three-part work (*Inferno, Purgatorio,* and *Paradiso*) collectively titled *Commedia,* offering a vision of Hell and Heaven from the perspective of an observer who witnessed a period of almost constant war, political conflict, and corruption in his home city of Florence. Revenge and retribution were the stuff of everyday life and inevitably shaped Dante's view of the universe and informed his writing. Part satire, part novel, and part journal (it is narrated in the first person), the *Divine Comedy,* as it is now usually known, was intended to be read aloud to an audience who would recognize the historical and political allusions that underpin what is essentially a gripping story. For dramatic effect, Dante creates a dialogue by introducing a companion on his journey to the 'horrid hole of Hell' (Alighieri & Kirkpatrick 2006, 32: 6); the Roman poet Virgil (70–19 BC) fulfills the roles of tourist guide, mentor, and protector.

Dante specified that Hell is a deep conical indentation, the lowest point of which is precisely at the center of the earth. The poor, tormented souls consigned to everlasting suffering occupy nine vast circular terraces that descend, in decreasing size, to the earth's core (Burge 2010). At the outer edge of the abyss is an area occupied by those who have committed no sin except that they were morally neutral and did not act or speak out against others' wrongdoings. Illustrating the statement later attributed to Edmund Burke (1729–1797) that all that is necessary for the triumph of evil is that good men do nothing,[4] the punishment suffered by these 'neutrals' might seem harsh to a contemporary reader. However, Bauman and Donskis have mapped the symbolic geography of evil through numerous modern atrocities and underline that evil is not confined to totalitarian ideologies: 'Today it more frequently reveals itself in failing to react to someone else's suffering, in refusing to understand others, in insensitivity and in eyes turned away from a silent ethical gaze' (2013, p. 8). Although writing principally about the Holocaust, Bauman and Donskis' words might be equally applied to carceral atrocities. Indeed, in the penal context, the more extreme the punishment, the more likely it is to recede from the public gaze and conscience, as this chapter will illustrate in its discussion of prison architecture and design.

The unfortunate occupants of the edge of the abyss observed by Dante and Virgil swirl in their masses moaning into the howling wind, naked and surrounded by attacking flies and wasps as their faces run with blood. Following this is the descent down through the nine circles of 'that profound pit of pain filled with the howl of endless woe' (Alighieri & Kirkpatrick 2006, 4:1). The field notes of two contemporary prison researchers, the first written inside a prison in Russia and the second as the writer emerged from the gloom of an American jail, contain powerful echoes of Dante's medieval vision of Hell, while at the same time suggesting that, at their most extreme, carceral environments are timeless and universal:

> I'm not sure I feel safe tonight. It's midnight. The noises from inside the zone are getting louder... It sounds like dogs yelping but it's not. It's prisoners moaning and swearing... It feels really creepy... [I] actually feel too scared to move (Piacentini 2005, p. 201).

> Shock of the daylight, the sun, the fresh air... I drive silently straight to the beach [of Santa Monica], to wallow in fresh air and wade in the waves, as if to 'cleanse' myself of all I've seen, heard, and sensed...but my memory is seared by what I've seen... Every time my mind drifts back to it, it seems like a bad movie, a nightmare, the vision of an evil 'other world' that cannot actually exist (Wacquant 2002, p. 381).

In the study from which the first quote comes, Piacentini (2005) describes her experience of 'deep immersion' in decaying Russian prisons, whose roofless buildings, crumbling walls, and rusting fittings challenge the aesthetic idea of the prison as a secure, sanitized environment. Stating that Russian prisons resemble a mutated, fantastical form of the Soviet ideal, industrial zones where daily life is divided between work and rest, Piacentini also reflects on the very specific melancholia and darkness that incarceration can instill. The abiding image of the Russian prison, she tells us, is one of a hostile and austere environment of multi-cells, acute overcrowding, faceless voices, appalling squalor, and death on a massive scale from freezing temperatures or from industrial accidents (Piacentini 2005).

Evoking similar notions of deep entombment in a cold, industrial wasteland, Wacquant's research diary records the 'overpowering feeling of emerging from a dive into a mine shaft...[a] murky factory for social pain and human destruction, silently grinding away' (2002, p. 381). These field notes, written on Wacquant's first day in the Men's Central Jail (part of Los Angeles County Jail), vividly capture the author's relief at breaking out of the hellish physical environment of a jail which comprises 'seven mega-houses of detention' holding more than 23,000 inmates (Wacquant 2002, p. 371). In an obvious echo of Dante's conical and subterranean rendering of Hell, the Men's Central Jail is organized into five floors, two of which are underground, and inmates are crammed in dormitories where up to 150 men live cheek by jowl on bunk beds, which form a human filing cabinet in 'conditions that evoke the dungeons of the Middle Ages' (Wacquant 2002, p. 372). Wacquant highlights three aspects which combine to form his vision of Hell: the noise ('deafening and disorienting'); the filth (both of the trash variety, which attracts rats and roaches, and promiscuity which, in this communal living environment, is 'pushed to the point of obscenity'); and the total absence of natural daylight, which leads Wacquant to describe the facility as 'a tomb. A subterranean grotto. A safe for men buried alive far away from society's eyes, ears, and mind' (2002, p. 373).

If he were writing about the jail now, Wacquant might add to his list of hellish experiences suffered by inmates at LA County the deplorable conditions under which prisoners with mental illnesses are kept, which have led to a dramatic rise in suicides; the horrifying abuse meted out to inmates by staff; and corruption on the part of management, which included a special hiring track—called FOS, or 'Friends of the Sheriff'—for friends and relatives of department employees, even if they themselves have criminal records.[5] More than a decade after Wacquant described his shock at what he saw there, the facility has been the subject of several critical reports by the US Department of Justice, and in December 2013, federal officials announced that 18 current and former Los Angeles County sheriff's deputies were under investigation for offenses including alleged 'unjustified beatings of jail inmates and visitors, unjustified detentions and a conspiracy to obstruct a federal investigation into misconduct at the Men's Central Jail' (US Attorney's Office, Central District of California 2013).

The unpleasant sensations described by both Piacentini and Wacquant in their field notes, and the graphic news reporting of prisoner despair in the face of staff cruelty and corruption in one county prison system, echo Dante's experience as he descends into Hell and describes slamming gates, vile odors, ditches full of excrement, suicides, mutilations, many languages and strange accents, brutal and sadistic guards, pain and rage, anguished cries for help, voices loud and faint, deviant sexual practices, and other degradations. Once again reminding us of the freezing conditions of post-Soviet confinement, Wacquant details how inmates at LA County are permitted one outing per week on the caged roof of the jail, which is

> the residents' only chance to see the sky, to know whether it's sunny, rainy or windy, to breathe for two hours outside of the cold draft of the air-moving system that operates round the clock (to contain the risk of tuberculosis)... The inmates commonly complain...about the cold: in many tiers, the ventilation is set too high and the units are swept by gusts of chilly air; in the disciplinary cells, the atmosphere is downright frigid (2002, p. 374).

This truly is the lowest level of Hell; the ninth circle of the Inferno is freezing cold, an icy waste in which the atmosphere atrophies the soul. As Dante puts it, 'I did not die but I was not living either' (Alighieri & Kirkpatrick 2006, 34: 25).

The architecture of prison Hell

> There are some prison administrators who stress the need to create small maximum security facilities for the most troublesome offenders—'maxi-maxi' institutions. Their plans read like the design of the inner circles of hell (Morris 1974, p. 88).

From Alison Liebling's British male prisoner respondent who describes the hell of being 'behind the slab' at HMP Whitemoor (2011, p. 538), an evocative phrase with both physical and experiential dimensions, to Eleanor Novek's (2005) exploration of the American female inmates who experience confinement as a living hell with no redeeming potential (especially for the incarcerated women who are forced to relinquish their babies just a few days after giving birth while restrained by handcuffs), images of Hell are never far from the surface of ethnographic studies of imprisonment. But arguably it is in prisoners' (auto)biographies, poetry, journalism, and creative writing that the hell of incarceration is most vividly conveyed, and where descriptions of poorly ventilated, putrid-smelling prisons have a distinctly Dantean quality. Here, foul gasses, decaying dirt, prisoners' blood and tears and a pervasive and permanent sense of fear ('The Beast') are all trapped within the porous walls (Hassine 2011). It is perhaps Victor Hassine who has most excoriatingly captured Hell from a prisoner's perspective. A 'lifer' in the US corrections system who committed suicide after nearly 28 years inside, after being denied a parole hearing, Hassine was an educated, scholarly man. His observations about the different prisons in which he served time, which varied considerably in age, size, and layout, tell us much about the effects that carceral design has on its occupants; in fact, Hassine states that many of the crises facing penal systems in the developed world—including overcrowding, violence, mental and physical illness, drug use, high levels of suicide and self-harm—are intrinsically related to the 'fear-suffused environments' created by prison architects:

> To fully understand the prison experience requires a personal awareness of how bricks, mortar, steel, and the endless enforcement of rules and regulations animate a prison into a living, breathing entity designed to manipulate its inhabitants.... Prison designers and managers have developed a precise and universal alphabet of fear that is carefully assembled and arranged—bricks, steel, uniforms, colors, odors, shapes, and management style—to effectively control the conduct of whole prison populations (Hassine 2011, p. 7).

Throughout Western penal history, from the separate and silent systems of the mid-19th century, when prisons were designed and constructed to prevent moral contagion (i.e., the belief that prisoners risked becoming 'worse' if allowed contact with other offenders), to the 1950s when the rehabilitation model paved the way for a raft of psychology programs aimed at treating the offender, commentators have noted the link between physical environments and operational regimes. Indeed, the origins of the supermax can be traced to both these penal experiments; its harsh conditions of solitary confinement are found in the 19th century separate (or 'Pennsylvania') system, but its penal ideologies were honed in the post-war era of behavioral psychology when various forms of sensory deprivation and social isolation were introduced in order to make prisoners susceptible to 'remoulding' through therapy and medication.

The supermax philosophy is also underpinned by the now infamous 'nothing works' doctrine (Martinson 1974), a statement intended to support a reduction in the use of imprisonment that was instead appropriated to support calls for more brutal regimes within psychologically numbing custodial settings. The supermax thus incorporates numerous architectural and environmental elements designed to have effects far beyond those engendered by architecture that is merely drab, institutional, and grindingly dull. The coercive use of architecture to instill total psychic and bodily control over prisoners designated 'threatening', 'non-compliant', or 'high-risk' might be regarded as modern versions of *Inferno*: physical separation of prisoners and guards, hi-tech monitoring equipment, constant surveillance, electronic controls, hermetically sealed interior environments protected by bullet-proof glass, windows positioned too high in the walls to see out of them, windows painted over to obscure the view and obstruct natural light, and areas of both sensory deprivation and sensory overload which, taken together, result in psychic and physical pain on a par with techniques of torture.

While the UK—indeed Europe—has not yet embraced the supermax, neoliberal, populist political agendas over the last few decades have intensified the punitive force of the experience of imprisonment (Brown & Wilkie 2002), and perceived public endorsement for rigorous and unpleasant conditions have resulted in new prisons being built with 'a level of security above "high security" and internal routines not seen for 150 years' (Johnston 2000, p. 4). As Drake (2012) describes, most recent developments in penal philosophy and practice in England and Wales, including prison design, can be traced back to the escapes from high-security conditions at Whitemoor in 1994 and Parkhurst in 1995, which ushered in a new regime of security and control, including fortified perimeters, increased use of closed-circuit television (CCTV) internally as well as externally, strict volumetric control of prisoners' property, and a dramatic reversal of policy on so-called 'privileges' (basically anything that could be presented by the media as inappropriately conceived indulgences to an anti-social population). In essence, the 19th century principle of 'less eligibility' has re-emerged, based on an understanding that prisoners should 'suffer' in prison, not only through the loss of freedom but also by virtue of prison conditions, which should be of a worse standard than those available to the poorest free workers.

It is against this backdrop that we must view much of recent penal policy introduced by a Conservative-led coalition government. A hardening of penal sensibilities has coalesced around new anti-terrorism legislation, resulting in the introduction or curtailment of countless everyday procedures and practices that have combined to form insidious and pervasive erosions of humanity (Drake 2012; see also Bosworth & Turnbull and Lynch in this volume, describing the hardening of immigration detention policies, often linked to anti-terrorism efforts). The current Secretary of State for Justice, Chris Grayling, has taken the politics of vengeance to a new level with a raft of petty restrictions, including limiting young offenders' television access and imposing a blanket ban on families sending small items to prisoners, including books.[6]

Grayling's colleague, Home Secretary Theresa May, sums up the UK government's attitude: 'Prison works but it must be made to work better. The key for members of the public is that they want criminals to be punished' (Moran, Jewkes & Turner, forthcoming (citing Travis 2010)). That their policies have precipitated a 69 percent increase in prison suicides— widely referred to as a 'secret death penalty'—does not seem to trouble these politicians (Dunt 2014); nor has a similar prevalence of suicide troubled US officials (as detailed by Reiter and Blair in this volume). They possess an unshakeable moral certitude that retribution is a greater goal than rehabilitation. For one commentator, the UK government's stance epitomizes the enduring appeal of *The Divine Comedy*: 'Vendetta still rules. Entire foreign policies, not to mention civil wars and terror campaigns, are based on ideas of revenge and polarities of good and evil just as primitive as anything in Dante' (Jones 2011).

In the current era of criminal justice, then, despite crime rates that broadly remain steady or are in decline, we might be said to be experiencing a similar synergy to that which underpinned Dante's worldview formed at the turn of the 14th century: a surge of populist punitiveness whereby sentiments driven from 'below' by an angry and anxious public collide with 'authoritarian populism' engineered by ambitious and manipulative politicians eager to capitalize on public fears and prejudices in order to maximize their electoral appeal (Hall et al. 1978). A foreshortened life on Death Row, an enforced state of limbo via an indeterminate life sentence, or 'life without parole' in a penal hell-hole, is simply a just and necessary consequence of a given activity. And all these have been supported by the media's 'terrifying counter-democratic language' of vengeance and dehumanization (Hartnett et al. 2011).

Contemporary penal architecture reflects these political, policy, and media contexts, transforming prison security and with it prisoners' quality of life (Liebling with Arnold 2004; Liebling, Arnold & Straub 2011; Drake 2012; see also Liebling this volume). Given that the 19th-century prison buildings still in service in the penal estate are usually considered the least desirable carceral environments, the 'new prisons for old' policy currently being rolled out by the UK Ministry of Justice might appear to be a humane intervention. After all, Victorian 'houses of correction' ensure inmates' restricted economy of space, light, and color, imprisoning them psychologically as well as physically. However, it has yet to be established empirically whether 'old' always means 'bad' in prison architecture and design, or whether the kind of contemporary prison currently being commissioned in the UK necessarily equates to 'progressive' or 'humanitarian' (Hancock & Jewkes 2010; Moran

& Jewkes forthcoming). Of course, clean, humane, and safe environments are unquestionably desirable for prisoners and prison staff, but, in recent years, UK prison new-builds have been driven by logics of cost, efficiency, and security. The preoccupation with 'hardening' the prison environment to design-out risk has arguably swung towards an understanding of the situational, rather than social, dependence of behavior, 'creating safe situations rather than creating safe individuals' (Wortley 2002, p. 4). There is also a need in prison architecture to comply with HM (Her Majesty) Prison Service Orders about the specification of prison accommodation, which lay out 'measurable standards' that can be applied consistently across the estate (HMPS 2001, p. 1).

In this context, the UK government has resurrected formerly shelved proposals for 'Titan' style prisons that may bear some of the hallmarks of the supermax. Frequently sited in remote locations and consisting of bland, unassuming, and uniform exteriors, with vast expanses of brick, a few small windows, and no unnecessary decoration, these prison warehouses may communicate a particular message about society's attitudes towards prisoners (Jewkes 2013; Jewkes & Moran 2014). At a conceptual level, moral drive is, as Bauman says, 'limited by the principle of proximity', and the distance we feel from our actions is proportionate to our ignorance of them (2004, p. 193–4). Therefore, while we expect punishment to be exacting and are acquiescent about a popular media that takes on the role of vigilante on our behalf (bringing wrong-doers to justice, naming and shaming, criticizing sentencers who are 'soft' on crime, and so on), we are content for punishment to be mediat(iz)ed and made visible, as it were, at one step removed. Indeed, the nondescript external appearance of new-build prisons with vast walls and discrete but omniscient security and surveillance technology, reducing the need for watch-towers and razor wire, could be regarded as a visual metaphor for the loss of public empathy for the excluded offender; the 'silent ethical gaze' that Bauman and Donskis (2013) referred to. Their 'municipal' architecture enables us to turn a blind eye to the plight of the confined, while our daily newspapers reassure us that prisons are suitably hellish places. Simultaneously, then, the visible manifestation of extreme but 'fitting' punishment salaciously reported by the media and the invisibility of prisoners banished to these prison warehouses that are sited in remote, hard-to-reach locations, reduces their humanness and reinforces 19th century ideas of offenders as outcasts. In this way, the UK is once again following the American example, and, while we do not have the landscape to expel convicted offenders to inaccessible islands or virtually uninhabitable deserts, it is becoming more common to site prisons in locations that lack transport networks and infrastructure. As a *Guardian* editorial puts it, 'even if your worldview can't compute a prisoner as a victim of anything, and sees his or her rights to justice as completely waived by the committal of any crime, however petty, you would nevertheless be able to see that prisoners aren't rehabilitated in these conditions' (Williams 2014).

Any hope of rehabilitation is further undermined by the requirement for prison architects and constructors to 'future-proof' their designs in order to avoid the need for expensive retro-fitting of security if, at some point in the future, a facility needs to be used to accommodate higher-security inmates. In other words, a medium-security Category C facility holding those prisoners deemed unlikely to try to escape will be built with all the security paraphernalia and controlling of movement associated with a high-security Category B institution designed to hold prisoners for whom the potential for escape should be made very difficult. This combination of warehousing and controlled movement represents a new and insidious kind of Hell, in the US as in the UK, as Victor Hassine (2011) underlines. After describing the bleak environments, dark tomb-like spaces and deafening noise of several old-style jails in which he was housed, Hassine described how the brand-new SCI Albion Pennsylvania, built in the 1990s, appeared (initially at least) to be the most comfortable, best designed, and most attractive prison he had ever seen; 'an ocean of plush green fields of grass with handsome geometric outcroppings of earth-toned brick buildings...generously spaced...to create an eye-pleasing and harmonious vision of tranquility that evoked safety and relaxation' (2011, pp. 113–4). Looking like it could work as a rehabilitative prison, SCI Albion is in fact the 'least effective prison of all', Hassine declares:

> It is a dysfunctional, mean-spirited facility that callously steeps you in despair while it lavishes you with physical comfort. Albion provides the inmate a sterile environment with faceless bells and voices precisely controlling time and movement for no apparent purpose other than order. It is a place where everyone is suspicious of each other and superficial friendliness is all that can exist. It is a place where perception is the only reality that matters and where induced poverty is used to generate illusory wealth (2011, p. 125).

This is the kind of model now followed in England and Wales. In the new prison warehouses, staffing costs are minimized; prisoner education, training, and work are limited; prisoners are locked in their cells for increasingly lengthy periods with 'privileges' such as in-cell phones; and prisoner homicides, suicides, and sexual assaults are rising (Williams 2014).

My field notes, recording my first visit to a new privately-run prison in England, illustrate the similarities between new-build facilities in England and America:

> Superficially it's 'nice' enough, but the atmosphere is peculiar. The [prison] complex is vast—it feels like a small town with 'streets' connecting the buildings and a high, yellow mesh fence everywhere you look. It's easy to become disoriented because it all looks the same—it's like Toy Town or an architect's model come to life. Except there is nothing 'playful' or vivid about it. It feels completely unreal. Artificial and sterile...numbing in its blandness. No landscaping or trees so no birds or wildlife. No litter, no people visible. Really odd. Sensory deprivation made to seem acceptable (Author, field note, 24th May 2013).

It might be surprising to some that levels of assault, suicide, and mental illness are rising in the very prisons characterized by the press as 'holiday camps'. Yet the kind of 'privileges' that give rise to such newspaper reports mask the harms that these 'warehouses in disguise' may inflict. Connection to the outside world via an in-cell phone or video link (to family overseas, to lawyers, and to court hearings) may be dressed up as a 'perk', but they make a poor substitute for real, human, interpersonal connection. The combination, then, of bland, sterile architecture and a regime that minimizes costs by reducing prisoner association time and authorizing staffing-at-a-distance via TV monitors, produce a sterile and dehumanizing atmosphere. As Hassine notes, such prisons take on a manufactured, assembly-line quality comparable to an ant farm, beneath which lies a 'violence and crushing hopelessness the trapped ants are actually forced to endure...more hopeless and indifferent than any prison' (Hassine 2011, p. 119).

An alternative approach

> Waves crash on to the beach, birds sing in clear blue skies and an idyllic nature reserve stretches as far as the eye can see. But this is no exotic holiday destination, it's Bastøy Prison, home to some of the most notorious criminals in Norway (*Mirror.co.uk* 2007).

Hassine's poignant observations about the seemingly benign SCI Albion alert us to the perils of architectural determinism and remind us that the success of any prison design must be viewed within the context of its operational dimensions, as well as the prevailing climate of opinion regarding prisons and prisoners. Even prisons which appear, to the outsider at least, relatively humane are rendered hellish by the extreme spatial and temporal limits they place on the confined, and by the close proximity in which individuals have to live with others not of their choosing. As Jean-Paul Sartre (1944) observed, Hell is other people, and there may be no more vivid expression of this than the prison, whether it is in a deeply conservative US state or on a Norwegian prison island.

Nonetheless, the design process is, as Wener notes, 'the wedge that forces the system to think through its approach and review, restate, or redevelop its philosophy of criminal justice' (2012, p. 7). In other parts of the world—in which the 'new punitiveness' of the US and UK has not taken hold—prison designers have focused on the rehabilitative function of imprisonment and have experimented with progressive and highly stylized forms of penal architecture. There, internal prison spaces exhibit soft furnishings, color zoning, maximum exploitation of natural light, displays of art and sculpture, and views of nature through vista windows without bars. Arguably, Bastøy, the Norwegian island prison, is the most famous custodial environment in Europe. With its simple wooden accommodation, stunning setting and eco-philosophy, it resembles—superficially at least—a tranquil holiday retreat. However, the prison usually held up as being a 'model' of international best practice in penal architecture and design is Halden in Norway, a high-security facility, opened in 2009. The first prison to employ interior designers, Halden's varied color palettes, natural construction materials, emphasis on maximizing daylight (there are no bars on any windows), and location in a scenic forest might be regarded as a physical manifestation of the Norwegian prison system's focus on human rights and normalization: it is, says the governor, 'the world's most humane prison' (Adams 2010).

Now, a number of other countries are following Norway's lead and building humane, sensuous, architecturally innovative facilities. In some cases, this approach goes well beyond avoiding an institutional feel and aims to design prisons that—perhaps not uncontroversially—might be described as beautiful. Architects' websites give a flavor not only of the leading-edge designs being employed but also the penal philosophies underpinning them (Moran et al. forthcoming). For example, a new state prison on the island of Falster in Denmark is to be built by C. F. Møller. They say:

We have deliberately created a very varied and stimulating environment of different spaces and landscape features—hopefully this will contribute to the re-socialization of the individual and to create renewed confidence in the community and mutual respect for society as a whole (Warmann 2010).

Another Danish architectural company, Schmidt Hammer Lassen, has won the competition to design Greenland's first closed prison, which aims to be the 'world's most scenic prison'. Set within a stunning, rugged landscape, the prison will exploit the 'contrast between the rough and the beautiful':

The whole idea behind the project is to add qualities to the complex that will enhance rehabilitation and diminish physical and psychological violence... The thought process behind this is that access to nature—watching the clouds, birds, daylight, weather and so on, can aid in rehabilitation (Furuto 2013).

Meanwhile, OOIIO Architecture set out to design a women's prison in Iceland that 'doesn't look like a prison, forgetting about dark spaces, small cells, and ugly grey concrete walls...we based the building design on natural light, open spaces, and natural green materials like peat, grass and flowers' (OOIIO Architecture 2012). Instead of designing one large building (like a 'typical repressive old prison'), they decided to break it into several 'human-scale, connected' pavilions, which must be efficient and functional to enable the spatial separation of prisoners, but must also have 'natural light and exterior views, to increase the feeling of freedom'. The architects also had an eye to the speed and ease of construction and to the eco standards of the building, planning to draw upon Icelandic vernacular architecture to insulate the building. With a facade constructed from peat-filled cages planted with local flowers and grasses, they intended to deliver a building 'that changes with the seasons', making prison life 'less monotonous and more human and natural related' (OOIIO Architecture 2012).

Conclusion

The sole purpose of prisons is not just any human waste disposal but a final, definitive disposal. Once rejected, forever rejected (Bauman 2004, p. 86).

Whether the lofty aesthetic considerations hailed by architects are significant matters of concern to prisoners is a moot point, although, as noted earlier, prisoner autobiographies suggest that architecture and design are intrinsically related to the pain and harms inflicted by incarceration. Perhaps, then, the kind of designs noted above in Norway, Iceland, and Denmark develop an alphabet of openness, flexibility, and 'humane' treatment, rather than one of fear. Perhaps they even encourage a different kind of inhabitation than their English and US counterparts: one that encourages intellectual creativity and maturity.

But as some countries of Northern Europe seek novel and creative solutions to the pains of imprisonment, both the US and UK appear to be returning to medieval ideas about expressive forms of punishment meted out by harsh but just authorities. In these countries, the popular media's construction of prisoners as 'evil monsters' or 'human waste' makes 'hellish' prisons the most appropriate containers for them and images of subterranean, tomb-like, penal 'hell-holes' play a large role in popular imagination. Prisons are necessarily heavily symbolic institutions, and the popular media perpetuate the notion that people commit crimes because 'they' are not like 'us'. In this context, Dante's depiction of eternal suffering may be unremittingly and mesmerizingly cruel, but arguably it is regarded by society at large as a 'half-desirable destination' (Nellis 2006, p. 226) for those designated 'evil'.

Moreover, the notion of a benign God who ordains cruel punishment is one that governments of liberal democracies hold dear. Divine justice is immutable, and there can be no more graphic and disturbing rendition of 'do the crime, do the time' (and be prepared to do the time in the circles of Hell) than *Inferno*. It is this moral absolutism that permeates cultural ideas about offenders and punishment. The folklorist images of devils and demons that formerly soaked up diffuse security fears have been transformed into images that construct the 'outsider' status of perpetrators as unequivocal and incontestable (Bauman 2004). Offenders are beyond redemption, human waste that must be banished to a fitting location. Consequently, while capital punishment is unlikely to ever be reintroduced in the UK and the 17 US states that do not currently have an enforceable death penalty, eternal damnation finds form in penal Hell—the ultimate punishment for those offenders designated the 'worst of the worst'.

Notes

1 Limitations of space preclude an analysis of the racial and ethnic dimensions of mass imprisonment here, but I provide an extended and more detailed analysis of prison Hell and cultural connotations of lightness and darkness as they

pertain to the racial demographics of the prison population in Jewkes, 2014, 'Punishment in black and white: penal 'hell-holes', popular media and mass incarceration', *Atlantic Journal of Communication* special issue on 'Reframing Race and Justice in the Age of Mass Incarceration' vol. 22, no. 1, pp. 42–60.

2   ESRC Standard Grant ES/K011081/1 'Fear-suffused environments' or potential to rehabilitate? Prison architecture, design and technology and the lived experience of carceral spaces' (with Dominique Moran, School of Geography, Earth and Environmental Sciences, University of Birmingham, and Jennifer Turner, Department of Criminology, University of Leicester).

3   The pagination of this quote from Dante's *Inferno* should be read as follows: the first number indicates the canto, and the second the lines the quote comes from in the designated canto.

4   This maxim, in modern times most frequently used in relation to the Holocaust, might also be pertinent to the crisis facing the prison systems of the US and UK. An anonymous reviewer of a book proposal for the *Palgrave Studies in Prisons and Penology* series wrote: 'Of all the things future generations will be shocked with in regards to our use of imprisonment in 2012 (and there is much to shock), probably the starkest will be the question of "where were all the voices shouting 'what is going on here?'"

5   A detailed news archive of the problems and abuses uncovered can be found at the *LA Times* website: http://www.latimes.com/local/la-me-jails-sg-storygallery .html.

6   This restriction was subsequently challenged by a prisoner and overturned by the high court, but not before several authors took revenge on the minister for banning books being sent to prisoners in new imaginings of Dante's *Inferno*. Announcing that they would impale him on their pens, Australian novelist Kathy Lette told the *New York Times* that her next book will feature a corrupt lawyer named after the British Minister of Justice who ends up in a prison where he is deprived of reading matter and goes insane. A *Guardian* blog reported this story under the headline 'Fire, torment and villainy await Chris Grayling in novel punishment for prison book ban' (http://www.theguardian .com/books/booksblog/2014/jul/04/chris-grayling-prison-book-ban-novelist -revenge-plots). Meanwhile, British novelist Margaret Drabble said that she would be including Grayling in her forthcoming novel titled *Death by Fire*, adding 'He could die in the fire' (http://www.politics.co.uk/news/2014/07/07/ author-s-new-book-features-villain-called-chris-grayling).

References

Adams, WL 2010, 'Norway builds the world's most humane prison', *Time Magazine*, 10 May. Available from: <(http://content.time.com/time/magazine/article/ 0,9171,1986002,00.html>. [10 January 2015].

Alighieri, D & Kirkpatrick, R 2006, *Inferno: the Divine Comedy I*, Penguin, London.

Alexander, M 2010, *The new Jim Crow: mass incarceration in the age of colorblindness*, The New Press, New York.

Bauman, Z 2004, *Wasted lives: modernity and its outcasts*, Polity, Cambridge.

Bauman, Z & Donskis, L 2013, *Moral blindness: the loss of sensitivity in liquid modernity*, Polity, Cambridge.

Brown, D & Wilkie, M (eds) 2002, *Prisoners as citizens: human rights in Australian prisons*, Federation Press, Australia.

Burge, J 2010, *Dante's invention*, The History Press, Stroud.

Davis, A 2000, 'From the convict lease system to the super-max prison', in *States of confinement: policing, detention, and prison*, ed J James, St. Martin's Press, New York, pp. 60–75.

Dolovich, S 2011, 'Creating the permanent prisoner', in *Life without parole: America's new death penalty*, eds CJ Ogletree & A Sarat, NYU Press, New York.

Drake, D 2012, *Prisons, punishment and the pursuit of security*, Palgrave, Basingstoke.

Dunt, I 2014, 'Even the MoJ admits it: the prison system under Grayling is falling apart', *politics.co.uk*, 31 July. Available from: <http://www.politics.co.uk>. [31 July 2014].

Furuto, A 2013, 'Ny Anstalt correctional facility winning proposal / Schmidt Hammer Lassen architects', *ArchDaily*, 20 May. Available from: <http://www .archdaily.com/375056/ny-anstalt-correctional-facility-winning-proposal-schmidt -hammer-lassen-architects/>. [10 January 2015].

Hall, S, Critcher, C, Jefferson, T, Clarke, J & Roberts, B (eds) 1978, *Policing the crisis: mugging, the state and law and order*, Macmillan, London.

Hancock, P & Jewkes, Y 2010, 'Architectures of incarceration: the spatial pains of imprisonment', *Punishment & Society*, vol. 13, no. 5, pp. 611–29.

Hartnett, SJ, Wood, JK & McCann, BJ 2011, 'Turning silence into speech and action: prison activism and the pedagogy of empowered citizenship, *Communication and Critical/Cultural Studies*, vol. 8, no. 4, pp. 331–52.

Hassine, V 2011, *Life without parole: living and dying in prison today*, 5th edn, Oxford University Press, New York.

Her Majesty's Prison Service [HMPS] 2001, *Prison service order 1900: certified prisoner accommodation*, HMPS, London.

Jewkes, Y 2013, 'On carceral space and agency', in *Carceral spaces: mobility and agency in imprisonment and migrant detention*, eds D Moran, D, N Gill & D Conlon, Ashgate, Farnham.

Jewkes, Y & Moran, D 2014, 'Should prison architecture be brutal, bland or beautiful?', *Scottish Justice Matters*, vol. 2, no. 1, pp. 8–11.

Johnston, N 2000, *Forms of constraint: a history of prison architecture*, University of Illinois Press, Urbana, IL.

Jones, J 2011, 'Lines of fire: Dante's vision of hell still has an afterlife', *The Guardian* 5 May. Available from: <http://www.theguardian.com/artanddesign/jonathan jonesblog/ 2011/may/05/dante-hell-poetry-divine-comedy>. [01 February 2013].

Leonard, T 2012, 'Is Hook at last heading for hell?', *Daily Mail* 11 October. Available from: <http://www.dailymail.co.uk/news/article-2216530/Tom-Leonard-Abu-Hamza-New-York-Is-Hook-heading-Hell.html>. [11 January 2015].

Liebling, A with Arnold, H 2004, *Prisons and their moral performance: a study of values, quality, and prison life*, Oxford University Press, Oxford.

Liebling, A, Arnold, H & Straub, C 2011, *An exploration of staff-prisoner relationships at HMP Whitemoor: twelve years on*, MOJ, London.

Loader, I 2009, 'Ice cream and incarceration: on appetites or security and punishment', *Punishment & Society*, vol. 11, no. 2, pp. 241–257.

Martinson, R 1974, 'What works? Questions and answers about prison reform', *Public Interest*, vol. 35 (Spring), pp. 22–54.

Mirror.co.uk 2012, 'Organic porridge', *Mirror* 10 December. Available from: <http:// www.mirror.co.uk/news/uk-news/organic-porridge-527257>. [11 January 2015].

Moran, D & Jewkes, Y forthcoming, 'Linking the carceral and the punitive state: researching prison architecture, design, technology and the lived experience of carceral space', *Annales de la Geographie*.

Moran, D, Jewkes, Y & Turner, J forthcoming, 'Prison design and carceral space', in *Handbook on Prisons*, 2nd edn, eds Y Jewkes, J Bennett & B Crewe, Routledge, London.

Morris, N 1974, *Future of imprisonment*, University of Chicago Press, Chicago.

Nellis, M 2005, 'Future punishment in American science fiction films', in *Captured by the media*, ed P Mason, Willan Publishing, Cullompton.

Novek, EM 2005, 'Heaven, hell, and here: understanding the impact of incarceration through a prison newspaper, *Critical Studies in Media Communication*, vol. 22, no. 4, pp. 281–301.

OOIIO Architecture 2012, 'Female prison in Iceland', *OOIIO Architecture website*. Available from: < http://www.ooiio.com/en/portfolio/female-prison-iceland/>. [2 February 2014].

Piacentini, L 2005, 'Cultural talk and other intimate acquaintances with Russian prisons', *Crime Media Culture*, vol. 1, no. 2, pp. 189–208.

Sartre, JP 1944, *No exit*, Vintage Books, London.

Travis, A 2010, 'Prison works, says Theresa May', *The Guardian* December 14. Available from: <http://www.theguardian.com/politics/2010/dec/14/prison-works -says-theresa-may>. [11 January 2015].

US Attorney's Office, Central District of California 2013, *Eighteen charged as a result of federal investigation into corruption and civil rights abuses by members of Los Angeles County Sheriff's Department*, US Attorney's Office, Central District of California. Available from: <http://www.fbi.gov/losangeles/press-releases/2013/ eighteen-charged-as-a-result-of-federal-investigation-into-corruption-and -civil-rights-abuses-by-members-of-los-angeles-county-sheriffs-department>. [11 January 2015].

Wacquant, L 2002, 'The curious eclipse of prison ethnography in the age of mass incarceration', *Ethnography*, vol. 3, no. 4, pp. 371–397.

Warmann, C 2010, 'Danish state prison by C.F. Møller', *Dezeen Magazine*, 7 January. Available from: <http://www.dezeen.com/2011/01/07/danish-state-prison-by-c -f-m%C3%B8ller/>. [10 January 2015].

Wener, RE 2012, *The environmental psychology of prisons and jails: creating humane spaces in secure settings*, Cambridge University Press, Cambridge.

Williams, Z. (2014) 'Prisoner suicides: the dire cost of Tory tough-guy posturing on crime', *The Guardian* 15 September. Available from: <http://www.theguardian .com>. [15 September 2014].

Wortley, R 2002, *Situational prison control: crime prevention in correctional institutions*, Cambridge University Press, Cambridge.

2
The Limits of Punishment

Emma Kaufman, Yale Law School
Sam Weiss, Ford Foundation Fellow, American Civil Liberties Union Center for Justice

Structures of punishment are infused with anxiety about national belonging. Since the mid-1990s, governments in the United States, Australia, and much of Western Europe have embraced the practice of immigration detention, building quasi-prisons for non-citizens at a breakneck pace (see Bacon 2005; Bosworth 2007; Kelly 2005; National Immigration Forum 2013). Criminal justice systems have also warped under the pressure of border control. In the past five years alone, both the United States and the United Kingdom have established special prisons to hold foreign nationals serving criminal sentences (Guttin 2010; Greene & Mazon 2012). In Britain, non-citizens convicted of criminal offenses are transferred to prisons 'embedded' with border agents (Kaufman 2013). In the US, more than half of last year's roughly 400,000 deportations started when a border agent entered a prison or a jail (American Immigration Council 2013).

These practices unfold at the edges of punishment. In the formal language of the law, many carceral activities are classified as regulation rather than punishment. Holding a detainee in a freezing jail cell (Americans for Immigrant Justice 2013), transferring a long-term resident to a prison 3,000 miles from home (Lonegan 2006), denying non-citizens access to rehabilitative programs (Bhui 2004; Guttin 2010): none of these practices is punishment in technical, legal terms. Every day, on both sides of the Atlantic, some of the most pernicious and punitive aspects of late modern incarceration take place beyond punishment, in the gray zone of the civil sanction.

This chapter explores the line between punishment and regulation. Drawing on fieldwork in Britain and the United States, we critique the growing gap between lived and legal notions of punishment. The chapter focuses in particular on non-citizens convicted of criminal offenses, a group whose experiences bring the punitive aspects of regulation to life. Building from prisoners' testimonies, we assert that incarceration—whether in a detention center, a prison, or any facility in between—is punishment for the people subject to it.

In making this claim, the chapter wades into an ongoing conversation about the proper scope of punishment. In recent years, legal scholars and criminologists have debated the merits of a narrow definition of punishment. Some argue that cabined legal definitions ensure procedural protections (see, e.g., Ashworth & Zedner 2014; Zedner 2013). Others contend that legal terms ought to expand to reflect lived experience (see, e.g., Bosworth & Turnbull this volume; Hernández 2014). This chapter joins that debate, and aims to advance it, by asking how the law comes to define carceral practices in ways that disguise their punitive force. Turning to landmark legal cases, we argue that the limits of punishment enable increasingly harsh carceral regimes.

This argument proceeds in three parts. Part I maps the boundary between civil and criminal sanctions. Part II draws on ethnographic fieldwork to contend that prolonged incarceration is punitive, no matter how courts define it. This second part of the chapter presents prisoners' testimonies about incarceration, and specifically, how confinement becomes a mode of punishment for having the 'wrong kind' of identity. Part III returns to the law to examine cases in which lived experience creeps into the formal definition of punishment. Paying close attention to the text of legal opinions, we conclude that the law, while often a limiting force, can also create space for a more empathetic conception of punishment.

Before advancing that claim, a methodological caveat is in order. This chapter draws on work by authors trained in different disciplines, namely sociology and law. It contains, on one hand, testimonies from a yearlong ethnographic study of British prisons, and on the other, observations from several concentrated months of work in a clinic based in an American law school. These are two quite distinct contexts of punishment; they clash at times, and each comes with its own academic mores. Ethnography permits more first-hand narrative, but lives at a distance from the law. The law shapes the possibilities of punishment, but the dictates of client confidentiality affect how personal and rich legal storytelling can be. Ultimately, this chapter displays the norms of our respective disciplines as much as the boundaries of punishment. In this respect, it encourages scholars and critics of incarceration to consider how interdisciplinary thinking might make punishment less extreme.

The rise of regulation

In the law, punishment has sharply defined boundaries. Anglo-American legal systems draw a formal distinction between criminal and civil proceedings and attach a slew of consequences to the difference between the two. Technically, sanctions that flow from the criminal law constitute punishment and cannot be imposed without certain protections, such as a lawyer. Sanctions derived from civil law, on the other hand, are forms of regulation, which come with fewer procedural guarantees.

This distinction can produce odd outcomes. Under the legal definition of punishment, many measures that look and feel punitive are forms of regulation. Lifetime placement on a sex offender registry (Carpenter & Beverlin 2012), indefinite incarceration in a mental institution (Tsesis 2011), permanent termination of parental rights (Buss 2002), discipline inside prisons (Robertson 1991), and imprisonment for failure to follow a court order (Patterson 2008) are all civil sanctions. The entire system of immigration detention—a system that puts hundreds of thousands of people behind bars each year—is civil (Simanski & Sapp 2012). Anglo-American law also treats deportation, a practice often preceded by incarceration and increasingly tied to the commission of a crime, as an instance of regulation (Bosworth & Kaufman 2011; see also Bosworth & Turnbull this volume). As a result, migrants facing expulsion, parents facing dissolution of their rights, and people subject to confinement in isolation can be sanctioned without lawyers, a jury trial, or a conviction by proof beyond a reasonable doubt (*In re Winship* 1970; see also Markowitz 2008; Reiter & Blair this volume). In these ways and others, rights cling to the borders of punishment.

This claim only extends so far. Particularly in the American legal system, reality tempers strong arguments about the protections that come with the criminal law. The distinction between punishment and regulation seems less stark in the context of a legal system in which most criminal defendants fail to receive the basic safeguards promised in the US Constitution. As capital defense attorney Steve Bright recently noted, 'every day in thousands of courtrooms across the nation...the right to counsel is violated' (Bright & Sanneh 2013, p. 2152). Criminal defendants in the United States are routinely convicted en masse, without adequate counsel or without lawyers at all. America's under-resourced criminal justice system makes it almost ironic to insist that classes of civil defendants ought to receive 'criminal' protections.

Yet it remains true that defining a sanction as civil insulates it from whole portions of the Constitution, and in a broader context, from

European legal protections (see, e.g., Article 3 of the European Convention on Human Rights). While etching a line between criminal and civil proceedings does not ensure the realization of rights, it does determine the kind of rights claims a person can make. The law is an expressive social force—a pronouncement about how justice ought to be conceived as much as a practical guarantee—and the civil-criminal divide produces a class of remarkably punitive 'regulations' (Sunstein 1996). In this sense, the line between punishment and regulation is both generative and surreal.

At the same time, the borders of punishment have concrete consequences for real people. The legal definition of punishment affects the nature of incarceration regimes, and in the case of border control, enables the existence of a vast network of non-criminal detention centers. In the United States, the Department of Homeland Security currently operates a web of immigration detention centers, which hold nearly 400,000 people a year, and more than 30,000 on any given day. Some of these detention centers are standalone facilities; others are prison wings or institutions run by private contractors. In the United Kingdom, 12 facilities constitute their own immigration detention estate, and British prisons hold a number of detainees under immigration powers (Kaufman forthcoming 2015). In both countries, immigration detention is a growing practice.

A narrow definition of punishment is crucial to the survival of these facilities. If immigration detention were punishment rather than regulation, detainees would have claims to the legal protections that accompany the threat of punishment. Those claims might not win in a court—look no further than the conditions in America's prisons to see the law's limits—but calling detention punishment would, at a minimum, prompt thousands of lawsuits and impose immense costs on governments that wish to detain immigrants. Perhaps more to the point, classifying immigration detention as punishment would render the detention centers scattered across the US and UK conceptually incoherent. Detention centers exist in contrast to prisons; we need them, the argument goes, because detention is different than punishment. The strict borders between regulation and punishment get this argument—and the jobs, institutions, and contracts that depend on detention—off the ground.

The boundaries of punishment also encourage prisons to become more like detention centers. Over the past two decades, as the United States government has rushed to build immigration 'removal' centers, penal institutions across the country have imported the principles of border control directly into the criminal justice system. Scholars have documented the ways in which migration control seeps into prison practices (Bosworth & Kaufman 2011; Eagly 2013; Legomsky 2007; Lynch this volume; McLeod 2012). As they note, the US government has recently expanded its effort to use prisons to identify and deport foreign nationals. Under the auspices of its 'Criminal Alien Program', the Department of Homeland Security now sends immigration agents into every state and federal prison in the country (American Immigration Council 2013). The Bureau of Prisons, which runs America's federal penal institutions, also operates 13 prisons that hold solely non-citizens serving criminal sentences (Barry 2011). Prisons, the paradigmatic institutions of punishment, have become key participants in border regulation.

The United Kingdom has witnessed a parallel transformation of its prison system (Kaufman 2013). Since 2009, the British Prison Service has deputized and trained its officers to act as quasi-immigration agents. Today, prison officials in England and Wales routinely work with the UK Border Agency to identify and report prisoners who might be subject to deportation. The British government sends immigration agents into prisons to find non-citizens, and, like the United States, has established 'foreign-national only' prisons to hold people subject to 'removal' during their criminal terms. In both countries, penal institutions are increasingly integrated into the migration control apparatus.

This development, too, depends on the limits of punishment. Because migration control is not legally punishment, doing migration control behind bars is merely a regulatory shift—a change in practice, rather than a change in kind. The law, with its formalist boundaries and counterintuitive distinctions, permits pockets of 'regulation' to rise up in the interstices of punishment. Both in and outside of prisons, harsh carceral regimes are able to emerge and expand precisely because they serve non-punitive ends. One of the more extreme aspects of much 21st century punishment, then, is that it is not punishment at all.

Punishing identity

Despite legal doctrine, incarceration often feels punitive to the people confined in prisons and detention centers. We learned this in practice through ethnographic fieldwork in British prisons and clinical work at Harvard Law School. Beginning in 2010, one of us spent close to a year interviewing more than 150 foreign nationals in five men's prisons in England. Those interviews, some of which are reproduced here, were part of a broader project on the punishment of non-citizens in Britain

(Kaufman forthcoming 2015).[1] The other half of this chapter stems from advocacy in an American clinic devoted to helping people navigate the immigration consequences of criminal convictions. Given the norms of legal representation, these clients' words remain confidential, but their experiences suggest an equally glaring gap between life and law.

In Britain, interviewees were serving criminal sentences, often for offenses unrelated to migration, but prison authorities had identified them as non-citizens. Once 'flagged' as foreign nationals, these prisoners entered a separate system within the larger British prison estate. In virtue of their citizenship status, all foreign nationals imprisoned in England and Wales are required to attend meetings in which border agents fingerprint, photograph, and question them. Prisoners with fewer than five years left on their criminal sentences can also be sent to one of Britain's newly established 'all-foreign' prisons, where prison staff work full time with immigration officials to coordinate the deportation process (Kaufman 2013).

Prisoners subject to these 'regulatory' regimes often felt that they were being punished for their nationality rather than their criminal offense. In interviews, the distinction between punishment and migration control blurred: 'They just want you to feel punishment. They just want to punish foreign nationals', one man, who asked to remain anonymous, explained. Another prisoner, Rus, was incarcerated for a drug offense but felt he was being punished for having 'abnormal' citizenship. Other prisoners described similar experiences:

> I think all 300 prisoners here would say they're being punished because they're foreign (George, a prisoner in an 'all-foreign' prison) (Kaufman forthcoming 2015).[2]

> Punishment? Yes, definitely. That's their tactic. Immigration separates you from your family—literally, they say that—so that you just sign and go (Anonymous).

While prisoners had divergent narratives and senses of whether or not Britain was home, they overwhelmingly felt that their treatment in prison was a form of punishment for their citizenship status, and at a more basic level, for who they were.

People facing deportation from the United States described a similar slippage between punishment and border control. Clients in the legal clinic, who were convicted of criminal offenses, wrote to lawyers seeking information and advice about what would happen to them in the justice system. In the United States, deportation begins with a Notice to Appear, a piece of paper that informs people that they must report to court for a hearing on their immigration status. Many of the clinic's clients received this notice while serving a criminal sentence. From behind bars, they learned that they would not leave prison; instead, on their release date, they would be transferred to a different but nearly indistinguishable carceral facility. Legal advisors explained that deportation is mandatory for almost everyone convicted of certain offenses and that detention, though not technically punitive, flows directly from criminal confinement. Yet, as one carceral institution bled into another, people often perceived detention as a further aspect and a seamless continuation of their punishment.

In some cases, non-citizen prisoners in the United States also experienced harsher punishment during their criminal time. Many American prison systems have reacted to the rise of migration control by integrating citizenship into their existing classification regimes. As a result, prisoners who receive a Notice to Appear often find that their custody status—whether minimum, medium, or maximum security—increases without any change in their behavior. Prisoners discover, in other words, that they have gone from a lower to a higher security level not because of their actions, or even their crime, but because the US government has signed an immigration document. Prisoners with heightened custody statuses live in more regimented and violent areas of prisons, with less privacy and, in some cases, less access to prison programs such as drug treatment or continuing education. Prisoners can also be forbidden from transferring to other less punitive facilities, including halfway houses, because they are non-citizens. As these respondents demonstrate, citizenship shapes imprisonment.

The relationship between citizenship and confinement is similarly fraught in immigration detention centers. Despite formidable barriers to access, scholars and human rights groups have documented the experience of incarceration in both American (ACLU of Arizona 2011; Caldwell 2013; Golash-Boza 2010; Human Rights First 2011) and British (Bosworth 2014) detention centers. Detainees in these facilities often present confinement as a mode of punishment (See Bosworth and Turnbull in this volume). In a report from the Center for Victims of Torture, for instance, a detainee compared her incarceration to criminal imprisonment: 'You are treated like a prisoner and threatened with solitary confinement' (2013). In another study, ethnographer Tanya Golash-Boza noted that most of the 156 detainees she interviewed felt that they were 'treated like prisoners, as if they were in a prison.' Golash-Boza concluded that 'nearly all of the deportees...felt as through their deportation was punishment' (Golash-Boza 2010).

The conditions inside detention centers contribute to the impression that these spaces are built to punish. The American Civil Liberties Union reports that most detention centers in the US have solitary confinement units and that unhealthy food, tainted water, overcrowding, and dangerous temperatures are common (ACLU of Massachusetts 2009). In short-term holding facilities along the US-Mexican border, Customs and Border Patrol agents place detainees in cells known as 'iceboxes', where temperatures drop below freezing (Americans for Immigrant Justice 2013). Even in less bleak facilities, the daily experience of confinement—of waking, living, and sleeping in a cell—has fundamentally punitive overtones. In the United States, detainees are routinely held in jails, and in facilities that look just like them. In England and Wales, some detention centers are constructed to the literal model of Category B (medium-security) prisons (Bosworth 2012). For centuries, criminologists have argued that the architecture of confinement is constitutive of its purpose and place in society (Bentham 2011; Foucault 2005; see also Jewkes in this volume). It is intuitive that migrants would experience detention in these spaces as punishment.

People facing deportation also describe the prospect of expulsion as a punishment of its own. In Britain, prisoners often reported that the hardest part of being identified as a foreign national was not that it led to additional incarceration, but that it changed the way they viewed themselves. One prisoner, Damian, had grown up in the United Kingdom and had conceived of himself as British for his entire life. His perspective changed after he was incarcerated:

> It wasn't until I got to prison that I realized I wasn't British. When all this started, they made me realize I wasn't British (Kaufman forthcoming 2015).

Damien was not imprisoned for an immigration offense, but the UK Border Agency identified him as a non-citizen shortly after he entered prison. Over time, he said, being treated as a foreign national by immigration agents and prison officers shifted his view of home.

George, another prisoner in a British prison, also experienced incarceration as a transformation in his sense of self. In one interview, George described how prison affected his national identity:

> If you asked me before I would've said I was Ghanaian. If you asked my mindset, my identity, I would've said Ghanaian. But since being here I've realized I'm not Ghanaian; I don't fit in with the Ghanaians. But I'm

not English. It messes with my identity. I've started questioning who exactly I am. I'm not Ghanaian; we have totally different aspirations. Before I would've said, 'no, I'm not English'. But I'm bloody English now and I have to accept it (Kaufman forthcoming 2015).

George was incarcerated in an 'all-foreign' prison in the southeast of England. Ironically, living in a space designated for foreigners affirmed his sense of Englishness.

Patrick, who was imprisoned in a Category A (maximum-security) prison in the center of England, felt neither British nor foreign during his incarceration. 'I wanna go home to my family', he explained:

That's the only home I know. I don't know what they're thinking. If I went to Congo, they'd call me a foreigner. Here I'm a foreigner; there I'm a foreigner. I don't know (Kaufman forthcoming 2015).

These testimonies capture the extent to which border control operates through identity. For prisoners like Patrick, George, and Damian, the meaning of punishment depends less on the criminal law than on the state's power to determine who they are.

Though these are only a few narratives from a year of research, they capture a common sense that regulating migration is, at its base, about policing the boundaries of belonging and punishing those who fail to conform. Research by American ethnographers hints at the same conclusion. In their writing on the conditions and experience of confinement in the United States, many scholars have recounted how the prospect of deportation alters personal and national identity (Brotherton & Kretsedemas 2008; Coutin 2005). Sociologists David Brotherton and Luis Barrios have written of the 'social-psychological crisis' that afflicts deportees who conceive of themselves as American, yet experience deportation to places they cannot identify as home (2009). In a similar vein, Barbara Yngvesson and Susan Bibler Coutin (2006) describe conflicts of subjectivity and self in interviews with long-term residents of the United States who were deported to El Salvador. Their work suggests that, whether in prisons or detention centers, the regulation of migration is one way to discipline identity.

Each of these narratives is contextual. Combining accounts from people incarcerated in different facilities and countries can be disjointed, and perhaps misleading. Comparing confinement in Britain and the United States threatens to flatten the degree to which incarceration is a particular cultural and historical practice. The legacies of migration into and out of these countries, and the relationship between xenophobia and national identity in each, are crucial to understanding the nature of contemporary confinement (Hernández 2006; Kaufman forthcoming 2015). It is also dangerous to pull quotations from months of fieldwork and to summarize on behalf of clients whose experiences are distinct. Yet, notwithstanding these limitations, the comparison between countries and facilities offers a wider glimpse of punishment in an era of citizenship paranoia.

There are clear echoes across the Atlantic in the stories people tell at the intersection of punishment and border control. Prisoners in Britain and the United States are subject to regimes, first in prisons and then in detention centers, in which citizenship affects the quality, nature, and duration of confinement. Even brief accounts of American and British penal practices demonstrate the intricate and growing relationship between crime and migration control. Caught at the center of these carceral trends, foreign nationals feel little difference between punishment and regulation. For people sent to segregated prisons, denied access to halfway houses, and separated from their families because of their nationality, the legal definition of punishment is its own mode of alienation.

Legal fiction

Legal scholars and criminologists often critique the lines between imprisonment, detention, and deportation (See Markowitz 2008; Hernández 2014). Citing the realities of confinement, ethnographers note that the conceptual distinctions drawn in statutes rarely make sense in people's lives (Markowitz 2008; Hernández 2014). As a result, the law delegitimizes non-citizens' experiences and fails to capture both the breadth and the texture of incarceration in nominally 'civil' spaces. Yet the law of punishment need not be so limited. Law is not an inherently or even consistently impersonal force. To the contrary, the way courts police the boundaries of punishment suggests that lived experiences shape the law, surfacing even where legal doctrines seem most out of touch with reality.

As a sociological matter, the line between punishment and regulation develops from the relationship between courts and political bodies. American law offers a particularly clear example of this institutional dynamic. In the United States, judges define the term punishment by focusing on politicians' intentions. To decide whether a practice counts as regulation or punishment, American courts ask whether the lawmakers that created it had a preference for one label or another (*United States v. Ward* 1980). Judges consider, in other words, whether the politicians who establish sex offender registries, detention centers, and specialized prisons want those practices to be called punishment. This method is extraordinarily deferential: in general, if legislators intend a sanction to be regulatory, it is; if they intend to create a punishment, they can. Courts have the power to interpret laws, and judges can conclude that a sanction is simply too punitive to be civil, but this rarely happens. Instead, the line between punishment and regulation tends to lie wherever politicians draw it.

Judges have resisted this approach to punishment for as long as it has existed. As early as 1896, one American Supreme Court Justice called the purportedly regulatory practice of sentencing migrants facing deportation to hard labor 'not only punishment, but punishment infamous in its character' (*Wong Wing v. United States* 1896). Half a century later, Justices clashed over a case involving Ignatz Mezei, an eastern European migrant who was denied entry at the border of the United States (*Shaughnessy v. United States ex rel. Mezei* 1953). No country would accept Mr. Mezei, and he was stranded at Ellis Island for nearly two years. Ultimately, the Supreme Court decided that his detention fell within Congress's 'plenary power' to regulate migration. Justice Robert Jackson excoriated the decision:

> Realistically, this man is incarcerated by a combination of forces which keeps him as effectually as a prisoner, the dominant and proximate of these forces being the United States immigration authority. It overworks legal fiction to say that one is free in law when by the commonest of common sense he is bound.

Thirty years later, Justice Thurgood Marshall would again question the legal boundaries of punishment. In another case about detention—this time, detention pending a criminal trial—Justice Marshall called the distinction between civil and criminal incarceration a 'magical' 'technique for infringing' people's rights (*United States v. Salerno* 1987).

These critiques represent a minority view in American law. Both Justice Marshall and Justice Jackson wrote in dissent, and neither theory of border control has been adopted in the dominant legal discourse. Nonetheless, their opinions reflect a consistent strand of resistance to the idea that incarcerating migrants is a legitimate means of border regulation. While the law can seem Manichean, and often is, legal definitions are also malleable and contested. In cases such as Ignatz Mezei's, judges indict the law for its odd and willing blindness toward the way that punishment feels.

In other instances, lived experience enters the law in tacit fragments. Take, for instance, the practice of sentencing criminal defendants to 'time served'. At any given time, more than half a million people, not yet convicted of any crime, sit in American jails awaiting trial (Minton 2012). As a formal legal matter, such pre-trial detention can only exist if it is regulatory rather than punitive, for the trial is what determines whether the state may punish. Following this logic, and faced with the possibility that the entire detention regime was unlawful, the Supreme Court declared in 1987 that pretrial detention was civil rather than criminal (*Salerno* 1987). Yet, if defendants are convicted at trial, courts typically subtract the time a person spent in pretrial detention from the sentence they impose (Kolber 2013). A prisoner sentenced to two years who spent six months in jail waiting for his trial will thus have his sentence reduced to eighteen months.

In moments like these, the law bears witness to its own erosion. When judges turn time served in detention into a criminal sentence, they retroactively transform civil incarceration into punishment (*Salerno* 1987). This is a performative act of creation. It is also an implicit recognition that punishment is made of lived experience, for detention could not count as part of a criminal sentence unless the two were practically the same.

The transformation of time served is not the only point where the law bends toward intuitive, affective notions of punishment. Courts have also taken a more human approach to detention in several recent cases concerning the treatment of migrants. In 2001, for instance, the US Supreme Court heard the case of Kestutis Zadvydas, a resident slated for deportation on the basis of drug and theft convictions. Zadvydas was born in Germany to Lithuanian parents, but was a citizen of neither country. As happens in many cases of statelessness, the United States attempted to deport him to multiple countries—first Germany and Lithuania, and then the Dominican Republic—but no nation would accept him. In an historic opinion, a closely divided court ruled that detention with no real prospect of 'removal' was unlawful (*Zadvydas v. Davis*, 2001).

Zadvydas' case is stunning for several reasons. For one, it establishes a rule against detention 'pending deportation' beyond six months. This development changed the lives of stateless people detained across the United States (GAO 2004) and set a precedent for places like the UK, where non-citizens who cannot be deported have been detained for upward of six years (Kaufman forthcoming 2015). While the legal structures in Britain and the United States are similar in many ways, including their embrace of a counterintuitive civil-criminal divide, the two systems diverge around the question of how long detention without an end can persist before a court intervenes. In this respect, the British system, so often the moderate alternative to American law, is more extreme.

The *Zadvydas* opinion is also significant because it undermines the distinction between civil and criminal incarceration. Wary of actually crossing the line between punishment and regulation, the US Supreme Court insisted throughout its opinion that detention was 'nonpunitive in purpose and effect' (*Zadvydas* 2001). Yet five Justices borrowed from the language of punishment to cap 'regulatory' detention and ultimately ruled that the government must release detainees it cannot deport. Some judges have critiqued the opinion, arguing that it conflates the law of punishment with regulation of the border (*Zadvydas* 2001, J. Scalia, dissenting). This may be true, but as Thurgood Marshall said thirty years ago, that distinction was 'magical' from the start (*Salerno* 1987). *Zadvydas* did not so much undo the law of punishment as unmask the legal fiction at its heart.

Courts have also imported lived experience into discussions of deportation. To take but one example, in 2010, the Supreme Court encountered Jose Padilla, a lawful permanent resident who had lived in the United States for more than forty years. After Padilla was arrested for transporting marijuana, his lawyer advised him to plead guilty without informing him that the plea made deportation virtually mandatory. Under traditional legal definitions, Padilla's lawyer had no obligation to inform his client about the "civil" consequences of his conviction, including the possibility of deportation. Nonetheless, the Supreme Court declared the attorney's performance ineffective and overturned Padilla's plea (*Padilla v. Kentucky* 2010). The opinion pierced the distinction between civil and criminal penalties:

> We have long recognized that deportation is a particularly severe 'penalty,' but it is not, in a strict sense, a criminal sanction. Although removal proceedings are civil in nature, deportation is nevertheless intimately related to the criminal process....Thus, we find it 'most difficult' to divorce the penalty from the conviction in the deportation context. Moreover, we are quite confident that noncitizen defendants facing a risk of deportation for a particular offense find it even more difficult.

Appealing to the experiences of 'non-citizen defendants', the Court presented deportation as a quasi-criminal sanction, and crucially, as an experience that feels like punishment. After Padilla's case, deportation became civil only 'in a strict sense'.

Cases like *Padilla* and *Zadvydas* mark the beginning of a conversation, and perhaps a sea change. They find both echoes and contradictions in American law and reflect tensions that persist in the British system as well. These cases capture how, as punishment and regulation grow less distinct, and as systems of border control become more severe, the law manages to make room for a more empathetic approach to punishment. While the division between criminal and civil sanctions remains blunt and brutal, the law's formalism is more precarious than it seems. In practice, courts often deviate from formality at the outer edges of punishment, when the law starts to feel most wrong. Affective conceptions of justice—the idea that law encompasses the way that confinement feels—already enter the law implicitly. The question is whether they can surface and develop into a more humane vision of punishment.

Conclusion

Our central contention is that the law of punishment does not have to be as it is. This may seem obvious, particularly to those who understand punishment as a set of social practices. Yet critics of incarceration often take the law's shortcomings for granted. For good reason, sociologists of punishment argue that life and law are mismatched (see Bosworth and Turnbull in this volume; Kanstroom 2000). At the same time, legal scholars describe the line between civil and criminal sanctions as harsh and ill conceived (Hernández 2014; Markowitz 2008). These critiques are right, and they foreground the law's failure to capture the full experience of state power. But a critical lens can also make the limits of punishment seem more stable and unyielding than they are.

Lucia Zedner calls this phenomenon 'the danger of dystopia' (Zedner 2002). In a brilliant review of intellectual trends in criminology, Zedner argues that critical narratives of punishment, though illuminating, can also obscure opportunities for less harsh carceral regimes. This insight applies to the law of punishment. On one level, the legal definition of punishment is inaccurate and destructive. Ambiguous penal institutions and painful carceral practices exist because the law numbs itself to the feeling of punishment. This problem has only amplified in recent years, as punitive but technically civil spaces of confinement have sprung up in the capacious zone of regulation.

On another level, however, the law of punishment has splintered as confinement practices have grown more extreme. The birth and expansion of immigration detention centers, 'all-foreign' prisons, and 'icebox' holding cells have pushed critics and courts alike to question what it means to confine a person in a cell. Faced with that question, the law makes space—not enough space, but some space—for the affective dimension of punishment. Building from this moment of recognition, scholars of punishment should revisit the gap between life and law. In charting the law's boundaries, we can begin to outline a less dissociated legal system. We can also acknowledge the lives of those whose confinement does not yet count as punishment.

Notes

1   For brevity, the chapter refers to 'British' practices to describe prison policies in England and Wales and legal practices in the United Kingdom. To be clear, there are three distinct legal jurisdictions in the UK. Scotland has its own prison system, and each part of Britain has its own legal culture. In the UK, as elsewhere, borders and national identities are contested.
2   All quotations from prisoners in this chapter are excerpted from Kaufman, forthcoming 2015. All names are pseudonyms chosen by prisoners.

References

Cases

In re Winship, 387 US 358 (1970)
Padilla v. Kentucky, 599 US 356 (2010)
Shaughnessy v. United States ex rel. Mezei, 345 US 206 (1953)
United States v. Salerno, 481 US 739 (1987)
United States v. Ward, 228 US 242 (1980)
Wong Wing v. United States, 163 US 228 (1896)
Zadvydas v. Davis, 533 US 678 (2001)

Secondary Sources

ACLU of Arizona 2011, *In their own words: enduring abuse in Arizona immigration detention centers*, ACLU. Available from: <http://www.acluaz.org/detention-report-2011>. [10 January 2015].
ACLU of Massachusetts 2009, *Detention and deportation in the age of ICE*, ACLU. Available from: <https://www.aclum.org/ice>. [10 January 2015].
American Immigration Council 2013, *The criminal alien program: immigration enforcement in prisons and jails*, Immigration Policy Center. Available from: <http://www.immigrationpolicy.org/just-facts/criminal-alien-program-cap-immigration-enforcement-prisons-and-jails>. [10 January 2015].

Americans for Immigrant Justice 2013, *AI Justice takes action against border patrol for abusing immigrant women,* Americans for Immigrant Justice. Available from: <http://aijustice.org/ai-justice-takes-action-against-border-patrol-for-abusing-immigrant-women/>. [14 March 2013].

Ashworth, A & Zedner, A 2014, *Preventive justice,* Oxford University Press, Oxford.

Bacon, C 2005, *The evolution of immigration detention in the UK: the involvement of private prison companies* (Working Paper No. 27), Refugee Studies Centre. Available from: <http://www.rsc.ox.ac.uk/publications/the-evolution-of-immigration-detention-in-the-uk-the-involvement-of-private-prison-companies>. [10 January 2015].

Barry, T 2011, *Pecos prison town blues: 'Contract Confinement' for BOP's immigrant inmates,* TransBorder Project, Center for International Policy. Available from: <http://borderlinesblog.blogspot.com/2011/05/pecos-prison-town-blues-contract.html>. [10 January 2015].

Bentham, J 2011, *The panopticon writings,* Verso, New York.

Bhui, H 2004, *Going the distance: developing effective policy and practice with foreign national prisoners,* Prison Reform Trust, London.

Bosworth, M 2014, *Inside immigration detention,* Oxford University Press, Oxford.

Bosworth, M 2012, 'Subjectivity and identity in detention: punishment and society in a global age,' *Theoretical Criminology,* vol. 16, no. 2, pp. 123–140.

Bosworth, M 2007, 'Immigration detention in Britain,' in *Human Trafficking,* ed M Le, Willian Publishing, Devon.

Bosworth, M & Kaufman, M 2011, 'Foreigners in a carceral age: immigration and imprisonment in the United States,' *Stanford Law & Policy Review,* vol. 22, pp. 429–454.

Bright, S & Sanneh, S 2013, 'Fifty years of defiance and resistance after *Gideon v. Wainwright,*' *Yale Law Journal,* vol. 122, pp. 2150–2174.

Brotherton, D & Barrios L 2009, 'Displacement and stigma: the social-psychological crisis of the deportee," *Crime Media Culture,* vol. 5, pp. 29–55.

Brotherton, D & Kretsedemas, P (eds) 2008, *Keeping out the other: a critical introduction to immigration enforcement today,* Columbia University Press, New York.

Buss, E 2002, 'Parental' Rights,' *Virginia Law Review,* vol. 88, pp. 635–683.

Caldwell, B 2013, 'Banished for life: deportation of juvenile offenders as cruel and unusual punishment,' *Cardozo Law Review,* vol. 34, pp. 2261–2311.

Carpenter, CL & Beverlin, AE 2012, 'The Evolution of unconstitutionality in sex offender registration laws," *Hastings Law Journal,* vol. 63, pp. 1071–1134.

Center for Victims of Torture 2013, *Tortured & detained – survivor stories of US immigration detention,* Center for Victims of Torture. Available from: <http://www.cvt.org/sites/cvt.org/files/Report_TorturedAndDetained_Nov2013.pdf>. [10 January 2015].

Coutin, SB 2005, 'Contesting criminality: illegal immigration and the spatialization of legality,' *Theoretical Criminology,* vol. 9, pp. 5–33.

Eagly, I 2013, 'Criminal justice for noncitizens: an analysis of variation in local enforcement,' *NYU Law Review,* vol. 88, pp. 1126–1223.

Foucault, M 2005, *Discipline and punish: the birth of the prison,* trans. A Sheridan, Vintage, New York.

Golash-Boza, T 2010, 'The criminalization of undocumented migrants: legalities and realities," *Societies Without Borders,* vol. 5, no. 1, pp. 81–90.

Greene, J & Mazon, A 2012, *Privately operated federal prisons for immigrants,* Justice Strategies. Available from: <http://www.justicestrategies.org/publications/2012/

privately-operated-federal-prisons-immigrants-expensive-unsafe-unnecessary>. [10 January 2015].

Guttin, A 2010, *The criminal alien program: immigration enforcement in Travis County, Texas*, Immigration Policy Center. Available from: <http://www.immigration policy.org/special-reports/criminal-alien-program-immigration-enforcement -travis-county-texas>. [10 January 2015].

Hernández, CCG 2014, 'Immigration detention as punishment,' *UCLA Law Review*, vol. 61, pp. 1346–1414.

Hernández, CCG 2006, 'The perverse logic of immigration detention: unraveling the rationality of imprisoning immigrants based on markers of race and class otherness," *Columbia Journal of Race & Law*, vol. 1, pp. 353–364.

Human Rights First 2011, *Jails and jumpsuits: transforming the US immigration detention system—a two year review*, Human Rights First. Available from: <http:// www.humanrightsfirst.org/wp-content/uploads/pdf/HRF-Jails-and-Jumpsuits -report.pdf>. [10 January 2015].

Kanstroom, D 2000, 'Deportation, social control, and punishment: some thoughts about why hard laws make bad cases," *Harvard Law Review*, vol. 113, pp. 1889–1935.

Kaufman, E 2015, *Punish and expel: border control, nationalism, and the new purpose of the prison*, Oxford University Press, Oxford.

Kaufman, E 2013, 'Hubs and spokes: the transformation of the British prison,' in *The borders of punishment: migration, citizenship, and social exclusion*, eds KF Aas & M Bosworth, Oxford University Press, Oxford.

Kelly, M 2005, *Immigration-related detention in Ireland*, Immigrat Council of Ireland. Available from: <http://www.immigrantcouncil.ie/research-publications/archive /321-immigration-related-detention-in-ireland>. [10 January 2015].

Kolber, A 2013, 'Against proportional punishment,' *Vanderbilt Law Review*, vol. 66, pp. 1141–1179.

Legomsky, S 2007, 'The new path of immigration law: asymmetric incorporation of criminal justice norms,' *Washington & Lee Law Review*, vol. 64, pp. 469–528.

Lonegan, B 2006, *Immigration detention and removal: a guide for detainees and their families*, Legal Aid Society. Available from: <http://www.nilc.org/document. html?id=211>. [10 January 2015].

Markowitz, P 2008, 'Straddling the criminal-civil divide: a bifurcated approach to understanding the nature of immigration removal proceedings,' *Harvard Civil Rights-Civil Liberties Law Review*, vol. 42, pp. 289–351.

McLeod, AM 2012, 'The US criminal-immigration convergence and its possible undoing," *American Criminal Law Review*, vol. 49, pp. 105–178.

Minton, T 2012, *Jail inmates at midyear 2011*, Bureau of Justice Statistics, US Department of Justice. Available from: <http://www.bjs.gov/content/pub/pdf/ jim11st.pdf>. [10 January 2015].

National Immigration Forum 2013, *The math of immigration detention*, National Immigration Forum. Available from: <http://immigrationforum.org/blog/the mathofimmigrationdetention/>. [10 January 2015].

Patterson, E 2008, 'Civil contempt and the indigent child support obligor: the silent return of debtor's prison,' *Cornell Journal of Law & Public Policy*, vol. 18, pp. 95–141.

Robertson, J 1991, 'Impartiality and prison disciplinary tribunals,' *New England Journal on Criminal & Civil Confinement*, vol. 17, pp. 301–335.

Simanski, J & Sapp, L 2012, *Immigration enforcement actions: 2011*, US Department of Homeland Security Office of Immigration Statistics. Available from: < http://www .dhs.gov/sites/default/files/publications/immigration-statistics/enforcement_ar _2011.pdf>. [10 January 2015].

Sunstein, C 1996, 'On the expressive function of law,' *University of Pennsylvania Law Review*, vol. 144, pp. 2021–2053.

Tsesis, A 2011, 'Due process in civil commitments,' *Washington & Lee Law Review*, vol. 68, pp. 253–307.

Government Accountability Office (GAO) 2004, *Immigration enforcement: better data and controls are needed to assure consistency with the Supreme Court decision on long-term alien detention*, United States Government. Available from: <http://www .gpo.gov/fdsys/pkg/GAOREPORTS-GAO-04-434/html/GAOREPORTS-GAO-04-434 .htm>. [10 January 2015].

Yngvesson, B & Coutin, SB 2006, 'Backed by papers: undoing persons, histories, and return,' *American Ethnologist*, vol. 33, no.2, pp. 177–190.

Zedner, L 2013, Is the criminal law is only for citizens? A problem at the borders of punishment, in *The Borders of Punishment: Migration, Citizenship, and Social Exclusion*, eds KF Aas & M Bosworth, Oxford University Press, Oxford.

Zedner, L 2002, 'Dangers of dystopias in penal theory,' *Oxford Journal of Legal Studies*, vol. 22, pp. 341–366.

3
Immigration, Detention, and the Expansion of Penal Power in the United Kingdom

Mary Bosworth, University of Oxford and Monash University
Sarah Turnbull, University of Oxford

Although not a new phenomenon (Bashford & Strange 2002), immigration detention is increasingly utilized around the world as a state response to unwanted migration (Fassin 2011; Flynn 2014). One among an arsenal of strategies of border control that draw on familiar penal technologies, imaginaries, and practices, immigration detention blurs the boundaries between immigration and criminal justice (Stumpf 2006; Aas 2011; Bosworth & Kaufman 2011; Barker 2012; Aas & Bosworth 2013; Aliverti 2013). In so doing, it challenges us to think afresh about the meaning and nature of penal power, its limits, and its purpose.

In the United Kingdom (UK), immigration detention is not a form of legal punishment. It is administrative in nature and geared toward the ejection of unwanted foreign citizens from British soil. Nevertheless, many of those who are detained for immigration purposes experience their confinement as punitive. Immigration removal centers (IRCs) look like prisons and are staffed by uniformed officers employed by many of the same custodial firms. The locked doors, roll counts, room searches, pat-downs, bars on windows, high fences topped with razor wire, and ubiquitous closed-circuit television (CCTV) cameras are not only constant reminders to detainees of the denial of their liberty, but also, in their similarities to the prison, reveal these institutions as quasi-penal establishments. Women and men find their separation from loved ones and their communities especially difficult, perceiving in it an excessive response to their legal status. Their pains of confinement are compounded by the absence of a statutory time limit on detention. Such uncertainty over the duration of detention engenders considerable fear and anxiety.

While mindful of Lucia Zedner's warnings over the importance of retaining a narrow view of punishment as a legal category in order to protect some of its judicial safeguards (Zedner 2013; Ashworth & Zedner 2014), we suggest that IRCs reveal the expansive nature of punitiveness (see Hannah-Moffat & Lynch 2012; Kaufman & Weiss this volume). In their rootedness in identity, such places both converge with and diverge from prison. In order to explore these matters, and thus to make sense of the 'exceptional nature' of immigration detention, we draw on fieldwork conducted as part of two distinct studies of life in British IRCs.[1] Using field notes and interview data, we examine women and men's experiences of confinement. Notwithstanding the legal definition of immigration detention as administrative rather than punitive, we suggest that such places reveal a troubling extension of the reach of penal power in the service of border control that is facilitated by and embedded in race, gender, and postcolonial relations. We begin the chapter with an overview of immigration detention in the UK before examining the ways in which this practice converges with and diverges from imprisonment. We conclude by considering how immigration detention serves broader state aims of regulating and casting out unwanted others from British soil, revealing the important role of penal power in forging an exclusionary view of national identity.

Overview

On any given day, 2,800 foreign national citizens are detained under Immigration Act powers in one of 11 IRCs scattered throughout Great Britain (Home Office 2013b). Over the course of a year, this number swells ten-fold as 30,000 individuals pass through the system (Home Office 2013b). Around 1,000 others can be found in prison, post-sentence, awaiting deportation. In addition, a hundred or so individuals are held for up to five days in short-term holding facilities (STHF) at ports and airports, and a further undisclosed number are held in police cells or hospitals. Lastly, the Home Office operates a so-called 'pre-departure accommodation' facility, Cedars, equipped to hold nine families, near Gatwick Airport, where they may be detained for 72 hours (or up to one week with ministerial authority).

Although the British government has had the ability to detain foreign citizens for immigration matters since the Aliens Act 1905, it rarely used these powers until the mid-1990s, except as a reaction to events elsewhere. Thus, during the two world wars, citizens of states at war with the UK were detained in prisons, and in the 1980s, Tamils fleeing unrest in Sri Lanka were held on a boat in Harwich Harbour. The first immigration detention units were established in 1970 at Harmondsworth and Dover Castle in response to the Immigration Appeals Act 1969, which had given Commonwealth citizens who had been denied entry on arrival the right to an in-country appeal (Wilsher 2011; Bosworth 2014). Other centers that opened in the 1990s, like Campsfield House (1993) and Tinsley House (1996), sought to contain growing numbers of asylum seekers who were clogging up the overcrowded penal system. In 2001, the government pledged to stop housing asylum seekers in prisons, a policy change that significantly expanded the detention estate. That year the government also renamed detention centers 'immigration removal centers' to signify their intended purpose more clearly. Such places have never been designed to hold anyone for very long but rather to provide short-term 'secure housing' prior to administrative removal or deportation.[2]

Whereas operation of the first detention units was contracted out to just one private security company (then known as Securicor, now G4S), these days institutions are run by a series of corporations—GEO, Serco, Mitie, and G4S—along with Her Majesty's (HM) Prison Service (see Bacon 2005). Most of these corporations are multinationals that run equivalent facilities in the United States and Australia.

In Britain, most IRCs are concentrated in the south of England, with a number surrounding the two main London airports of Gatwick and Heathrow. There are additional short-term holding facilities lining the northern coast of France, designed specifically to hold migrants seeking to enter the UK by train or ferry (HM Chief Inspector of Prisons and Contrôleur Général des Lieux de Privation de Liberté 2013). Anyone subject to immigration detention in Britain can also be confined for up to five days in a police cell or for up to 24 hours in an immigration processing center. Those having come to the end of their criminal sentences may be detained under Immigration Act powers in prison. In each case, decisions to detain are not subject to automatic judicial review. Consequently, even though detainees can apply for bail from an immigration judge, or submit their case for judicial review, IRCs operate with fewer oversight mechanisms and lesser legal standards than those available under the criminal law (O'Nions 2008; Bosworth 2011).

For persons without a legal right to be in the UK, removal centers are meant to be the final point in their migration. Foreign citizens may be detained once their criminal sentence is complete, for over-staying a visa, for failing to possess a visa, or for breaching the terms of a visa. They may also be held to determine their identity or to establish the basis of their claims where there is a risk of absconding. A small group of asylum seekers whose cases have already been determined as 'straightforward' may be held in two particular centers (Harmondsworth for men and Yarl's Wood for women) under the Detained Fast-Track Process, while former asylum seekers whose claims have been rejected may be detained prior to removal (Silverman & Hajela 2013).[3] A number of detainees in all categories are long-term British residents, some with significant ties to the UK, having grown up in the country. Many have family members in Britain.

Like prisons, immigration detention centers are highly racialized and gendered institutions (Bosworth & Kellezi 2014). The vast majority of those confined are young men of color, while those who guard them are predominately white men. In 2013, women comprised 15 percent of those entering detention in the UK (Home Office 2013b). Women officers can also be found in all establishments.

Male or female, detainees are drawn from all over the world but tend to originate from the global South and, more particularly, from those countries where the UK either currently has an active military presence or has in the recent past. Most hail from former colonies, particularly from the so-called collection of 'New Commonwealth' nations that achieved self-government from Britain after 1945.[4] There are very few 'Old Commonwealth' (i.e., Australian, New Zealand, or Canadian) citizens detained (Home Office 2013b). In addition, all detention centers hold a significant number of Chinese and a smaller sum of Vietnamese nationals, as well as citizens from Eastern European states like Albania that are not part of the European Union.

The stated purpose of immigration detention, under Section 3(1) of the Detention Center Rules 2001, is 'to provide for the secure but humane accommodation of detained persons in a relaxed regime with as much freedom of movement and association as possible, consistent with maintaining a safe and secure environment, and to encourage and assist detained persons to make the most productive use of their time, whilst respecting in particular their dignity and the right to individual expression'. This description conjures notions of rationalized, ordered spaces and regimes (Hall 2010). Yet, detention is highly affective and emotional, complex, and ambiguous (Bosworth 2014). As Khosravi (2009) aptly observes, immigration detention is simultaneously caring and punitive, coercive and empowering, hospitable and hostile. Detainees are both infantilized as needing guidance and responsibilized as adults who are in control of their choices and futures (Khosravi 2009). In the remainder of the chapter, we attend to these complexities and contradictions by drawing on the lived experiences of those subject to detention.

Penal convergences

Although IRCs are not, officially, places of punishment, there are many points of intersection between them and the prison system in their population (poor and racialized), the companies that run them,[5] their architectural design, their security features, and the conditions of everyday life (see also Kaufman & Bosworth 2013; Kaufman & Weiss this volume). At any given time, approximately one-third of those in detention in Britain have previously spent some time in prison (Home Office 2013a) or have a criminal record.[6] So, too, many center managers are former prison governors, from both the public and private sectors, while a number of facilities, particularly those run by Her Majesty's Prison Service, are formerly or currently part of penal institutions.

All of the IRCs built since 2002 have followed prison security design. Surrounded by high fences and razor wire, they may only be entered via imposing gates, through which detainees must pass in armoured vans. Detainee mobility is highly controlled as well. Whereas in some establishments—like Campsfield House, Tinsley House, and Yarl's Wood—detainees may wander around largely at will, elsewhere—in Colnbrook, Brook House, and Harmondsworth, built to Category B, high-security prison design—their movements are restricted. Men (as well as the handful of women housed in the short-stay unit in Colnbrook) spend considerable portions of each day locked in their housing units as though they were in prison.

Staff and detainees spoke at length about the penal nature of these institutions and how it affected their sense of identity. Some, like Isis[7] (Maldives, Yarl's Wood), were shocked by the high gates and barbed wire, wondering where they had been taken (ST field notes 06/02/14; see also McGregor 2012). Others had no doubt. In Morton Hall, a center that at the time of research had recently been converted from a low-security women's prison to a men's IRC, Charles hissed angrily: 'It's a cell, not a room! It's got bars on the windows, what room has that?' (Nigeria, Morton Hall). In Yarl's Wood, Jennifer felt the same. '*It is a prison*', she lamented. 'This is exactly like prison' (Barbados, Yarl's Wood).

The secure buildings also blurred the distinction between detainees and offenders for staff. Although officers knew that detainees were not serving criminal sentences, the securitization of the environment in which they worked raised questions about the dangers posed by the people within them. 'At the end of the day', Jonathan pointed out, 'these guys are deemed to be innocent, not committed any crimes, same as civilians. But', he stumbled on, 'they're in detention. They're held in a secure environment'. The custodial surroundings, Jonathan recognized, cast the detainees as dangerous and guilty of something, although he was unsure of exactly what. Struggling to reconcile this paradox, he stuttered, 'I don't, I don't actually, I don't look at them as criminals, but… they have committed, they have done wrong, because they're in the country without…[pausing] A lot. Not all of them. A lot of them are here because they shouldn't be' (Detention Custody Officer (DCO), Morton Hall; see also Bosworth & Slade 2014).

Detainees responded to the penal architecture and security practices in a similar fashion, fearing that such institutions housed dangerous people. In a language in which he was not fluent, Yoet tried to explain: 'We are here, strange people. Like somebody from prison… It's different, some drug addicts and…it's no good. No supposed to be together. If some people who say long prison sentences supposed to be in another place, not here. Or we're supposed to be in another place. But we are together and we are not safe' (Moldova, Colnbrook). Many were anxious to differentiate themselves from those with criminal records, or any others who might otherwise be considered less deserving of a right to remain in Britain. Even people who had been convicted sought to soften their image. 'I no killed somebody', insisted Yi-Ling, who had been convicted of a string of shoplifting offences. 'I no do something wrong. I have address' (Singapore, Yarl's Wood).

In their testimonies, people's fears of stigmatization became apparent, as they recognized the implicit meaning of their treatment at the hands of the state. 'When you're in this place, in Colnbrook', Joao complained, 'and you're going to the [immigration] court, they obviously think you're a killer or you're a rapist or you're, or you do something serious' (Angola, Colnbrook). Such treatment, women and men complained, made them feel (and appear to be) less than human. 'This [detention] make us be the worst creature in the world, you know', Luiza said angrily. 'No rights, no nothing, no dignity' (Brazil, Yarl's Wood). Whatever its legal status, staff and detainees made clear, immigration detention felt punitive. Those confined in institutions that so closely resembled prisons often felt criminalized, while the staff who worked with them were not immune, wondering both about the identity of those in their care and about their own role. In their resemblance to prison, the physical spaces of detention centers and their mode of governance drew upon and engendered similar feelings of stigmatization and punishment (see also the chapter by Jewkes in this volume).

Penal divergences

In spite of their physical and operational similarities to prison, Immigration Removal Centers are governed by a different structure of administrative law; they are not part of the criminal justice system. Daily life is also subject to specific rules and expectations. Some of these differences amplify the punitive experience of detention. Others, however, reveal the specificity of this form of confinement. Crucially, while prisons and IRCs are both shaped by everyday indignities (Turnbull 2014), the purpose and legitimacy of detention, unlike imprisonment, are contested and unclear (Bosworth 2013). Additionally, unlike a prison sentence, a period of detention has no statutory limit in the UK. Although the majority of those in detention are held for less than three months, each center houses some women or men for over six months and a handful for some years (Stefanelli 2011).[8]

In addition to not knowing *when* detention will end, most detainees do not know *how* it will end. Will they be released into the community? Or will they be forced to leave the country? Deportation itself may not resolve the matter. The government delivers individuals only to particular ports in their country of origin. From there, women and men must make their own way 'home'. Some may face further legal action or detention in their country of origin.

Not surprisingly, such uncertainty is difficult to endure and often feels punitive. Although IRCs meet their basic material needs, without knowing when or how detention would end, many detainees found it difficult to 'do' their time. Aroleoba described matters this way:

> You don't really know, it's even more torturing than a prison, because in a prison, if you're there for two years, you know you're there for two years. After two years, you'll be out... So you already know when you're going in, you already know your date... This is the highest I can, you know, this is the longest I can be in. But in a detention center, where your case is being decided, you don't know. You're just like that, hoping for the next day can bring something rapid, you know, different (Nigeria, Campsfield House).

Like other sites of indeterminate duration with which they might be usefully compared, such as the Guantánamo Bay detention facility (see Koenig this volume), remand centers or jails where people await conviction or sentencing for a criminal offence, and death row (Abu-Jamal 1996; Toch 1999), IRCs are especially damaging to the mental and physical health of those within (Silove et al. 2007; Robjant et al. 2009; Coffey et al. 2010; Steel et al. 2011).[9] 'Being here [in detention]' Aroleoba complained, 'is like, you can't go forward; you can't go back; you're stuck in the middle, and you don't even know what's gonna happen next. Drives people crazy' (Nigeria, Campsfield House). Under these circumstances, everyday matters like sleeping and eating were often adversely affected. Some, like Pascal (Rwanda, Colnbrook), were prescribed sleeping tablets, while others, like Paul (Jamaica, Campsfield House), coped by 'sleep[ing] the day away' because he could find no rest at night. Many reported that they struggled to eat and endured a number of physical ailments like headaches, stomach pains, and rashes—all of which they connected to their emotional distress. 'If I'm not depressed I eat normal food, small food, and I go to the gym, I do exercise', Hali noted. 'But if I'm depressed I eat and I don't exercise, I just keep on putting away just like that. Because I don't just have interest in going to a gym, Internet café. I don't, you know, I don't have interest, yeah. Doesn't nothing interest me. Nothing interest me because you don't know what future hold for you any longer. You know, before I was thinking "Oh, I have a future." Well, now I don't know what the future hold' (Nigeria, Yarl's Wood).

Matters generally worsened the longer people remained behind bars. 'This place is killing me', Naimah complained. 'I cannot eat. You see my skin [acne]. When I arrived I was very fresh. I am not fresh anymore' (Pakistan, Yarl's Wood). Priya concurred. Not only had she lost six kilograms, she reported, but her character had changed. 'Here, it's depressing, though. And I'm very fun-loving girl. I like to laugh and crack jokes, always make fun of each other. Like friendly with everyone. But in this one and half month, I've seen a different, different side of me, quieter side of me' (India, Yarl's Wood).

The indeterminacy and uncertainty of immigration detention in the UK worried staff as well as detainees. Officers in all centers regularly criticized the duration of confinement. Many were adamant: 'It should be six months, no more', Leah argued. 'Then they should tag them and release them. They can call them back in when they get their travel documents' (DCO, Yarl's Wood). Ryan, her senior officer, who had worked for many years in prisons, agreed: 'They just need to change the law to get rid of indefinite detention. We don't hold any prisoners like that. It doesn't make sense' (senior management team (SMT), Yarl's Wood).

Staff members were not just concerned about the unsettling effect on detainees but also about the way uncertainty prevented the centers from developing meaningful regimes. According to the Operating Standards (UK Border Agency 2008), all centers must offer lessons in English as a second language (ESOL), arts and crafts, a library, space for faith-based worship, and leisure activities, including a gym, and make available Internet access and some level of IT training. Unlike in prisons, however, there is no requirement that IRCs provide opportunities for paid work, vocational training, or higher education. Neither are there routine drug treatment programs, psychological counseling, or an equivalent of 'sentence planning'. 'They [prisoners] know how long they're gonna be in prison for', Scot explained. 'A lot of the activities and education they do can be structured around, around their length of stay. Whereas here, you know, our residents don't know how long they're going to be at the center for. And it's really hard to actually give them any kind of structured activity or education, you know, to be ongoing while they're here. And it's... If we start something, they're not necessarily going to finish it' (SMT, Yarl's Wood).

For those confined, the limited range of *meaningful* activities made detention boring and monotonous. Designed to facilitate expulsion, these institutions have no inherent reason to train or educate. Like those on remand (or in jail in the United States), detainees find it difficult to fill their time. As in these other custodial institutions, the lack of meaningful activities feels punitive and unfair; it also exacerbates the pains of confinement. 'There's nothing much to do', Paul observed. 'It's like they [center staff] think it's so much to do but it's just getting, you know, repetitive after a while. The same old thing every day, the same old food, same old people you see' (Jamaica, Campsfield House). Many, like Buddy, feared they were stagnating:

> Generally, there is nothing much to do for me. I'm a computer-literate person. Generally, I'm very, very busy person, because I'm always dealing with computers, doing this, sitting, busy all the time. But here, nothing much to do. This really frustrates me. Because you keep away from your main job for a long time, you actually start losing grip on things. You start forgetting most of the stuff. So it's quite, quite alarming situation for me (Pakistan, Yarl's Wood).

To keep busy, some detainees threw themselves into religious worship. After describing how the Home Office had issued—and then canceled— 'removal directions' (airplane tickets) on five separate occasions, Mary Jane said: 'My source of strength is from God. If I didn't believe in God... because that's where I get my strength from. Cos I'm pretty sure when you're being tortured like that, you have to have some kind of...you know, another strength. Because if you're just not relying on anything, there's no way...you'll go crazy' (Zimbabwe, Yarl's Wood). Others, like Mia from the Gambia, questioned their faith. What kind of God, they wondered, would leave them in such limbo? 'I still pray, but don't think God is listening. I'm not sure I believe', Mia confided sadly (Gambia, Yarl's Wood).

In each center, a small group took advantage of the limited offerings, in a bid, like Phillip, to stay active and avoid thinking too much about their uncertain and precarious situations. 'I keep myself very busy, very busy', he said. 'In the mornings I'm in the gym. In the afternoon I come and work in the Diversity Office, and in the evenings I go to chapel. I'm really involved with the services, I help out' (Nigeria, Morton Hall). Not everyone could act in this way, however. Many were simply too worried about their immigration case to participate in anything. Anxious about their future and often nervous of those around them, many spent the bulk of their time in their rooms. As with their physical health, their mental states tended to worsen the longer they were detained (Bosworth & Kellezi 2013). 'When I first came here I would even come to the library and practice English, but my brain does not work and I can't concentrate', Mia sighed. 'I write and I don't even know what I am writing. I don't feel like doing anything' (Gambia, Yarl's Wood).

Detainees across all the centers complained of being considered 'less than' a 'normal' human being. As Joel put it, 'Being here at all you ain't being treated like a human being' (Jamaica, Colnbrook). In their explanations, many turned again to the prison as a comparator to describe the punitive nature of detention. 'They treat us worse than their own criminals', Emmanuel asserted bitterly (Togo, Colnbrook). Bored and anxious, angry about the perceived illegitimacy of his treatment, he searched for a means of expression, finding clarity only in the lack of criminal justice restrictions and due process. Such views reveal the affective impact of the different procedural requirements under immigration law under which detainees' status as non-citizen denies them the same legal protections available to British criminals.

Many bridled against the stigma of their (immigration) status as unwanted and unwelcome, recognizing how it seeped into all aspects of day-to-day life and limited their capacity for agency. 'It's very depressing', Evelyn lamented.

> Yeah, life in [detention], very, very depressing. Because everything you're saying, you are not believed. Even the officers, maybe you asking for something, they think that you are lying. You know, you become a liar, even about your health. I was, the other day, I was

asking the nurse, 'Why would I lie about my health? It's my health. Why would I say I have this? I don't want to be sick. But if I say I feel like this, why would I lie?'... So it's very, very depressing. And they don't treat you like a normal human being. ... This is different treatment, not like a normal human being. That's what I'm feeling (South Africa, Yarl's Wood).

Such complaints, while by no means specific to immigration detention (see, for example, Koenig this volume), were exacerbated in this environment where so many found the constraints on their liberty unjustified and illegitimate. For Evelyn, a diabetic used to self-care, the center's restrictive environment was exceedingly frustrating and one that dominated her time. Banned from injecting herself with insulin as she was used to doing, she became dependent on healthcare staff for access to medication, professionals whom, she complained, did not believe her when she felt unwell (weak and dizzy) due to her condition.

Indeed, a lack of agency affected all aspects of daily life. Sometimes problems sprang from the manner in which detainees arrived. Those taken into custody unexpectedly, for instance, while signing in as an asylum seeker, or in a work raid, did not always have a chance to bring with them personal belongings such as clothing or towels. Even those who did were prevented from bringing all their items, limited by the weight restrictions of airline luggage policies. Under these circumstances, many depended on the institution for everyday provisions from clothing to razors, sanitary towels, and footwear. According to Luiza, such items were often inadequate. 'To be honest, the towel that they give to us is very disgusting. You get it, how can you, to dry your body with that towel? Not hygienic [...]. Some of them [other detainees] put on the floor, and then they [staff] give that dirty thing to us to use. This is dignity, no' (Brazil, Yarl's Wood).

Those fortunate enough to have brought personal items to detention were not always able to access them since, like prisons, the number and kind of possessions allowed in detainees' rooms are restricted. Anything additional or considered contraband has to remain in the induction unit for collection en route to the airport or upon release. This arrangement, Amira made clear, felt

[d]egrading. I've asked for my bags when I was about to move here [Yarl's Wood]. And I said, 'Can I please get my suitcases?' Because [...] I was about to go on my plane. And to put my clothes in it. And they gave me some kind of see-through bag and they said 'There you go'.

I said 'No, I've got suitcases. No, I don't need to move like some, I'm some sort of homeless person, whatever'. They said to me, 'This is what we've got right now' (Oman, Yarl's Wood).

Luiza, who had lived in the UK for 11 years, agreed. Adamant against returning to Brazil in what she called a 'shame situation', she stated angrily: 'I don't want to go back like I'm ashamed. I don't want to go back with my plastic bag, even without a right to have your luggage, your things' (Brazil, Yarl's Wood). For these women, the institutional restrictions on their possessions was unfair and dehumanizing; why did their lack of citizenship permit such intimate intrusion?

In detention, the denial of agency has a unique temporal quality. Like other confined populations, detainees must follow the daily routines of the institution. However, it is not just their present but also their futures and their pasts which detainees are unable to control. The unexpected and indefinite nature of their confinement means they are largely prevented from determining their futures. Their pasts are also seized since, in order to be deported or removed, their time in Britain, their connections to family and community, and their experiences of trauma are officially labeled irrelevant. As detention uproots them from their pasts and determines what comes next, it both undermines their sense of self and fixes their identities as strangers, no matter how familiar.

This aspect of detention adds another layer of pain to the experience of confinement in these institutions and is, as a result, often perceived as intentionally punitive. Detainees feel personally rejected and affronted by the administrative response to their immigration status. Being identified as someone who is unwelcome hurts. In this affective response to their confinement and expulsion, we see a further parameter of the expansion of penal power through identity and the effect of migration control. Notwithstanding the legal boundaries separating the administrative confinement of detention from the criminal punishment of imprisonment, detention felt punitive for detainees.

Casting out the strangers among us

As the preceding discussion emphasizes, much of the 'extreme' nature of immigration detention springs from its divergence from what we commonly understand as punishment: a term of imprisonment following a criminal conviction. As an exercise of administrative power that aims to immobilize and expel those without the right to remain, immigration detention emerges as a unique type of custody. Whereas other institutions of confinement restrict agency in a bid to 'responsibilize' or 'cure' inmates who will eventually be returned to the community, immigration detention does not aim to govern detainees through neo-liberal strategies of producing 'good citizens' (Bashford & Strange 2002; Bosworth 2012). Because detainees are ostensibly going to be removed, detention is not oriented around (re)integration (Leerkes & Broeders 2010). Such people, the Home Office and politicians insist, no matter how long their residence in the UK, do not belong. Despite statistics that say otherwise, they are not coming back.[10] Under these conditions, the denial of agency facilitates the objectification of detainees. They become somehow less than human, a troublesome pest unwanted by the British state. This shift is facilitated by familiar racialized narratives and path-ways. Such matters are amplified in the resemblance of these centers to prison (i.e., the pains associated with confinement) as well as in the manner in which IRCs diverge from prison (i.e., the illegitimate, uncer-tain, and indefinite nature of detention). The role and effect of detention becomes clear: identifying the strangers among us and casting them out.

The fact that the bulk of detainees in Britain have migrated from the global South is not surprising, particularly as legalized migration routes are increasingly closed off and restricted to all but the most 'desirable' of migrants (van Houtum 2010). It is also understandable that many detainees are from former British colonies given patterns of familial migration and the enduring influences of empire and colonization that shape migration trajectories. Detention is one among many techniques that maintain the whiteness of the nation by separating those who 'belong' in Britain from those who do not (see, for example, Hernandez 2008; Lawston & Escobar 2009). The government's attempt to isolate and excise these strangers through immigration detention reflects a con-venient act of disconnecting the past from the present and the future. In so doing, the government enables what Stuart Hall (2001, p. 218) labeled 'colonial amnesia', effectively denying Britain's role in setting up pathways of migration by enclosing and then expelling those who do not fit its legal requirements (see also Bosworth & Kellezi 2014; Kaufman & Bosworth 2014).

The racialized and postcolonial nature of immigration detention was the subject of a number of conversations with detainees and the cause of considerable frustration. Commenting on his detention, Ravindar (India, Campsfield House) observed bitterly that Britain came to India and took his forefathers' land. Twice dispossessed, he was detained, cast out as an unwanted migrant from the country which had irrevocably changed his own. Women and men from Jamaica, Nigeria, Pakistan, and

Dominica told similar stories. Several referred to immigration detention as a contemporary form of slavery in which they were being used to generate profit for private companies. In these accounts, and the emotions that accompanied them, we witness how removal centers disavow shared postcolonial membership and also the pain such policies engender. The racialized nature of belonging and exclusion is experienced as unfair and punitive.

Such matters are also highly gendered. Men worried about their ability to support their families and to parent their children from afar. 'I know what it's like to grow up without a father', De'ron warned. 'My mother struggled to raise nine children. She was mother and father to us both. So they want my children to grow up without a father?' (Jamaica, Tinsley House). 'How am I supposed to live without my kids?' Adashe wailed (Zimbabwe, Morton Hall). Women spoke of having their hopes for safety, autonomy, and self-development dashed. Many of them were explicit, citing the oppressive nature of traditional gender norms in their home countries. Fleeing violent husbands, fathers, brothers, they longed to stay in the relative safety of Britain. Yet it was precisely their aspiration to set the terms of their own lives that detention prevented. In so doing, it became clear that although not ostensibly part of the detention's rationale, gender inequalities and violence are both key effects of this form of penal power.

Conclusion

In their overlaps with prison and in their differences, IRCs challenge fundamental assumptions about punishment, requiring us to think critically about how coercive state power may reproduce penal techniques and logics within non-criminal justice settings. For, despite failing to adhere to the usual goals of punishment, immigration detention is experienced as punitive by those who are confined as well as by some of those who work there. Immigration detention is not punishment, but it is a type of penalty applied on the basis of identity to those without British citizenship or legal status—the vast majority of whom are men of color from the global South.

In multicultural liberal democracies such as Britain, the use of detention centers as a strategy of border control reveals the racialized and gendered nature of penal power under conditions of globalization. The convergences in the populations confined in the country's prisons and in its detention centers highlight the need to consider how identities matter to state practices of punishment and the criminalization of 'unwanted' people, citizens and non-citizens alike. That immigration detention is not applied evenly to all foreigners on British soil underscores the inequitable access to citizenship—or merely a regularized status—along lines of race, gender, socioeconomic status, and country of origin.

By drawing on detainee testimonies, this chapter has offered a textured and embodied account of the punitive nature of immigration detention. The pains that detainees make clear are connected to fundamental issues of belonging and dignity, to their sense of self, and their rights as human beings. As the state identifies and then casts out those who do not belong, we see how the administrative power to detain extends penal power down new and familiar pathways, identifying the usual suspects: poor, young men of color. Instead of integration and inclusion, these individuals are immediately defined as strangers, already destined for elsewhere.

Notes

1 Since November 2009, we have, separately and together, conducted research across the British immigration detention estate, including fieldwork in seven of the 11 IRCs that currently make up the British system: Campsfield House, Morton Hall, Dover, Yarl's Wood, Colnbrook, Brook House, and Tinsley House. More details can be found on the website http://bordercriminologies. ox.ac.uk. Parts of this chapter draw on Bosworth (2014).

2 Though the effect of these two methods of ejection is the same—the person is expelled from the UK and denied re-entry for a certain period of time—those who are held in detention for overstaying a visa or following a failed bid for asylum are, usually, 'removed', whereas those with a criminal record are 'deported'.

3 In July 2014 the UK Supreme Court found the operation of the Detained Fast Track system unlawful. Since then, the government has been adjusting how it identifies appropriate cases. Legal attempts are still underway to have the system ended (for a description of the system see Vine 2011).

4 These countries include, but are not limited to, India, Pakistan, Jamaica, Nigeria, Bangladesh, and Sri Lanka.

5 In addition to operating prisons, some of the private companies running detention centers run the vans that transport prisoners and suspects to court or between prisons. The same companies also provide electronic 'tagging' for the Ministry of Justice—a venture in which both Serco and G4S were found to be overcharging the government (see Travis 2014)—as well as assisting the police and the probation service.

6 Since 2008, non-European Economic Area (EEA) citizens sentenced to 12 months custody or more (or whose sentences over the past five years add up to this amount) plus EEA members sentenced to 24 months or more face mandatory deportation. Those with a deportation order may be detained. There are no statistics on the kinds of crimes these populations have committed. Those we interviewed had been accused or convicted of gun crimes, drug offences, immigration crimes, shoplifting, domestic and other violence, rape, and fraud.

7   Not her real name. All participants have been allocated pseudonyms and some have been given a different country of origin to ensure anonymity.

8   Although the majority (62 percent) of detainees in 2013 were held for less than 29 days, a third (33 percent) were detained for over one month, and 6 percent—nearly 1,900 individuals—were in detention for over four months, with 199 detained between one and two years and 50 for two years or longer (Home Office 2013b). For the latter group, the length of detention may extend due to court and bureaucratic processes and the simple fact that some people are not straightforwardly deportable or removable from the UK.

9   Indeed, data from 2010–11 found that over 80 percent of those surveyed in Tinsley House, Brook House, and Yarl's Wood were depressed according to the Hopkins trauma scale (Bosworth & Kellezi 2013).

10 Not all non-citizens are easy to expel from British soil. In 2013, 56 percent of detainees were removed from the UK, while 36 percent were granted temporary admission or release (Home Office 2013b).

References

Aas, KF 2011, '"Crimmigrant" bodies and bona fide travelers: Surveillance, citizenship and global governance', *Theoretical Criminology*, vol. 15, pp. 331–346.

Aas, KF & Bosworth, M (eds) 2013, *The borders of punishment: citizenship, crime control, and social exclusion*, Oxford University Press, Oxford.

Abu-jamal, M 1996, *Live from death row*, Harper Perennial, New York.

Aliverti, A 2013, *Crimes of mobility: criminal law and regulation of mobility*, Routledge, Abington.

Ashworth, A & Zedner, L 2014, *Preventive justice*, Oxford University Press, Oxford.

Bacon, C 2005, *The evolution of immigration detention in the UK: the involvement of private prison companies*, Refugee Studies Center Working Paper [Online]. Available from: <http://www.rsc.ox.ac.uk/publications/working-papers-folder_contents/RSCworkingpaper27.pdf>. [5 May 2014].

Barker, V 2012, 'Global mobility and penal order: criminalizing migration, a view from Europe', *Sociology Compass*, vol. 6, pp. 113–121.

Bashford, A & Strange, C 2002, 'Asylum-seekers and national histories of detention', *Australian Journal of Politics and History*, vol. 48, pp. 509–527.

Bosworth, M 2011, 'Human rights and immigration detention', in *Are Human Rights for Migrants? Critical Reflections on the Status of Irregular Migrants in Europe and the United States*, eds MB Dembour & T Kelly, Routledge, Abingdon.

Bosworth, M 2012, Subjectivity and identity in detention: punishment and society in a global age. *Theoretical Criminology*, vol. 16, pp. 123–140.

Bosworth, M 2013, 'Can immigration detention be legitimate?' in *The borders of punishment: citizenship, crime control, and social exclusion*, eds KF Aas & M Bosworth, Oxford University Press, Oxford.

Bosworth, M 2014, *Inside immigration detention*, Oxford University Press, Oxford.

Bosworth, M & Kaufman, E 2011, 'Foreigners in a carceral age: immigration and imprisonment in the United States', *Stanford Law & Policy Review*, vol. 22, pp. 429–454.

Bosworth, M & Kellezi, B 2013, 'Developing a measure of the quality of life in detention', *Prison Service Journal*, vol. 205, pp. 10–15.

Bosworth, M & Kellezi, B 2014. 'Citizenship and belonging in a women's immigration detention center', in *New Directions in Race, Ethnicity*, eds C Phillips & C Webster, Routledge, Abingdon.

Bosworth, M & Slade, G 2014, 'In search of recognition: gender and staff-detainee relations in a British immigration detention center', *Punishment & Society*, vol. 16, forthcoming.

Coffey, GJ, Kaplan, I, Sampson, RC & Tucci, MM 2010, 'The meaning and mental health consequences of long-term immigration detention for people seeking asylum', *Social Science & Medicine*, vol. 70, pp. 2070–2079.

Fassin, D 2011, 'Policing borders, producing boundaries: The governmentality of immigration in dark times', *Annual Review of Anthropology*, vol. 40, pp. 213–226.

Flynn, M 2014, *How and why immigration detention crossed the globe*, Global Detention Project. Available from: <http://www.globaldetentionproject.org/publications/working-papers/diffusion.html>. [19 May 2014].

Griffiths, M 2013, 'Living with uncertainty: indefinite immigration detention', *Journal of Legal Anthropology*, vol. 1, pp. 263–286.

Hall, A 2010, '"These people could be anyone": fear, contempt (and empathy) in a British immigration removal center', *Journal of Ethnic and Migration Studies*, vol. 36, pp. 881–898.

Hall, S 2001, 'Conclusion: the multicultural question', in *Un/Settled multiculturalisms: diasporas, entanglement, transruptions*, ed B Hesse, Zed Books, London.

Hannah-Moffat, K & Lynch, M 2012, 'Theorizing punishment's boundaries: an introduction', *Theoretical Criminology*, vol. 16, 119–121.

Her Majesty's Chief Inspector of Prisons & Contrôleur Général des Lieux de Privation de Liberté 2013, *Report on unannounced joint inspections of Coquelles and Calais non-residential short-term holding facilities, 6–7 November 2012*, Her Majesty's Inspectorate of Prisons. Available from: <http://www.justice.gov.uk/downloads/publications/inspectorate-reports/hmipris/short-term-holding-facility-reports/calais-coquelles-2012.pdf>. [14 May 2014].

Hernandez, DM 2008, 'Pursuant to deportation: Latinos and immigrant detention', *Latino Studies*, vol. 6, pp. 35–63.

Home Office 2013a, *Foreign National Offenders in detention and leaving detention*, Home Office. Available from: <https://www.gov.uk/government/publications/foreign-national-offenders-in-detention-and-leaving-detention/>. [14 May 2014].

Home Office 2013b, *Immigration statistics, October to December 2013*, Home Office. Available from: <https://www.gov.uk/government/publications/immigration-statistics-october-to-december-2013/immigration-statistics-october-to-december-2013#detention-1>. [14 May 2014].

Kaufman, E & Bosworth, M 2013, 'Prison and national identity: citizenship, punishment and the sovereign state', in *Why prison?*, ed D Scott, Cambridge University Press, Cambridge.

Khosravi, S 2009, 'Sweden: detention and deportation of asylum seekers', *Race & Class*, vol. 50, pp. 38–56.

Lawston, JM & Escobar, M 2009, 'Policing, detention, deportation, and resistance: situating immigrant justice and carcerality in the 21st century', *Social Justice*, vol. 36, pp. 1–6.

Leerkes, A. & Broeders, D 2010, 'A case of mixed motives? Formal and informal functions of administrative immigration detention', *British Journal of Criminology*, vol. 50, pp. 830–850.

McGregor, J 2012, Rethinking detention and deportability: removal centers as spaces of religious revival, *Political Geography,* vol. 31, pp. 236–246.

O'nions, H 2008, No right to liberty: the detention of asylum seekers for administrative convenience, *European Journal of Migration and Law,* vol. 10. Available from: <http://booksandjournals.brillonline.com/content/10.1163/157181608x 317336>. [14 May 2014].

Robjant, K, Robbins, I & Senior, V 2009, 'Psychological distress amongst immigration detainees: a cross-sectional questionnaire study', *British Journal of Clinical Psychology,* vol. 48, pp. 275–286.

Silove, D, Austin, P & Steel, Z 2007, 'No refuge from terror: the impact of detention on the mental health of trauma-affected refugees seeking asylum in Australia', *Transcultural Psychiatry,* vol. 44, pp. 359–393.

Silverman, SJ & Hajela, R 2013, *Immigration detention in the UK,* The Migration Observatory. Available from: <http://migrationobservatory.ox.ac.uk/briefings/ immigration-detention-uk>. [10 January 2015].

Steel, Z, Momartin, S, Silove, D, Coello, M, Aroche, J & Tay, KW 2011, 'Two year psychosocial and mental health outcomes for refugees subjected to restrictive or supportive immigration policies', *Social Science & Medicine,* vol. 72, pp. 1149–1156.

Stefanelli, JN 2011, 'Whose rule of law? An analysis of the UK's decision not to opt-in to the EU asylum procedures and reception conditions', *International & Comparative Law Quarterly,* vol. 60, pp. 1055–1064.

Stumpf, J 2006, 'The crimmigration crisis: immigrants, crime, and sovereign power', *American University Law Review,* vol. 56, pp. 367–419.

Toch, H 1999, *Prison madness: the mental health crisis behind bars and what we must do about it,* Jossey-Bass Inc, San Francisco.

Travis, A 2014, 'G4S agrees to repay £109m for overcharging on tagging contracts', *The Guardian,* 12 March. Available from: <http://www.theguardian.com/busi ness/2014/mar/12/g4s-repay-overcharging-tagging-contracts>. [13 May 2014].

Turnbull, S 2014, 'Blurred boundaries: experiencing immigration detention as punishment'. Paper presented at the Penal Boundaries Workshop, University of Toronto, Toronto.

UK Border Agency 2008, *Operating Standards for Immigration Removal Centers,* Home Office. Available from: <https://www.gov.uk/government/uploads/system/uploads /attachment_data/file/257352/operatingstandards_manual.pdf>. [14 May 2014].

Van Houtom, H 2010, 'Human blacklisting: the global apartheid of the EU's external border regime', *Environment and Planning D: Society and Space,* 28, 957–976.

Vine, J 2011, *Asylum: a thematic inspection of the detained fast track.* Independent Chief Inspector of the UK Border Agency. Available from: <http://icinspector.inde pendent.gov.uk/wp-content/uploads/2012/02/Asylum_A-thematic-inspection -of-Detained-Fast-Track.pdf>. [6 October 2014].

Wilsher, D 2011, *Immigration detention: law, history, politics,* Cambridge University Press, Cambridge.

Zedner, L 2013, 'Is the criminal law only for citizens? A problem at the borders of punishment', in *The borders of punishment: migration, citizenship, and social exclusion,* eds KF Aas & M Bosworth, Oxford University Press, Oxford.

4

(Im)migrating Penal Excess: Sheriff Joe Arpaio and the Case of Maricopa County, Arizona

Mona Lynch, University of California, Irvine

In 1992, Joe Arpaio was elected Maricopa County (AZ) Sheriff as a candidate of 'integrity and administrative ability' who offered 'the best chance of reforming our clownish sheriff's department' (*Arizona Republic* Editorial 1992). Maricopa County is the fourth-largest county in the nation (Eagly 2011) and home to Phoenix, a nationally influential new-right political hub (Shermer 2013), yet the sheriff's office had previously been headed by men characterized in the press as 'good ol' boys' and 'Keystone Kops' (*Arizona Republic* Editorial 1992) prone to botched investigations, scandals, and publicity stunts. Touting Arpaio's long career in federal law enforcement with the Drug Enforcement Administration, the endorsement that he received from Arizona's largest and most important newspaper concluded that he 'would bring none of this baggage to the office of sheriff' (*Arizona Republic* Editorial 1992).

Yet, within months of taking office, Arpaio had outdone his predecessors, gaining worldwide publicity for his cartoonish brand of law and order. As I have detailed in prior work (Lynch 2004; 2009) and will describe more fully below, Arpaio erected the infamous 'Tent City' jail in his first year of office; instituted a number of degrading, harmful, and cruel policies and practices in the county's jail facilities; and began an aggressive law enforcement campaign that included buying a military tank to use in his own local war on drugs. One issue not on his punitive agenda, however, was immigration.

That changed after the millennial turn, once political winds brought immigration squarely into the law and order tempest, both in the state and nationally. In response, Arpaio expanded his regime, transforming his law enforcement operation into 'a sort of freelance immigration-enforcement agency' (Finnegan 2009) and further diversifying his jails, which became extremely punitive immigration containment zones for hundreds of undocumented arrestees. An especially powerful force in that transformation came in 2007 when the Maricopa County Sheriff's Office (MCSO) entered into a Memorandum of Agreement with Homeland Security to participate in the 287(g) program, which delegates federal immigration enforcement powers to state and local law enforcement agencies.

This chapter explores the ramifications of the 'decentralization of immigration law' (Litwin 2011, p. 399) that attends the 287(g) program through a close examination of the MCSO's deployment of delegated federal immigration enforcement powers. Using a series of primary and secondary documents to trace the genealogy of Arpaio's foray into immigration enforcement,[1] I demonstrate how federal legal power was absorbed, reconstituted, and redeployed as part of an extreme local regime of punitive crime control. Specifically, I use this case to illustrate how the 287(g) program imparts immense and relatively ungovernable new power to local law enforcement that expands both legal and physical jurisdictions of the participating agencies; and I examine how and why, once delegated, these expanded powers are difficult to take back. The risk of these complications is present in the very design of the program, but it is exacerbated by the self-selection of participating agencies into the program. Because participation garners few tangible benefits for local agencies other than expanded enforcement powers, those agencies that do sign on may well do so specifically for the accretion of power.

While this case may be an outlier in its particular manifestation of the 287(g) partnership, it offers important analytic insights for understanding how law is localized. First, to the degree that Arpaio's office represents an 'alien culture' (Darnton 1984, p. 78) relative to most urban law enforcement agencies, it provides analytic entry into the opacity of the extreme practices, revealing their logics and meanings (see Darnton 1984). Moreover, if we think of penal practices (among other social phenomena) as falling along a continuum, the end points are critically important to understanding the bounds of possibility in a given culture. As innovators like Arpaio push those end points, they can and do have ripple effects in jurisdictions that look to such 'leaders' for policy insight.

The chapter proceeds as follows: In the next two sections, I briefly describe the 287(g) program, including its mandates, delegation procedures, and participation requirements, and I provide some background context on Arpaio's extreme law and order regime in the MCSO. I then delineate my theoretical framework for my analysis, drawn from socio-legal, criminological, and punishment and society scholarship, to help explain the legal extremism at play in this case. I follow with the meat of this analysis, by illustrating three interconnected phenomena that ultimately result in the subsumption of the federal into Arpaio's local regime: 1) how immigration enforcement is 'localized'; 2) how the ideologies and technologies of the local crime control regime are then deployed via immigration enforcement; and 3) how jurisdictions get expanded, exposing new populations and landscapes to Arpaio's war on immigration (see Figure 4.1). I conclude by asking more generally about the consequences of delegating legal power, using this case as a cautionary tale. I suggest that such power is much easier to give than take away, and will transmute, proliferate, and metastasize in potentially unpredictable ways.

The 287(g) program

In 1996, the Illegal Immigration Reform and Immigrant Responsibility Act was passed into law, which, among other things, provided a formal mechanism by which local law enforcement agencies could enter into an agreement with the federal government to assist in federal immigration enforcement. This provision, though, was not operationalized until after 11 September 2001, when the federal government expanded and transformed immigration law enforcement within its larger 'Homeland Security' mission (Litwin 2011). In 2002, the Department of Justice issued a memorandum declaring that local and state law enforcement agencies could be delegated the power to enforce immigration law under certain circumstances during the course of their own law enforcement activities. This would be accomplished through a Memorandum of Agreement (MOA) via the 287(g) program (Litwin 2011).

Beginning in 2005, Immigration and Customs Enforcement (ICE) began actively recruiting state and local agencies to partner through 287(g) agreements. The 287(g) program had two basic models for delegation of authority: the Task Force Officer model, which provided trained officers from participating agencies the power to investigate citizenship status in the course of responding to criminal matters, and the Jail Enforcement model, which bestowed trained custodial officers in participating agencies the power to process, interrogate, and detain suspected aliens within their facilities. In order to participate in this partnership, local agencies had to designate officers who would then meet some very minimal training requirements in immigration law, policy, and procedure over a four- to five-week period. Importantly, both of these programs were designed to help identify undocumented persons among those who were suspected of criminal involvement, so the authorization of enforcement powers was to be limited to those otherwise identified as criminal suspects.

The 287(g) program did not offer much to local agencies, and the Task Force model was often a hindrance to other law enforcement priorities as it had a chilling effect on immigrant communities who became less trusting of local police in participating jurisdictions. Moreover, there was no funding stream attached to the program, and, therefore, participation ended up costing the local entities, in large part by diverting resources to this effort. The peak year for the program was 2009, with 91 signed MOAs, including a mix of Task Force, Jail Enforcement, and Hybrid models blending the two, in force (Watson 2013). The Task Force program was phased out in 2012, and as of 2014, just 36 agencies provided Jail Enforcement under 287(g) (US ICE 2014).[2]

Sheriff Arpaio's trajectory in penal extremism

Sheriff Arpaio took office in January 1993, and by late summer, he had installed 'Tent City', a compound of 37 donated open-air military tents on a strip of Phoenix desert neighboring the city dump and local animal shelter. Originally designed to house up to 1,000 jail inmates (Bermudez & Casey 1993),[3] that compound became ground zero for the Arpaio punitive regime. It was not enough to house inmates in facilities subject to extreme heat in the summer[4] and occasional freezing conditions in winter (Slinger 2013), however. All aspects of life inside the facility were transformed over the next few years: meals were reduced to two a day, and hot meals and coffee were eliminated; post-expiration date food provisions (including the now-infamous 'green bologna') were purchased at cut-rates to feed inmates; since 1995, inmates have been issued pink underwear and are dressed in retro black-and-white-striped uniforms; chain gangs were instituted for men, women, and children; and nearly all recreational activities have been curtailed or eliminated (see Lynch 2004 and Finnegan 2009 for more details). These dehumanizing conditions seemed to catalyze widespread abuse by guards, who have been found in multiple investigations to systematically mistreat, degrade, and harm inmates (Amnesty International 1997; US Department of Justice 2011 [also noting a 1995 DOJ investigation]).

Arpaio transformed the law enforcement arm of the MCSO as well, deploying deputies and a huge 'posse' comprised of citizen volunteers to launch a number of operations in the county. These forces patrolled shopping malls in search of carjackers (Sanchez & Fiscus 1993); conducted road blockades to search cars for illegal drugs (Fritze 1993); made highly publicized prostitution sweeps (Fiscus 1994); 'ambushed' graffiti vandals (Leonard 1995); and went after parents behind on child support (Tyler 1995). Arpaio also used his law enforcement powers against personal and political foes, eventually formalizing this tactic through the creation of an anti-corruption task force, MACE, of which fully half of all investigations targeted known opponents of Arpaio and others in his office (Hensley & Wingett 2009). During his years in office, he has investigated and/or arrested journalists, citizens, county supervisors, judges, the state attorney general, and other law enforcement officials who have publicly opposed or criticized him or his office (Hagan 2012; Hensley & Wingett 2009).

All of these practices have been fodder for Arpaio's insatiable publicity machine. The MCSO issues press releases for nearly every policy move, scheduled event, and deployed operation. Arpaio regularly appears on local, national, and international news programs and talk shows and has been featured in major newspapers and magazines worldwide (Finnegan 2009; Hagan 2012; Lynch 2004). Such practices have cost the county more than $50 million in payouts to settle hundreds of lawsuits over wrongful deaths, injuries, and unlawful arrests, among other harms imposed by the MCSO (Hagan 2012). Between 2003 and 2007 alone, $30 million was paid out on claims against Arpaio and MCSO (Bolick 2008).

Arpaio turned to immigration soon after the 2005 election of Andrew Thomas as Maricopa County Attorney; Thomas had successfully campaigned on a hardline anti-immigration platform. Their first joint effort, in 2006, involved arresting and prosecuting defendants under a new state law making it a felony in Arizona to smuggle or conspire to smuggle humans for profit (AZ Stat. 13-2319). Stretching the law well beyond its intent, Arpaio created a 'Human Smuggling Unit' (HSU) comprised of deputies and posse members tasked with seeking out and arresting both smugglers and undocumented immigrants who had paid for border crossing assistance, on the theory that they co-conspired to commit the human smuggling of themselves (Archibold 2006). In the first eight weeks of operation, the HSU arrested 146 people under the statute (Archibold 2006) and held them in Tent City until their cases were resolved (see Eagly 2011 for a full discussion of this law's enactment and enforcement in Maricopa County). Just months later, Arpaio and the county signed the 287(g) Memorandum of Agreement with Homeland Security and sent 160 deputies off to South Carolina to be trained with ICE on federal immigration law. This became the single largest authorized officer group among all the 287(g) participating agencies; the MCSO then supplemented the 287(g) force with unauthorized deputies and posse members to focus on immigration enforcement.[5]

Arpaio's embrace of immigration enforcement triggered a major reprioritization of agency resources. Two local newspapers and the conservative Phoenix think tank the Goldwater Institute issued reports based on analyses of internal records indicating that all of MCSO's core missions suffered due to immigration-related 'misplaced priorities' (Bolick 2008, p. 1). In two years, MCSO response times to service calls dramatically increased, arrest and clearance rates fell, service of warrants in non-immigration cases declined, and numerous violent crimes went uninvestigated, including 432 sexual assault and child molestation crimes over a three-year period (Bolick 2008; Gabrielson & Giblin 2008; USDOJ 2011). Furthermore, the immigration enforcement efforts cost the county millions of dollars in overtime for officers assigned to those duties, racking up a $1.3 million budget deficit in three months (Bolick 2008).

Arpaio's practices also came under fire for the discriminatory and abusive manner in which they were implemented. Within the jails, Spanish-speaking detainees were denied jobs, basic services, and access to legal resources for not using English and were called derogatory names and racial slurs in both English and Spanish (USDOJ 2011). Law enforcement efforts not only targeted people well beyond the intended scope of the 287(g) program, as will be detailed below, but also relied on unconstitutional racial profiling techniques (*Melendres v. Arpaio* 2013).

Delegation or transformation of law?

The underlying logic of the 287(g) program assumes a direct and clean dispersal of legal mandates—put simply, that local and state participants become de facto federal immigration agents, extending the power and reach of Homeland Security's version of legal policy. Specifically, ICE characterizes the delegation as one in which 'designated officers…perform immigration law enforcement functions, provided that the local law enforcement officers receive appropriate training and function under the supervision of ICE officers' (US ICE 2014).

Several lines of scholarship suggest that logic does not comport with empirical realities of policy in action. The devolution of federal power to state and local actors conceptually overlaps with what Garland (1996) calls a 'responsibilization strategy' whereby the state devolves powers and responsibilities down to local, primarily non-profit organizations and institutions as a new mode of governance. The responsibilization process, in its ideal form, 'leaves the centralized state machine more powerful than before, with an extended capacity for action and influence' (Garland 1996, p. 454) through its coordination and partnership with new organizational entities. In the case of the 287(g) program, while the transfer of responsibilities occurs between traditional state actors, rather than to non-public entities, it does breech formerly impermeable jurisdictional borders via the federal government's deployment of a 'multi-agency/multi-authority approach that encompasses federal, state and local resources, skills and expertise' (US ICE 2014). Thus, similar logics drive this devolution of power and responsibility, in that the federal government hands off direct management of its duties to autonomous agencies, while (ideally at least) extending its own power through that move.

Such a strategy has the strong potential to take shape quite differently than its idealized form. Goddard's (2012) ethnographic work on the devolution of youth crime-prevention efforts to community-based organizations is particularly instructive. He found that while the devolution process does indeed extend and reinforce state governance through non-state partners, it was a symbiotic process since 'the [s]tate's power is dependent upon the local agencies' acquiescence to act' (Goddard 2012, p. 359). Moreover, the agencies imbued with responsibilities at times subverted the goals of the state by mimicking the appropriate rhetoric while acting in ways that served local needs.

In a wholly distinct line of work, 'legal endogeneity' scholars have argued that 'law should be considered, at least in part, as endogenous, constructed in and through the organizational fields that it seeks to regulate' (Edelman, Leachman & McAdam 2010, p. 656). Researchers in this area have delineated a process by which often-ambiguous legal mandates are interpreted, institutionalized, and legitimized by those organizations subject to them, which in turn feeds back to shape legal institutions' interpretations of compliance. Law in this model is a 'continuously evolving institution that is shaped and given meaning through its interaction with organizations' (Edelman, Leachman & McAdam 2010, p. 656.). Thus, this line of work makes clear that law is dynamic in meaning and contextually constituted, so an unadulterated imposition of a legal mandate, or as in this case, transfer of legal power, can be nothing more than an ideal.

While both of these lines of work focus on the devolution, dispersal, and transformation of legal power and responsibilities into non-state fields, they suggest an analytic starting point for the kind of relationship authorized by the 287(g) program. First, both sets of insights push beyond the policy-practice, or law-on-the-books/law-in-action scholarship by highlighting the dynamic features of how law moves across fields and actors. The work on legal endogeneity also resists a top-down model whereby the reshaping of legal meanings and practices begins and ends with on-the-ground organizational practices. Rather, this work demonstrates how law's articulation by recipient organizations feeds back to even the loftiest law-making institutions through the former's construction of procedures and policies meant to satisfy law's demands (Edelman et al. 2011).

In the coming analysis, I build on these insights in two ways. First, by examining the conferral of legal power (as opposed to the imposition of legal mandates, as has been the substance of the legal endogeneity literature) between differently situated *state* actors (as opposed to the state-private relationships addressed in both the responsibilization and legal endogeneity literatures), I demonstrate how localized enforcement powers are immediately amplified and extended. Because local law enforcement agencies begin the relationship with deeply institutionalized legitimacy, well-developed organizational structures, and considerable resources, they are able to incorporate the federal law into their organizations with little expenditure or effort. This, then, can lead to subsumption to the local (or localization) whereby the local organization absorbs the new law into its preexisting logics, structures, and modes of action, an effect contrary to the idealized logic of 287(g). Put simply, local officers do not become federal agents; federal law becomes a new tool for local officers to use in their existing regimes.

This leads to my second contribution, which is to delineate how, in this kind of arrangement, the legal power in motion can be remade such that it is difficult to identify, contain, or rescind. Thus, once the law is localized, the federal powers bestowed may be formally revoked, but the institutional practices they spawned can be maintained and dispersed to new locales. Indeed, in this case, the delegation of federal immigration law enforcement powers directly contributed to the growth of an extreme punitive regime, making it that much more formidable an opponent when the federal government sought to exit the partnership, and when the federal court attempted to rein in Arpaio's anti-immigration practices.

Figure 4.1 illustrates the proposed process of how the federal law becomes incorporated locally, as illustrated by this case. The federal immigration authority, rather than functioning as a distinct and specialized subfield of practice in the larger organization, enters into the

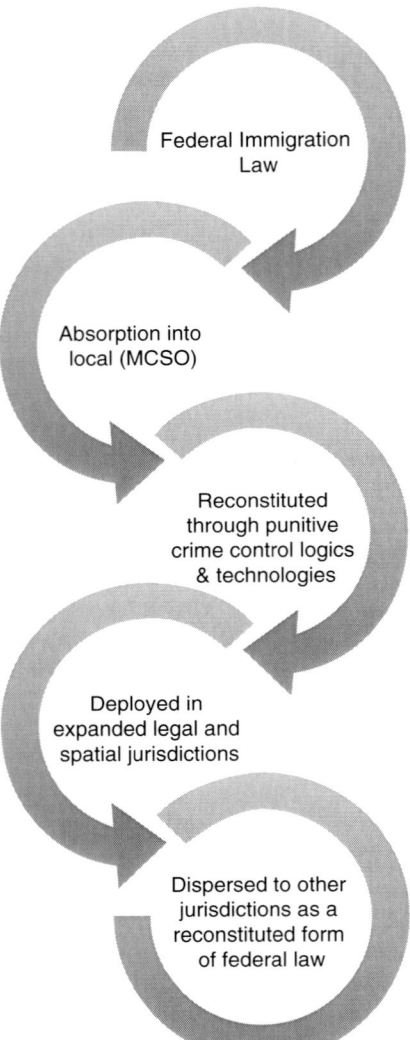

Figure 4.1   Flow and Transformation of Federal Immigration Law under 287(g)

local operation and is deployed through the logics and technologies of MCSO, thereby contributing to the 'crimmigration' (Stumpf 2006) of federal immigration law while simultaneously beefing up the local organization through the absorption of the powers that uniquely attend federal immigration enforcement. The reconstituted model of immigration law is then dispersed first within MCSO's jurisdiction as a new law and order weapon. It is also dispersed outside of the MCSO boundaries, in part through the publicized drama produced by this case and propelled by Arpaio through his ubiquitous press releases (Hagan 2012).

The marriage of 287(g) and Arpaio

The absorption into the local

As noted above, by the time Arpaio signed the 287(g) MOA, the MCSO had already begun to build an institutional infrastructure within its law enforcement operations that was devoted to enforcement of the new state human smuggling law. That infrastructure reproduced Arpaio's extreme version of law enforcement while directly extending the regime to encompass 'illegals' as criminal targets (Pomfret & Geis 2006). The agency applied the well-established law enforcement strategy of specialized units—one that Arpaio had creatively used throughout his tenure—when it devised the Human Smuggling Unit (HSU) in 2006.

While the HSU was initially comprised of just two deputies (supplemented by hundreds of volunteer posse members), this unit became a building block for a new and larger configuration, the 'Illegal Immigration Interdiction strike force' (affectionately referred to as the 'Triple I'), which was created in 2007 once MCSO joined the 287(g) program. Triple I was devised as the parent structure of all MCSO immigration enforcement, so HSU became a division within that structure and was ramped up in size. Soon after the ratification of the 287(g) MOA, Arpaio issued a press release announcing the new Triple I strike force, comprised of 'a community action team (CAT), a human smuggling unit, and a specialized jail operation [that...] will investigate, detain and arrest illegal aliens in the community and inside the jail facilities' (Arpaio 2007a). Thus, the federal powers allowed the MCSO to build out its nascent anti-immigration enforcement structure, but within the existing logic and methods of MCSO's local model of crime control.

The local absorption process is also evident in how Arpaio extended his penal regime to his new war on immigrants. Three months into the MCSO's pre-287(g) state immigration enforcement efforts, Arpaio contrasted his penal approach to that of the federal government's: 'If you get caught by [federal] immigration you get a free ride back to Mexico in an air-conditioned bus. A free ride? Not in my county. I'm going to put them on chain gangs, in tents, and feed them bologna sandwiches' (Pomfret & Geis 2006). This set the stage for how Arpaio managed immigration detention once in the 287(g) program, through an intensification in punitiveness as vastly more immigration-related arrestees were brought into custody. For example, in early 2009, he issued a press release announcing a planned relocation of 200 'illegal aliens to be chained and marched' for an hour-long journey on foot from a regular jail facility to a newly expanded, segregated section of Tent City, 'their new place of incarceration until their sentences are served and the illegal aliens are deported to their home countries' (Arpaio 2009a). The 'perp walk' was widely covered by media, adding a new debased group to Arpaio's publicity repertoire. So rather than creating an insulated unit of specialists within the jail enforcement program that treated 287(g) arrestees like federal immigration detainees, this program facilitated the expansion of existing local practices by bringing new bodies into MCSO's punitive machine.

It also inspired punitive innovation that built on the longstanding degradation strategy within the jails, in this case via a form of nationalism that seems directly designed to denigrate undocumented persons in custody. For instance, Arpaio ordered that undocumented inmates, once housed in Tent City, be educated on American immigration law so they could understand the gravity of their offenses. If found to violate rules in Tent City, they were also subject to time on a special immigrant-only chain gang that cleans up garbage in the desert on known border crossing/human smuggling routes (Arpaio 2009a). Additionally, beginning in 2006, as anti-immigration became his focus, Arpaio instituted a 'patriotism' program in the jails, so inmates begin and end the day with the Star Spangled Banner and God Bless America playing over the PA system (Arpaio 2007b; Karimi 2014). Within the regular jail facilities, inmates are now required to display American flag decals on the walls, and if they remove or deface them, are punished with a diet of bread and water (Karimi 2014). Finally, in direct contraversion of the 287(g) policies that the MCSO was required to uphold, jail staff enforced an English-only policy on prisoners, even refusing to meet sanitary and medical care needs if requests were not made in English (USDOJ 2011).

Immigration and 'crime control' meld, ideologically and technologically

The absorption process melds federal immigration control and local law enforcement, resulting in ideological and technological outputs that mimic the localized norms, discourses, and practices, but that target new subjects. In this case, the local-federal meld can be observed in how the immigrant subject is rhetorically constructed by the MCSO, as well as in the modes of enforcement deployed in the field and in the custodial treatment within the jails. First, the target of enforcement and punishment is deemed a criminal, independent of any criminal behavior. Referred to as 'illegal aliens' or 'illegals' in official documents and press releases, the undocumented are imbued with criminal risk by virtue of status. Indeed, their status elevates their criminal risk, as reflected in Arpaio's explanation of the move of undocumented inmates to Tent City, which is fortified by a surrounding electric fence: 'This is a population of criminals more adept perhaps at escape. But this is a fence they won't want to scale because they risk receiving quite a shock—literally' (Arpaio 2009a; see Bosworth & Turnbull this volume for a detailed discussion of this criminalization process in a UK detention setting).

Because the undocumented are deemed per se criminal, the end goal is to use available law enforcement tactics to identify and arrest those in that status category regardless of criminal conduct. Accordingly, even before the 160 officers assigned to 287(g) duties had entered their initial training, Arpaio made clear that he was not going to follow the terms of the agreement that limited enforcement to major criminal offenders. In a press conference held soon after signing on to 287(g), he stated: 'Ours is an operation where we want to go after illegals, not the crime first. It's a pure program. You go after them and you lock them up... We want to stop illegals coming into this country and put them in jail' (Ruelas 2007, p. 10). Moreover, aggressive law enforcement tactics in this regime are justified as a means to that end goal of arresting undocumented persons, including targeting on the basis of racial characteristics and the widespread use of pretext stops to catch 'illegals' (Ruelas 2007, p. 10).

The MCSO's tactics included a number of well-developed organizational practices that were simply redirected toward undocumented immigrants. Predominant among these was the regular use of 'saturation patrols' and 'crime suppression sweeps' in which anywhere from dozens to hundreds of officers and posse members descended upon designated locales—including highways, deserts, towns, neighborhoods, and business districts—and proactively sought out the targeted offenders. Especially early in the regime, 'roving patrols' (Giblin 2008) were regularly used, where the sheriff's officers patrolled, after dark, the lightly traveled highways in and out of the county for cars suspected of holding immigrants. This tactic was highly reminiscent of the kind of race-based pretext stops used by agencies to identify narcotics transporters, characterized as 'driving while Black' (Harris 1997). Arpaio himself described how his deputies used this tactic in a rural corner of the county, which he characterized as 'prime hunting grounds' (Arpaio &

Sherman 2008, p. 36). He detailed how officers 'learned to spot which vehicles were most likely carrying illegals' (Arpaio & Sherman 2008, p. 36), then looked for any one of myriad reasons, from broken tail lights to out-of-date license tags, to make the stop.

The suppression sweeps, likewise, aimed to find any ostensible violation to justify intervention. In July 2007, Arpaio described an early saturation sweep in a press release:

> [M]ore than 200 armed Sheriff's deputies, reserves and volunteer posse along with the full resources of the Sheriff's Office including SWAT, aviation, electronic surveillance, night vision, and hi tech weaponry, will saturate valley cities as well as roadways and highways commonly used as transportation corridors for human trafficking.

> Sheriffs (*sic*) personnel will be targeting vehicles commonly used to move human cargo to destinations inside and outside the county. If a vehicle is stopped for cause, anyone inside who is determined to be an illegal alien by the Sheriff's immigration trained experts will be arrested and jailed (Arpaio 2007b).

Not only were enforcement strategies redirected toward immigrants, investigative technologies were as well. In July 2007, Arpaio initiated an 'illegal alien' tip hotline, which was advertised all over the county via banners attached to MCSO-owned semi-tractor trailers (Arpaio & Sherman 2008), which were 'driven on valley streets and roadways to familiarize the public with the hotline number' (Arpaio 2007b). Citizens were encouraged to report '*any* illegal' (emphasis in original), and the MCSO promised to pursue the case (Arpaio & Sherman 2008, p. 43). The hotline generated hundreds of calls, and as promised, the agency followed up on all tips, opening up new areas of enforcement, as detailed below.

Expanded enforcement powers open up new territories of control

There are three planes on which the 287(g) powers both widened and deepened the reach of Arpaio's extreme crime control and punishment regime. The first and most straightforward one is the expansion of legal jurisdiction that comes through the 287(g) delegation process. While the state human smuggling law had provided the entrée into immigration enforcement, even under the very broad interpretation under which Arpaio operated, the enforcement was still limited to suspected instances where money was exchanged in the furtherance of border crossings. The 287(g) authority allowed investigations into citizenship status in the course of criminal investigations, which Arpaio stretched to include infractions, which were then proactively sought as pretexts to identifying undocumented aliens.

That legal expansion thus brought new categories of potential 'illegals' into the gaze of MCSO, which represents the second plane of expansion in Arpaio's war on immigration. No longer limited to smuggling contexts, which led to the roving patrol model of enforcement, the MCSO moved into residential areas of the county in its search for undocumented subjects, utilizing saturation tactics to confront and arrest 'suspects'. Many saturation patrols were conducted in areas with high concentrations of Latinos and other minorities.[6] The patrols were typically several-day operations in which officers and posse members arrived at the designated location by vehicles, horseback, and helicopter and stopped hundreds of people in search of the undocumented. The town of Guadalupe, whose population of 5,000 is predominantly Latino and Yaqui Indian, was subject to one of these 'crime suppression sweeps' in April 2008, over the protests of the town's mayor and residents (Lemons 2008).

The hotline intensified this expansion, bringing several new suspect groups into the spotlight: day laborers, service workers (especially kitchen workers and cleaners), food vendors, and Latinos residing in crowded homes. Day laborers were the first and most highly sought target group, as announced in a press release titled 'Sheriff Arpaio goes after Day Laborers', issued soon after the hotline went into operation (Arpaio 2007d). The release credited the hotline for bringing this group to the attention of MCSO: 'Since the tip line was implemented, over 120 calls of 2,100 have been received specifically about day laborers' (Arpaio 2007d).

In a later press release, MCSO conflated day laborers with both crime and illegal status, as it announced an upcoming 'crime suppression operation…to help business owners…with the growing amount of crime associated with illegal immigration' (Arpaio 2008b). The business owners reported that the two-day laborer centers in the planned suppression area were 'magnets for more illegal aliens', which created 'an atmosphere detrimental to business'. Those who protested the targeting of day laborers also became subject to the Arpaio regime. Promising to 'intensify' MCSO efforts at one locale subject to weekly suppression sweeps, Arpaio announced he would increase the deployment of the Triple I 'as pro-illegal immigration demonstrators and illegal immigrant day laborers continue to protest [Arpaio's] illegal immigration policies' (Arpaio 2007e). Latino street vendors, too, became a sought-after target, prompting the MCSO to begin using county health code violations as a mode of uncovering undocumented persons (Arpaio deposition 16 November 2010; Collum 2008).

The third expansion catalyzed by the 287(g) partnership was territorial. While the sheriff's enforcement power does, on the books, extend to all localities within the jurisdiction, primary policing duty is usually limited to unincorporated areas of the county and those municipalities without their own police forces. Such was the traditional arrangement with the MCSO. This changed once Arpaio's office was empowered with 287(g) enforcement authority, however. Arpaio expanded his primary enforcement territories to include the two largest cities in the county, Phoenix and Mesa (along with some smaller cities with police forces), even though each has its own major police agency. Many of his press releases included a version of the following self-congratulatory refrain that positioned the MCSO as having the responsibility to enforce these laws, even if its peer agencies would not: 'The Maricopa County Sheriff's Office is and continues to be the only Arizona law enforcement agency enforcing all aspects of the Arizona human smuggling law and federal immigration laws' (Arpaio 2007c).

Politics was a driving force in this; Arpaio characterized leaders in both Phoenix and Mesa as unwilling to enforce immigration laws, and he called them out in his press releases in announcing his enforcement incursions into their jurisdictions. While both of these cities' police departments entered into 287(g) jail and task force partnerships (Capps, Rosenblum, Rodríguez & Chishti 2011), neither deployed those powers as aggressively as the MCSO. City leaders and the police chiefs in both cities publicly expressed concern about eroding relations with the large Latino communities in their jurisdictions and so used the 287(g) powers sparingly (Capps et al. 2011). In a press release announcing one anti-immigration incursion into Mesa, Arpaio justified his imperialistic enforcement as follows: 'Since no one else will enforce state and federal immigration laws, my deputies have gone into the City of Mesa for the third time. Sheriff's deputies will continue to enforce state and federal immigration laws everywhere in the county, including Mesa and Phoenix' (Arpaio 2007e). Indeed, Arpaio imposed immigration enforcement on these previously off-limits locales in what was clearly a power play to, in part, publicly ridicule municipal officials. For instance, in regard to enforcement efforts/incursions in Phoenix, press releases specifically mentioned that Phoenix citizens and business owners call upon the MCSO because they 'receive little help from the city of Phoenix' (Arpaio 2008b) and 'have more faith in the Sheriff's office' (Arpaio 2008a) to address illegal immigration.

Putting the genie back in the bottle?

The immigration enforcement practices of the MCSO prompted wide-ranging backlash, including protests, condemnation by state and national political figures, a class-action lawsuit filed in 2007 alleging the MCSO engaged in racial profiling, and an investigation, beginning in 2008, by the US Department of Justice into allegations of civil rights violations. In 2009, ICE decided not to renew its task force agreement with Arpaio, because 'his sweeps were not consistent with [ICE's] priorities' (Lemons 2009).[7] The DOJ investigation concluded in 2011, finding multiple, serious civil rights violations in both the enforcement and jail divisions' immigration-related practices. When Arpaio refused to cooperate with the DOJ to remediate the problems identified in its investigation, the Civil Rights Division filed a lawsuit against the sheriff, his office, and the county.[8] Concurrently, the *Melendres v. Arpaio* lawsuit proceeded to trial in federal district court, ultimately resulting in 2013 in a sweeping judgment against Arpaio finding that under his leadership, the MCSO engaged in racial profiling. The court permanently enjoined the MCSO from enforcing the state or federal immigration law as it had been doing, especially its traffic enforcement practices.

Despite these multiple blows to his immigration law enforcement authority, Arpaio has defiantly continued to seek out undocumented people to arrest, using substantially similar practices. The day after the task force authority was rescinded, Arpaio issued a press release titled 'Nothing Changes', in which he announced a planned two-day suppression sweep that would 'incorporate all aspects of illegal immigration laws, such as employer sanctions, human smuggling, and crime suppression' (Arpaio 2009b).[9] He made two conceptual moves of note in this release. First, he cited two *state* laws to be enforced using the same methodology that had been in use for two-and-a-half years under 287(g) enforcement. Second, 'crime suppression' here became synonymous with illegal immigration, as the two had been tightly linked in numerous press releases throughout the 287(g) period. The press release went on to report the numbers in that regard, noting that 'this office has arrested and detained over 33,000 illegal aliens since the inception of the 287(g) program in 2007' (Arpaio 2009b).

Six months later, Arpaio issued a press release announcing his 14th county-wide crime suppression sweep, which would focus on 'illegal alien'-related enforcement. The release reported that, in the wake of losing 287(g) authority:

> Arpaio...ordered that all 900 sworn deputies be properly trained to enforce illegal immigration laws, a move made necessary after the recent decision by Department of Homeland Security to take away the federal authority of 100 deputies, all of whom had been formally trained by ICE (Immigration and Customs Enforcement) to enforce federal immigration laws.

> 'They took away the ability of 100 federally trained deputies to enforce immigration laws and so I replaced them with 900 sworn deputies, all of whom are now in a position to enforce illegal immigration laws in Maricopa County', Arpaio said (Arpaio 2010).

Thus, Arpaio not only reclaimed his right to enforce immigration law, he localized it outside of the confines of 287(g) by deputizing all of his officers as immigration law enforcers. Once localized, the federal enforcement power that had been bestowed was difficult to isolate and extract.

Moreover, in defiance of the *Melendres* court order, and under the ongoing threat of the Department of Justice lawsuit, Arpaio has continued to authorize crime sweeps, even if less blatantly characterizing them as focusing on illegal immigration. By 2013, Arpaio regularly chastised the federal government for its failures in closing the US-Mexico border, while his office concentrated on enforcing (ostensibly) state immigration laws. In one such press release, he derided the federal government for losing track of hundreds of MCSO-identified 'illegal immigrants', then described how his office continued to successfully tackle immigration using state law: 'The Maricopa County Sheriff's Office is closing in on 6,000 arrests under the Human Smuggling statute, which was passed into law by the Arizona State Legislature' (Arpaio 2013). The office has also adopted a more aggressive strategy, continuing into the present, of raiding cleaning companies and restaurants in order to identify and arrest, on state ID theft and forgery charges, those using false identification to work (Arpaio 2014).

Conclusion

In many ways, the potential consequences of this delegation of power were evident, or at least should have been, before the conferral of power ever happened. Arpaio was a known quantity to the federal government well before 2007. He had been investigated by the Department of Justice in the mid-1990s regarding conditions in Tent City, his extreme practices were internationally infamous, and his defiant stance toward any effort to rein them in was fundamental to his public persona. While the original 287(g) arrangement was ratified under a very different federal executive branch (one that virtually ignored civil rights as a Department of Justice concern, for instance), it would take willful ignorance to not see the potential for abuse by conferring power to this sheriff.

The effect of this federal-local partnership is not limited to the extremity of its realization in Maricopa County, nor to the difficulty of reining in the enforcement powers once conferred, however. The partnership elevated Arpaio's platform and authority by first inviting him into the world of federal immigration enforcement, providing him with additional credentials in the immigration arena, then pushing him out. The rebuff predictably motivated Arpaio to publicly declaim the federal government, bolstered by the added legitimacy that came with his experience with the 287(g) program. Consequently, his brand of the war on immigration has helped shape immigration law within Arizona and around the nation. Arpaio's slant on immigration is evident in the text of SB 1070, the state's sweeping anti-immigration law, introduced by Arpaio's former chief deputy, Senator Russell Pearce, and passed by the state legislature in 2010. As passed, the legislation looked very much like Arpaio's interpretation of 287(g), providing officers with the ability to intervene into the business of nearly anyone who looks suspiciously 'illegal'.[10] Political candidates around the nation, including Rick Perry during his presidential primary campaign, actively sought Arpaio's endorsement, specifically for his anti-immigration credentials (see Hohmann 2010). Indeed, Arpaio has emerged as a central spokesman for the national far-right about the problem of immigration, most recently in debates over Central American youth entering the US in large numbers (see Hannity 2014). And while his practices are extreme relative to peer organizations, they are not qualitatively distinct. Over half of all 287(g) detentions in 2010 were of suspected misdemeanants, traffic violators, or non-criminals, indicating that local enforcement has not hewed to federal directives. In some jurisdictions, especially in the South, only a fraction of detainees are suspected of serious crimes, and accounts of racial profiling and over-zealous enforcement, similar to the MCSO's practices, have emerged (Capps et al. 2011).

Finally, and more fundamentally, this case highlights the importance of the 'local' in understanding why law takes the particularized shape it does in any given time and place (Lynch 2011). The 287(g) program may have produced any number of implementation styles, but these styles are *necessarily* going to be propelled by the pre-existing structures, conditions, and ideologies of the local recipient agency. And, to return to the notion of endogeneity of law, the subsumption process should be expected to culminate with the reconstitution of the law, which is spit back out to the world in its new formation. While Arpaio, as immigration enforcer, now sits in an oppositional position to the current configuration of federal immigration authority, rather than as an extension of it (reflected most pointedly in the rescission of his enforcement powers and the ongoing DOJ case), his vision of federal immigration law and policy has infiltrated the legal and political landscape across the nation. And through his extremity, he has expanded the universe of possibility in a punitive war against immigrants, leading to innovation transfer outside the borders of Maricopa County and cultivating new tensions and debates about what immigration enforcement should look like.

Notes

1 I rely substantially on MCSO's press releases, many of which were entered into evidence in the *Melendres v. Arpaio* racial profiling trial that concluded in 2013. Many of his press releases are available on the MCSO website (http://www.mcso.org/PressRelease/Default.aspx); however, most of those relevant to this case have been removed from the site. These documents are on file with the author.

2 The Secure Communities program is functionally replacing much of the 287(g) function.

3 The original name of the compound was In-Tents Jail (Bermudez & Casey 1993), but Tent City was the name that caught on. As of 2014, Tent City is occupied by 2,000 inmates.

4 Temperatures, as measured inside the tents, have reached 145 degrees in the summer, 30 degrees above the outside temperatures, because the tents can 'mimic ovens or hot cars' (Scott 2011).

5 The number of additional unauthorized members was event-driven. Major sweeps involved hundreds of extra officers and posse members, whereas more targeted operations may include just a handful.

6 There was also another model occasionally used by MCSO that might be best characterized as a purification model—targeting day laborer congregations in 'lily-white' areas (Lemons 2008), especially when vocal constituents or political allies requested intervention. Arpaio orchestrated one such sweep in his own upscale hometown of Fountain Valley.

7 The jail enforcement contract was renewed in 2009 but was subsequently terminated in 2012.

8 The case against Arpaio and the county are still pending as of this writing.

9 Early on in this battle, he asserted a continued right to enforce federal immigration law even without 287(g) authorization as he continued his immigration enforcement regime. He cited a non-existent federal statute, erroneously provided by one of his sergeants, in support of this position. See Melendres 'Findings of Fact' at 129. See Eagly (2011) on local police authority to enforce federal *criminal* immigration violations.

10 See Shahani (2010) for an immigration rights advocate's analysis in just these terms, essentially blaming Napolitano for creating the Arpaio 'monster' that helped spawn controversial and expansive state-level anti-immigration law, SB 1070. Indeed, Arpaio named the immigrant-only Tent City section 'Camp 1070'.

References

Amnesty International 1997, *USA: Ill-treatment of inmates in Maricopa County jails, Arizona*, Amnesty International. Available from: <http://www.amnesty.org/en /library/info/A>. [10 January 2015].

Archibold, R 2006, 'Arizona county uses new law to look for illegal immigrants', *New York Times* May 9. Available from: <http://www.nytimes.com/2006/05/10 /us/10smuggle.html? pagewanted=print&_r=0>. [08 January 2015].

Arizona Republic Editorial 1992, 'Our choices: Arpaio for sheriff', *Arizona Republic* 1 November. Available from: <http://www.azcentral.com/news/articles/1992 /11/01/ 19921101joe-arpaio-for-sheriff.html>. [08 January 2015].

Arpaio, J deposition 2010, 'Videotaped deposition of Sheriff Joseph M. Arpaio, Phoenix, Arizona, November 16' *Melendres v. Arpaio*, Exhibit 15, CV 07-2513-PHX-GMS.

Arpaio, J (Sheriff, Maricopa County) 2007a, *Arpaio deploys first of 160 deputies & officers in comprehensive fight against illegal immigration*, press release, Maricopa County Sheriff's Office, 29 March.

Arpaio, J (Sheriff, Maricopa County) 2007b, *Sheriff's crackdown on illegal immigration heats up: hundreds of deputies/volunteers targeting profile vehicles; Arpaio opens hotline for citizens to report illegal aliens*, press release, Maricopa County Sheriff's Office, 20 July.

Arpaio, J (Sheriff, Maricopa County) 2007c, *Sheriff's anti-human smuggling unit arrests 8 more illegals*, press release, Maricopa County Sheriff's Office, 8 August.

Arpaio J (Sheriff, Maricopa County) 2007d, *Sheriff Arpaio goes after day laborers*, press release, Maricopa County Sheriff's Office, 4 October.

Arpaio J (Sheriff, Maricopa County) 2007e, *Arpaio intensifies presence at pro-illegal immigration protest at Pruitt's*, press release, Maricopa County Sheriff's Office, 5 December.

Arpaio J (Sheriff, Maricopa County) 2008a, *Sheriff mobilizes posse in central Phoenix. Crime suppression operation. Illegal immigration arrests anticipated*, press release, Maricopa County Sheriff's Office, 18 January.

Arpaio J (Sheriff, Maricopa County) 2008b, *Arpaio's crime suppression operation migrates north to Bell Road*, press release, Maricopa County Sheriff's Office, 27 March.

Arpaio J (Sheriff, Maricopa County) 2009a, *Arpaio orders move of hundreds of illegal aliens to their own Tent City: electric fence to minimize escape risk*, press release, Maricopa County Sheriff's Office, 3 February.

Arpaio J (Sheriff, Maricopa County) 2009b, *Sheriff Arpaio: 'nothing changes' crime suppression operation underway in Northwest Valley*, press release, Maricopa County Sheriff's Office, 16 October.

Arpaio J (Sheriff, Maricopa County) 2010, *Arpaio announces 14th Crime Supression (sic) Operation as human smuggling arrests have dramatically increased this year*, press release, Maricopa County Sheriff's Office, 18 March.

Arpaio J (Sheriff, Maricopa County) 2013, *Maricopa County Sheriff Breaks up Human Smuggling Ring*, press release, Maricopa County Sheriff's Office, 27 February.

Arpaio J (Sheriff, Maricopa County) 2014, *83ʳᵈ criminal employment/ID theft case leads Sheriff's office to state capitol complex. Arrested nine illegal immigrants involved in state crimes*, press release, Maricopa County Sheriff's Office, 13 June.

Arpaio, J & Sherman, L 2008, *Joe's law: America's toughest sheriff takes on illegal immigration, drugs and everything else that threatens America*, Amacom Books, New York.

Bermudez, F & Casey, RF 1993, 'Tent City: canvas replaces bars for inmates', *Arizona Republic* 4 August. Available from: <http://www.azcentral.com/news/articles/2010/03/ 13/20100313joe-arpaio-tent-city.html>. [08 January 2015].

Bolick, C 2008, *Mission unaccomplished: the misplaced priorities of the Maricopa County Sheriff's Office*, Goldwater Institute Policy Report. [2 December 2008].

Capps, R, Rosenblum, M, Rodríguez, C, & Chishti, M 2011, *Delegation and divergence: a study of 287(g) state and local immigration enforcement*, Migration Policy Institute. Available from: <https://www.migrationpolicy.org/research/delegation -and-divergence-287g-state-and-local-immigration-enforcement>. [08 January 2015].

Collum, L 2008, 'Police: food cart vendors did not have permits', *Arizona Republic* 1 August. Available from: <http://www.azcentral.com/news/articles/2008/08/0 1/20080801permits 0801.html>. [08 January 2015].

Darnton, R 1984, *The great cat massacre*, Basic Books, New York.

Eagly, I 2011, 'Local immigration prosecution: a study of Arizona before SB1070', *UCLA Law Review*, vol. 58, pp. 1749–1817.

Edelman, LB, Leachman, G & McAdam, D 2010, 'On law, organizations, and social movements', *Annual Review of Law and Social Science*, vol. 6, pp. 653–85.

Edelman, LB, Krieger, LH, Eliason, SR, Albiston, CR & Mellema, V 2011, 'When organizations rule: judicial deference to institutionalized mployment Structures', *American Journal of Sociology*, *117*, 888–954.

Finnegan, W 2009, 'Sheriff Joe: Joe Arpaio is tough on prisoners and undocumented immigrants, what about crime?', *New Yorker* 20 July.

Fiscus, C 1994, 'Prostitution posse set for duty', *Arizona Republic* 24 March. Available from: <http://www.azcentral.com/news/articles/1994/03/24/19940324joe -arpaio-prostitute-posse.html>. [08 January 2015].

Fritze, D 1993, 'Sheriff plans drug blockade' *Arizona Republic* 17 December. Available from: <http://www.azcentral.com/news/articles/1993/12/17/19931217joe -arpaio-drug-blockade.html>. [08 January 2015].

Gabrielson, R & Giblin, P 2008, 'MCSO evolves into an immigration agency', *East Valley Tribune* 10 July. Available from: http://www.eastvalleytribune.com/ special_reports/ reasonable_doubt/>. [08 January 2015].

Garland, D 1996, 'The limits of the sovereign state: strategies of crime control in contemporary society', *British Journal of Criminology*, vol. 36, pp. 445–71.

Giblin, P 2008, 'Human smuggling unit in action', *East Valley Tribune* 10 July. Available from: <http://www.eastvalleytribune.com/special_reports/reasonable _doubt/>. [08 January 2015].

Goddard, T 2012, 'Post-welfarist risk managers? Risk, crime prevention, and the responsibilization of community-based organizations', *Theoretical Criminology*, vol. 16, pp. 347–63.

Hagan, J 2012, 'The long, lawless ride of Sheriff Joe Arpaio: locking up the inno-cent. *Rolling Stone* 2 August. Available from: <http://www.rolingstone.com/culture/news/the-long-lawless-ride-of-sheriff-joe-arpaio-20120802>. [08 January 2015].

Hannity, S (television host) 2014, 'Sheriff Joe Arpaio on what's behind the bor-der surge' (transcript), Fox News 16 June 2014. Available from: <http://www.foxnews.com/on-air/hannity/transcript/2014/06/17/sheriff-joe-arpaio-whats-behind-border-surge>.

Harris, DA 1997, 'Driving while black and all other traffic offenses: the Supreme Court and pretextual traffic stops', *Journal of Criminal Law and Criminology*, vol. 87, pp. 544–58.

Hensley, JJ & Wingett, Y 2009, 'Does MACE unit fight corruption or political foes?' *Arizona Republic* 19 July. Available from: <http://archive.azcentral.com/arizonarepublic/news/articles/2009/07/19/20090719mace0719.html>.[08January 2015].

Hohmann, J 2010, 'Immigration foes like Arpaio in high demand', *Arizona Republic* 14 May. Available from: <http://www.azcentral.com/news/articles/2010/05/14/20100514immigration-foes-like-arpaio-in-high-demand.html>.[08 January 2015].

US ICE 2014, *Delegation of immigration authority section 287(g) Immigration and Nationality Act*, US Immigration and Customs Enforcement. Available from: <http://www.ice.gov/ news/library/factsheets/287g.htm>. [08 January 2015].

Karimi, F 2014, 'Sheriff Joe Arpaio: 38 Arizona inmates who defaced flag to eat only bread, water', *CNN* 24 January. Available from: <www.cnn.com/2014/01/24/justice/ arizona-inmates-bread-water/index.html>. [08 January 2015].

Leonard, S 1995, 'Arpaio will ambush graffiti vandals', *Arizona Republic* 23 March. Avail-able from: <http://www.azcentral.com/news/articles/1995/03/23/19950323joe-arpaio-graffiti-vandals.html>. [08 January 2015].

Lemons, S 2008, 'Guadalupe made it clear that Joe Arpaio's attacking anyone with brown skin', *Phoenix New Times* 29 May. Available from: <http://www.phoenixnewtimes.com/2008-05-29/news/guadalupe-made-it-clear-that-joe-arpaio-s-attacking-anyone-with-brown-skin/>. [08 January 2015].

Lemons, S 2009, 'Joe Arpaio scores 287(g) jails agreement in ICE announcement, ICE head says Arpaio has no federal authority to continue sweeps', *Phoenix New Times* 16 October. Available from: <http://blogs.phoenixnewtimes.com/bastard/2009/10/joe_arpaio_gets_ jails_agreemen.php>. [08 January 2015].

Litwin, M 2011, 'The decentralization of immigration law: the mischief of §287(g)', *Seton Hall Law Review*, vol. 41, pp. 399–426.

Lynch, M 2004, 'Punishing images: jail cam and the changing penal enterprise', *Punishment & Society*, vol. 6, pp. 255–70.

Lynch, M 2009, *Sunbelt justice: Arizona and the transformation of American punish-ment*, Stanford University Press, Redwood City, CA.

Lynch, M 2011, 'Mass incarceration, legal change and locale: understanding and remediating American penal overindulgence', *Criminology & Public Policy*, vol. 10, pp. 671–698.

Melendres v. Arpaio 2013, PHX-CV-07-02513-GMS.

Pomfret, T & Geis, S 2006, 'One sheriff sees immigration answer as simple', *Washington Post* 20 May. Available from: <www.washingtonpost.com/wp-dyn/content/article/2006/05/19/ AR2006051901856.html>. [08 January 2015].

Ruelas, R. (2007) 'Arpaio Stays Silent on Real ICE Plan', *Arizona Republic*, 2 March, p. 10.

Sanchez, R & Fiscus, C 1993, 'Sheriff's posse on mall patrol', *Arizona Republic* 18 November. Available from: <http://www.azcentral.com/news/articles/1993/11/18/19931118joe-arpaio-mall-carjackings.html>. [08 January 2015].

Scott, E 2011, 'Temperatures rise to 145 inside Tent City', *Arizona Republic* 3 July. Available from: <http://www.azcentral.com/arizonarepublic/local/articles/2011/07/03/20110703tent-city-temperatures-rise-145.html>. [08 January 2015].

Shahani, A 2010, 'In Arizona, feds are fighting a monster they built', *Colorlines* 26. Available from: <http://colorlines.com/archives/2010/07/in_arizona_feds_struggle_to_slay_an_ immigration _monster_they_built.html>. [08 January 2015].

Shermer, ET 2013, *Sunbelt capitalism: Phoenix and the transformation of American politics*, University of Pennsylvania Press, Philadelphia.

Slinger, A 2013, 'Tent City Inmates Brace for Freeze', ABC News 15 January. Available from: <http://www.abc15.com/news/region-phoenix-metro/central-phoenix/tent-city-inmates-bundle-up-for-freeze>. [08 January 2015].

Stumpf, J 2006, 'The crimmigration crisis: immigrants, crime, and sovereign power', *American University Law Review*, vol. 56, 367–419.

Tyler, L 1995, '50 deadbeat parents lassoed', *Arizona Republic* 30 July. Available from: <http://www.azcentral.com/news/articles/1995/07/30/19950730joe-arpaio-deadbeat-parents.html>. [10 January 2015].

US Department of Justice 2011, 'Letter to Bill Montgomery, County Attorney, Maricopa County. RE: United States' Investigation of the Maricopa County Sheriff's Office', 15 December.

Watson, T 2013, 'Enforcement and immigrant location choice', *National Bureau of Economic Research*, working paper no. 19626.

5

A New 'Ecology of Cruelty'? The Changing Shape of Maximum-security Custody in England and Wales

Alison Liebling, University of Cambridge

[T]he new prison sentences share with the death penalty this [life trashing] quality...shattering any possibility of common ground between agents of punishment and subjects of punishment.... Such sentences are cruel because they are undisguisedly aimed at causing despair in their targets (Simon 2001a, p. 129).

The whole system has changed. What controls everything is, like, inference. Before, you had to do stuff to be that person. Now you just have to say you'll do it, or someone else has to say you might do it. Nothing is real—it's not real anymore (Prisoner, in Liebling, Arnold & Straub 2011).

Interviewer: Can you think of five words that would describe what your life is like for you at Whitemoor?
Prisoner: I would say struggle. Perseverance. Solitude. Anxiety...and... just...what's the word...? Reflecting.[1]

Introduction: high-security imprisonment, risk, and danger

This chapter describes prisoners' accounts of their experience of the changing shape of high-security prisons in England. Their analysis of a new crisis of trust and recognition is powerful, troubling, and dangerous. The prisoner above who said, 'what controls everything is, like, inference.... Nothing is real', describes a world of diffuse suspicion, with assumptions of unworthiness, which have damaging effects on individuals and institutional dynamics. I describe how prisoners' existential and emotional needs were neglected in a spiral of liberty deprivation and distant reporting and how this constitutes a form of cruelty. Prisoners described anxiety, frustration, fear, anger, and resignation: 'feeling traps' in the face of arbitrary or administrative power. The effects of these dynamics include emotional harm, damage to 'agentic capacities' (Jacobs 2014), and the undermining of a civic disposition.

The study drawn on in this chapter constitutes a repeat of a research project conducted 12 years earlier in the same maximum-security prison during 1998–99. The repeat study was requested by the Home Office in 2008 following an Inspectorate (HMCIP) report describing apparently distant relationships between staff and prisoners. Since the original study had found positive relationships at the establishment, the finding of distance was a matter of concern to senior managers and external bodies. The second or repeat study was, like the first, broadly ethnographic. The fieldwork took place over the period of one year (2009–10). The research team[2] drew on four sources of data: sustained observation; a weekly thematic dialogue group with a regular group of prisoners; long interviews with 52 prisoners and 36 staff; and quality of life surveys with 159 randomly selected prisoners and 194 staff. The approach adopted was 'slow entry' into the field, building relationships with prisoners and staff over time before requesting long interviews. This proved helpful and appropriate and resulted in in-depth, high-quality interviews, often conducted over more than one sitting (see Liebling, Arnold & Straub in press).

The prisoners we interviewed were mainly young men, but some were in their 60s and 70s, requiring assistance from other prisoners to get to or from work in wheelchairs. A disproportionate number were Black or mixed race. Most were serving indeterminate life sentences, with minimum tariffs (the period of time to be served before becoming eligible for release) of 20 years or more. Many were beyond their tariffs by many years. Some were serving 'whole life' sentences, with no prospect of release. Many were facing periods in custody longer than they had been alive. Many would still be in prison in 25 years' time. Their sentences were 'awesome': unthinkable and overwhelming. They did their sentences 'one day at a time', by 'going to the gym', 'taking up yoga', or 'cooking'.

The study found that an all-consuming ideology of risk and danger had squeezed out humanity and trust, which had been present and flowing in the first study, in 'guarded' but significant ways.

Activities that permitted psychological growth among prisoners were now known as 'pampering' and so were restricted. Prisoners described experiencing crises of identity and survival, violence and the fear of violence, and religious and other forms of discrimination. They described being trapped: unable to access, or ineligible to take, the courses they were required to take in order to move on. They were 'too risky' to downgrade but not risky enough for intervention; and they were regarded as 'manipulative' if they engaged in positive behaviors. Few prisoners understood the logic or practice of 'getting off Cat A' (the highest and most restrictive security category). They lived for many years, often beyond their original tariff, or minimum sentence, in a Kafkaesque world of the social construction of danger. Some were, or clearly had been, violent. But the question of how continuing dangerousness was addressed, assessed, or understood, was, as prisoners, said, 'murky':

> *Interviewer:* Do the staff in here 'trust intelligently'? Do they know who to trust and who to worry about?
> *Prisoner:* I think they haven't got a clue about who to trust. There's not enough interaction for anyone to know who to trust.

These findings (see Liebling, Arnold & Straub 2011) resonated in surprisingly clear ways with accounts of supermax custody and extreme punishment emerging from the US (see, for instance, Reiter & Blair and Pittendrigh this volume). The new absence of trust, hope, and meaning had led to distancing from staff, inauthentic relations, and increased fear and violence in the prison compared to the situation as described only 12 years earlier (Liebling & Price 2001). What made this newly emerging form of imprisonment extreme was the length and indeterminacy of prisoners' sentences, the circumstances of their convictions, the lack of respect or recognition prisoners experienced in prison, and the lack of access to meaningful activities, including relevant work and further education. In response to a changing population composition, staff were newly fearful as well as distant. One of the 'situational pathologies' to arise was a new and complex use of faith identities by prisoners to gain recognition and power. This led to a complex rearrangement of the prisoner hierarchy and to acute forms of violence.

In his book, *Reforming Punishment*, Haney (2009) illustrates the many 'situational pathologies' created by harsh prison conditions and the destructive legacies they create. He identifies the 'flawed logic' that lies at the heart of worsening prison conditions in supermax prisons in the

US, describing the damaging impact of these depriving environments on individual identity and emotional range. He outlines the problematic set of ideological beliefs that encourage this extremely depriving and 'soul destroying' climate, fostering cruelty and a destructive set of interpersonal dynamics between prisoners and staff (Haney 2008). His analysis, as well as those of others working in the field of US and Canadian penology, is applicable to a form of long-term high-security imprisonment emerging in England and Wales in response to a series of major prison escapes, a rising fear of terrorism, and the imposition of increasing, disproportionate, and indeterminate sentence lengths on mainly young men of color. The effects of increased punitiveness, segregation, 'risk-informed logics', and 'narrow organisational understandings' of the person on institutional behavior and dynamics are stark, widespread, and deeply troubling (see Hannah-Moffatt & Klassen, Reiter & Blair, and Koenig this volume; see also Rhodes 2004; Shalev 2009). Our findings resonated with Craig Haney's (2008) account of the 'ecology of cruelty' arising in modern US supermax prisons, despite higher levels of movement and interaction in the English high-security prison. What resonated was the link between dehumanizing penal policies and the dysfunctional and damaging social climate created when staff and prisoners are subjected to them.

The prisoner cited above, who was 'reflecting', was describing a form of inner contemplation on the nature of his treatment. He could not act, or protest, for fear of major consequences relating to his 'progression', or movement down the security categories toward eventual release, but he observed, and inwardly digested, the state of play:

> I do generally think that the majority of staff here would like to see you being punished. I'll give you an example. Sometimes we eat outside. On the Ones [first landing] we put the tables out and everyone gets together, we eat together. So the officers will come and stand right opposite us and observe, and it's quite obvious they're doing that to intimidate us. I mean, there's always a...there's always an issue to hide behind... OK, 'we're doing it to observe'...there's nothing's going on. Well, fine, you do that, but we know, really, why you're standing there? And I think it's got to the point where people are actually self-censoring to the point where some of the people are reluctant to be on the Ones, they say, look we're going to get attention to ourselves, blah, blah, blah, and all we're doing is sharing a meal together. So, it's got to the point where if you're actually in a good mood or you're having a good laugh, you have to conceal

that from the officers. In case you get moved around or you get into trouble (Prisoner).

A social shift toward risk aversion, and the 'atmosphere of suspicion', meant that staff were 'always on red alert'. Staff felt under pressure from intelligence units within the Prison Service and the police to investigate, monitor, and report on prisoners. Officers were required to observe and manage prisoners 'for intelligence' on a daily basis. Prisoners were aware of the intelligence gathering and security measures taking place around them:

> Inmates have to be individualistic, because nowadays if you seem to... get too close to somebody, they look into it as something negative... If I get something from you, you get something from me, it's either bullying or we're planning a gang or we're doing something negative. They're looking at us negative... So nowadays, even if you want to help somebody, you have to be careful who you help out, where before it was no problem (Prisoner).

'Looking at us negative', a 'stripped down conception of the penal subject' (Dolovich 2012) had consequences for individuals and the prisoner community (see also Maruna et al. 2004).

Maximum-security prisons and the crisis of trust

> It's all about trust, innit? (Prisoner)

Scholarly interest in the treatment of long-term prisoners in conditions of high security has historically been precipitated by major events in England and Wales: major disturbances in the 1970s and 1980s and high-profile escapes in the 1990s. Problems of order and security have preoccupied those tasked with managing high-security prisons since their inception in the 1970s. The more recent interest has emerged less as a result of events, as both disorder and escapes have dramatically declined in the wake of improved management and staff practices, but rather in light of concerns in the media and elsewhere about gang-related violence and the risks of radicalization. I argue in this chapter that while these concerns need to be taken seriously, as do the potential links between them, this is not the right place to start in order to understand the contemporary problems of high-security imprisonment. The current 'crisis' is a crisis of trust, out of which a new ecology has formed.

High levels of distrust, between staff and prisoners in particular, led to further escalation of mutual suspicion and hostility over the relatively short period between the two studies (12 years). A 'fear and loathing' (Simon 2001b) of offenders convicted of acts of terrorist violence in particular, and of increasing numbers of young Black and mixed-race men convicted (often on joint enterprise charges) of gang-related violence involving drugs, guns, and heated local rivalries, made all prisoners 'objects of suspicion'. Rehabilitative aspirations had been subsumed by concerns about present and future 'vivid danger' (Padfield 2002). As one prisoner described:

Prisoner:	The problem is they're seeing inmates in the same way... it's not good to...for inmates to be seen talking to an officer for too long. So what happens is you've got this overriding culture between officers and inmates that inhibits having any meaningful relationship between inmates and staff.
Interviewer:	What one thing would improve the quality of your life here?
Prisoner:	The one thing? I think just...the belief in prisoners. I think that's lacking. I think sometimes it's easy to be cynical 'cause your job's on the line. Sometimes you just have to trust and have good expectations of people. So I'd say a culture shift towards being more positive. A very revealing incident for me was I managed to see what officers were writing...for my appeal interview I need to have some paperwork. In there I saw some of the comments that the staff were writing and you could see quite clearly there's quite a lot of racism, or negative beliefs, and it comes through in their writeups. For me it's quite upsetting to see...it's not only incorrect, it's just... it's quite scandalous. It's almost malicious.

The ideology staff expressed in action rendered prisoners, and specific groups of prisoners in particular, 'inherently untrustworthy':

Prisoner:	The problem I have is I'm in a minority...on top of that I'm a Muslim. So you get a lot... I know a lot of these people are ex-army, ex-police, ex-firemen, it's all one sort of family. So what you're going to find is a lot of people carry that ideology through together, like. So I think what happens is, they're looking...they see us through a certain prism and it taints the way they view us and...on the news

something happens in Afghanistan or Iraq, immediately if there's a Muslim walking down the corridor with a beard or a long shirt who looks like an Arab, he's going to get it.

Interviewer: Really?

Prisoner: I think what it is, there's a traditional form of racism, which I think is slowly fading out, to be honest. But I think there's a new form, which is, I mean, if you look at society as a whole, it's very anti-Islamic at the moment. It's difficult enough wearing a scarf outside without being assaulted, so you can imagine a guy who's come into prison who's found religion, then he's, like, I'll decide to grow a beard and have a long flowing shirt. These guys, and, like, they flick on the news, this guy's killed ten soldiers. They could come into work tomorrow morning, your typical Sun reader, right, it's him, his people...and so... Here you're at the mercy of officers and if they've got a problem with you, then you've got problems. I get stereotyped into that group of not wanting to be British, not sharing British values, inherently untrustworthy (Prisoner in Liebling, Arnold & Straub 2011).

That this trust has existed in UK high-security prisons, albeit in guarded and limited forms, is well established (see, e.g., Sparks et al. 1996; Liebling 2002). Prison staff at their best operate in a highly skilled and professional manner, distributing degrees and varieties of trust to many prisoners (choosing who to unlock, who to support, who to provide positive reports for, who to believe, and so on), and this form of trust is developed via enduring relationships with individual prisoners. This skilled use of discretion brings risks, but it is preferred to (that is, regarded as more legitimate than) blunt rule enforcement. The rules and their enforcement can be reasonable, and have tended to become more so in prisons in England and Wales, following a period of liberal reforms precipitated by the Woolf Report into a series of disturbances in the 1990s (Home Office 1991), and a subsequent emphasis on 'decency' in official discourse (Liebling, with Arnold 2004).[3]

This trajectory was interrupted in the wake of a rapidly changing social and political context characterized by increased punitiveness and emphasis on risk, drastically rising prison population size, shifting population composition, longer and more complex sentences, increasing gang membership and inter-prisoner violence, increasing accommodation of (and raised expectations among) minority religious groups in prison, and fears of radicalization in the wake of terrorist attacks. A new penological shift away from staff-prisoner interactions on prison landings toward security information reporting, governing-from-a-distance, actuarial methods of offender management, and achieving performance targets, meant that new generations of high-turnover managers were less visible in prison. Senior managers worked toward a 'hard-edged' model, meaning that the basic priority was custodial and cautious ('I don't want my staff to *like* prisoners, I want them to manage them with appropriate scepticism'; senior manager, in Liebling, Arnold & Straub 2011).

These dynamics altered the contours of daily prison life, making daily routines uncomfortable for staff and prisoners and full of caution on both sides. Staff no longer 'recognised their audience', in the terminology used by Bottoms and Tankebe (2012) in their analysis of legitimacy in criminal justice. Some groups of prisoners were especially subject to assumptions of risk, aggravating already existing social disparities (see Harcourt 2007). The proportion of Black and mixed-race prisoners had grown between the two research projects from 21 to 55 percent of Whitemoor's population. The proportion of Muslim prisoners had grown from a small and 'uncounted' number to 40 percent of Whitemoor's population. Half of this number were 'in-prison conversions'—a particularly feared or 'risk-laden' group. Many of these prisoners felt they were 'under constant scrutiny' (HMCIP 2008). Fewer prisoners were making their way out of the high-security prison or off the highest security level (Category A).

By 2008, far from constituting the 'oil' that made day-to-day life in prison 'work', staff-prisoner relationships were regarded as highly risky. Anxieties about 'conditioning' or manipulation, breaches of boundaries, or failures in security, made extended contact between staff (of any kind) and prisoners a matter of concern. Contact was monitored, and discouraged, in the wake of concerns about becoming unduly influenced by powerful prisoner 'leaders'. This preoccupation with the risks of relationships had reached extreme levels at the time of our research (in 2009–10):

> The best interaction in this jail, as far as I'm concerned, is with the teachers… On Monday, I was speaking to a teacher in my class. When I left the class, I heard an officer say something to her… I didn't hear exactly what he said, and I heard her say 'No, we were speaking about…' and that's the end of the conversation and I went. The next day I came back. I said to her, 'What…was he asking you about what

we was talking about?' and she said 'Yeah' and I said 'Why didn't you just tell him to get off...like, you're a teacher, that's your job. You're supposed to talk' but she said 'no, I just explained to him what we were talking about...' and I said, 'That's like bullying. He's not supposed to ask you what you're talking about. You're a teacher' (Prisoner).

Lengthy conversations—with teachers, chaplains, and officers, had become 'suspicious':

They can't move in this job...this job's all about security. That's why I think a lot of the communication...a lot of the relationships are not there... They can't talk to you for too long. If they're seen talking to you for more than 30 seconds, something's going on (Prisoner).

Staff were 'skating on ice', trying to find the right kind of relationship without taking risks. They were uncertain of their role, and they also had to absorb and make sense of a number of serious assaults on their colleagues. They were 'present' rather than 'engaged', completing tasks 'lightly' rather than forming relationships during the operation of day-to-day procedures (Crewe, Liebling & Hulley 2014). Staff and prisoners encountered each other 'in role' rather than out of it, but this meant that they often did not 'know each other' well enough to discard fears and stereotypes.

The problem of being regarded as 'inherently untrustworthy' was not confined to Muslim prisoners, but their experience illustrated a more general ideological shift away from a view of long-term prisoners as redeemable, worthy of investment (a view represented in several official reports, including Home Office 1968, 1984), and believable— toward an ideology of danger and unworthiness. This ideology had not been explicitly stated but was carried in the culture and practices of prison officers, senior managers and officials, and political discourse. Long-term prisoners were no longer a 'priority' for offending behavior courses. Their increasing distance from any prospect of release became an argument for neglect as well as an indicator of their dangerousness. The human consequences of this development were dire.

While the English high-security prison is not an exported 'supermax', transferred from the US, our research suggests that their tone and aspects of their operation have evolved and transformed in unexpected ways, which are recognizable in accounts of US supermax custody (see Rhodes 2004, 2009) and in descriptions of 'tough on crime' penal policies in the US more generally (see Simon 2014). The 'new logic of imprisonment' described by Simon in relation to California, but recognizable in our research in England, 'produced a zero sum contest between the dignity of prisoners and public safety' which promotes 'indifference to the needs of prisoners' (2014, p. 11). This 'social and moral indifference' (Rhodes 2009), or 'institutional thoughtlessness' (Crawley & Sparks 2005), excludes prisoners' existential and emotional needs.

Prisoners in Whitemoor described 'an intensification of enclosure' (Rhodes 2009, p.193) relating to the length and nature of their sentences, the prominence of risk assessments, and the pressures they faced in navigating their circumstances in an environment still social and 'liberal' in relation to each other, and yet constraining, exclusionary, and potentially violent. In addition to long and indeterminate sentences, prisoners were subjected to internal administrative procedures, particularly security categorization, sentence planning, transfer, and administrative segregation, processes that could lengthen their stay, increase their risk profile, and both deepen and 'tighten' their experience of custody (see Liebling et al. 2011; Crewe 2009; Lazarus 2006). These processes were mysterious and the decision-making diffuse and often the result of *inference*. *Getting in* to and struggling to *get out* of high security had major effects on the length of time spent in prison, but these processes were distant and opaque. Many prisoners did not 'deserve' to be in high-security conditions but were sent to fill spaces, or to complete a course, as a result of police information, or as a result of 'trouble' elsewhere in the system. One young mixed-race male, serving a 20-year sentence he had not expected, explained at four years into his sentence how he came to be Cat A:

> *Prisoner:*   I don't really know how it happened. I know I was in my cell one day, they came to me, they said 'You're going to the Seg'. 'Why?' They said 'We've been told that you're a potential Cat A. We have to hold you in the Segregation 'cause there's no...we don't hold Cat As in this prison'. They took me to the Seg...I was there for two days and then one morning, the third morning, they said 'Yeah, you're going' and [another prison's] officers were there and they took me to [that prison] and I was on the Cat A Wing. And ever since I've been Cat A.
>
> *Interviewer:* Have you had Cat A review boards?
>
> *Prisoner:*   I've had one Cat A review, and it didn't say anything on it. It just said 'you will remain Cat A'.
>
> *Interviewer:* OK. I mean, police intelligence is the other...
>
> *Prisoner:*   Yeah, police intelligence... Yeah, that's what they said... 'police intelligence...'

In a spiral of liberty deprivation, and the confounding of judicial with administrative decision-making, the lengthy tariff was in itself a reason to 'stay on Cat A': 'it is too soon—he's still got 20 years' (see Lazarus 2006 for an important critique of this logic). Prisoners compared their circumstances and speed of progress with others—there seemed to be no obvious relationship between culpability, risk, and the route to freedom. Compliance with sentence planning required active engagement with specified offending behavior courses. These requirements could change over time, as new courses were developed. The assessment documentation was frequently the subject of complaints relating to inaccuracies, lack of context, and the recording of casual conversations or remarks which 'stayed on file' for years. Prisoners were skeptical and reluctant to engage in the process, to their disadvantage:

> To tell the truth, until my last sentence planning, which was July, all the ones before that have just been rubbish, but I have to say that...I wouldn't say that I wasn't co-operating with it, but I weren't as... interested in it as I was the last time 'cause this last one, now, I've been doing...I've been having a lot of input, 'cause obviously I've been here a while now, seen how everything goes and I've realized that you have to go through certain avenues...so my last one they recommended certain courses. I've been trying to get on courses. I've been writing letters. I've been very involved. ... My offender manager's had to change my OASys (risk assessment) paper about seven times...because I've gone through it and...things were wrong and wrong information, whereas the ones before...I hadn't even been going through them, so they'd been putting wrong things on there... (Prisoner).

Prisoners were highly critical of the quality and tone of these reports. One prisoner brought his risk assessment document to a Dialogue group discussion to point out, to the other prisoners' amusement, that the information contained in it did not relate to him. It referred to his wife and children—but he was not married and had no children. Prisoners waited years to be assessed for recommended programs, sometimes only to be told they were not eligible—as they put it, 'not violent enough'. False information was impossible to erase. Even overturned adjudications reappeared as 'the reason you are not eligible for a family visit'. There were traps everywhere.

As a result of continuous monitoring and assessment, self-censorship was an art form. Prisoners checked their demeanour, their contact with others, their networks, and their expressed emotional range. Every move had consequences. Those who had not learned the skills and self-control required to contain their frustration were doomed. One prisoner said of another, whom he had grown up with and who was regarded as requiring special administrative measures:

The picture that's painted of him is all wrong. 'Cause they don't know him. At the same time, yeah, I understand why that picture gets painted of him. He doesn't know how to communicate. That's all it is. It's like I keep saying, if you don't know how to communicate in a middle-class fashion in a middle-class institution, you're not going to get anywhere. He's got no education. He only knows how to communicate on a street kind of level. You are going to frighten them. That's all it is. Jerome [pseudonym] is a mouse. He's just—he just doesn't know how to communicate. Intimidation is the only thing he knows, so he's become good at it. He can look frightening. That's the one style of communication he has encountered. That's all he's got, really. It's making it all bad for him... There's much worse people than him in here. It becomes a self-fulfilling prophecy. It's like going to court—if they bring out armed police, everyone thinks you are really dangerous. When you are in here, you have to know how to deal with people, how to not get those labels. Jerome is not even in here for a violent crime. The other day they knocked him back for his Cat A review. They won't let him do the CALM (anger management) course—because he's got no violence on his record. Then they knock him back on his Cat A review because he's dangerous! He's been in jail nine years. If he was as bad as they say he is, he'd be in the unit. He's all mouth. He wouldn't understand why he comes across as being dangerous. He's just telling them (Prisoner).

Being 'all mouth' was fatal. Prisoners were being punished for a life-style they did not choose: for structural disadvantages and related cultural practices or codes that became indicators of dangerousness. Some prisoners talked at length with us about their experiences of poverty, hardship, and exclusion: the learning of aggression and posturing to survive, 'acting street' (Fader 2013). In long interviews, they revealed complex and contradictory values, emphasizing fatherhood, material striving, and loyalty. As many qualitative penal scholars have argued:

I can conclude only that even youth who are the most embedded in street culture are well aware of and in fact aspire to mainstream values of work, family, and above all, dignity (Fader 2013, p. 33; see also Shapland & Bottoms 2012).

Yet the conditions of their confinement seemed to provoke prisoners in ways that made preserving any grain of autonomy compelling. The more prisoners fought, the more their isolation and punishment 'tightened around them' (see Rhodes 2009).

Race, religion, and the crisis of trust

Prisoners faced other major difficulties in this new ecology. Rates of conversion to Islam (particularly among younger Black and mixed-race prisoners) were high, but the pathways were varied and complex. Faith identities were being adopted and used in many ways, including for meaning and protection. The main motivations for turning to faith or faith identities included dealing with the pains of long-term imprisonment; seeking 'anchored relations' and protection; seeking meaning and identity development; rebellion; and in some cases, coercion. Whatever else was going on, prisoners found that faith practices offered a new form of both 'salvation' and power. A lower level of professional confidence among staff meant they kept a distance from some prisoners, fearing accusations of discrimination on religious grounds, so they were reluctant to 'police' faith-related claims. Lack of knowledge in a new multicultural context led to a risk of faith becoming the new 'no go area' in prison. Many prisoners exploited this gap, asking for adaptations to the regime, pressing others to pray at inconvenient times, or imposing rules prohibiting the cooking of pork in kitchens.

A reduced information flow between staff and prisoners and its replacement by assumptions of dangerousness and 'policing-from-a-distance' (that is, the removal of prisoners arousing concern to segregation units or special units) left prisoners at the mercy of each other. In an opaque mixture of attraction, exploitation, and protection, a new prisoner community was taking shape. 'This Muslim thing' was talked about endlessly on the wings:

> *Interviewer:* So how would you describe relationships like between prisoners in here?

Prisoner: It's divided, isn't it? I'm not a Muslim…yeah, but I'm here. I can see this Muslim thing. I can see everything what's going on…

Interviewer: Yeah. So what's going on?

Prisoner: It's a proper hard subject to say what is going on. All right then, I'm going to break it down to you. You've got…the vulnerable people who see this Muslim thing… strategically, yeah? And if you feel…a bit vulnerable, that's the best thing for you to do… Because obviously, there's a big number of them, they are sticking together, or most of them are trying to stick together, so if you feel vulnerable or anything like that in a prison, the best thing for you to do is to join up, and that's what a lot of people are doing. A lot of people are not Muslims, they're just…under the umbrella. Then you've got a handful of people which most of them are in for terrorist crimes anyway, who are the strict, real Muslim type of guys. Now, as far as all this bullying and going to people to be Muslim and that, that's not true. You've got these ones that are the real strict ones. Now these vulnerable ones are coming to these strict ones because being with these strict ones is the…the middle of the umbrella… 'Cause these guys are really…they are the proper…they're serious about what they're doing. They've grown up in it, they're born into it…this is their whole core beliefs, morals, everything. Yeah? They're not forcing them to do anything, but if you decide that you're Muslim and you're coming to me and asking me for things, then I'm obviously going to tell you, aren't I? If I am born in this and I've grew up in this and I'm a Muslim, and you come to me and you say I want to be Muslim, I want to learn how to do it, then I'm going to show you, because even in the Muslim faith itself, it tells you that you should…if people want to learn…you should teach them, and you should show them what to do. So obviously, people are coming to them, they're showing them… Get me? But then, because these guys are not real Muslims, and they're coming to them, they're getting wrapped up with these geezers…but they're not real. They're doing other little things that they're not supposed to be doing… So then they're getting into conflicts now… Then they find out that you're doing other things, well, obviously they're going to have something to say 'cause you've gone to them. And then...when people are having something to say, then these guys are running off now, running to the officers. 'Ah, they're bullying me. They're making me do this'... Well, they're not making you do anything. You've gone to them... Then, obviously, you have got the knob heads that are using it for power... And I wouldn't say mostly that them are the strict ones... It's not them... really. It's mostly...the Black geezers what are...got this, kind of, more, type of...gang type of mentality...who are... using it...because obviously they all have to look a bit... it says wherever it says in that they're supposed to look after each other and no one else should be able to harm a Muslim and all this kind of stuff... So that kind of...that is, like, breeding gang rules...like, in the street, where you'd say 'You can't touch him 'cause he's with me'. It kind of sets them kind of things up easily...you can, sort of, twist it in a way... But even though this group are using it like that, they're also sticking to it very strictly... So these ones under the umbrella, because they're actually doing everything they're supposed to do...these ones are not going to go against them because...they are told as they've learned that if he's a Muslim and if he's doing everything right...whatever is going on, you have to embrace that person. And what they ignored is, these guys that are doing this, they know this, so...they will pray five times a day, they will do all the right things, but at the same time, in the little back of behind it, they're also using it to do other things.

Interviewer: OK. And then where does that leave anyone who's not Muslim and doesn't want to be...?

Prisoner: Like me...

Interviewer: Yes.

Prisoner: It leaves you like me, having to fight for yourself... It's hard, isn't it? It leaves you in a hard position. Yeah. Leaves you in a hard position...

This attempt at description by a mixed-race prisoner often assumed by staff to be Muslim illustrates the complexities of risk, identity, and survival for individual prisoners in a new environment characterized by fear, absence, and 'phantoms': Muslim prisoners were the new 'folk devils', but they were also a new source of power and influence. 'Muslim gangs' were present *and* imagined, but no one knew who was who. An empty and soul-destroying climate offered few alternative avenues for power or meaning. Religion was often a source of hope and atonement. But distortions of religious identity could also provide 'an umbrella'.

Extreme punishment and its effects

The demise of humanity, the new bureaucracies of risk, extremely long and indeterminate sentences, and the difficulties prisoners faced in accessing any of the activities or courses they were required to complete to be downgraded from maximum security, created a bleak environment. Hope, identity, and meaning were scarce. Prisoners described anxiety, frustration, fear, anger, and resignation, and many expressed the pains of their circumstances in ways that were both moving and deeply troubling. In one interview, a prisoner reported that he would throw away drawings or poems after producing them while in his cell because he was afraid he could be negatively judged on their basis. Even our talk, in interview, was 'risky':

> I'm not free to make that piece of art, I'm not free to write that poem, I'm not free to write that story, I'm not free to send them things off to that competition, I'm not free to buy them magazines, I'm not free to talk about this (Prisoner in Liebling et al 2011).

Sixty-eight percent of prisoners agreed that their 'time at Whitemoor' felt 'very much like a punishment': that is, that this experience was more than the deprivation of liberty. Prisoners were suffering from frustration and distress. Despair and desperation were not always 'frenzied' (Haney 2009, p. 70). Some prisoners adapted: 'You know what. You get used to it. I don't like it…but I can deal with it. It's not your own life, or it feels like it's not your own life' (Prisoner). Others remained uncomfortable and fearful: 'In every way you're vulnerable, ain't you? Vulnerable to anything…to assaults, just to being mistreated, to anything' (Prisoner).

Many prisoners talked about the need for 'space' in the tiniest areas of the wing and its operations, in order to forge a manageable life. Without a degree of freedom to choose when or what to eat, who to mix with, how to pass the time, every day was hard. Being subject to disparate, new, or unnecessary uses of authority—not being trusted to comply with the routine without pressure—was experienced as deeply painful, frustrating, and an affront to dignity:

Prisoner: I tell you one thing I really don't like. I don't like...being told to do things that I'm...that I've got enough sense to do anyway. Like...I've been on this wing a long time now...so when it comes to things like bang up and that, they're not supposed to...this rule came out last year some time...they're not supposed to turn your lock in. So basically you...the big part of your lock goes into your door. They have to flick it out so it stays out all the time so your door can't push shut... So you couldn't go into you cell and shut your door yourself...'cause that lock's out the time. So when it's bang up, they have to go aro d and when you go into your cell, they have to loc that thing. So until you go into your cell, they can't loc that door. So they tend to...a lot of these new ones... stand by your door...and call you, and keep calling you so that they can flick that thing off. Whereas, I've been here quite a while now and some of these officers know me. What they'll do with my door, they'll just flick it... Because they know that I know it's bang up anyway. I'm not running off. I'm going to go in my cell anyway. So... little things like that. It sounds like a little thing...but it is actually a big thing. If somebody's standing by your door saying 'Come in your cell now', it changes everything...

Interviewer: It's an area where they're using their authority where they don't need to...?

Prisoner: Yeah. That's what it is...that's exactly what it is.

There were countless examples of these kinds of interactions: how prisoners were called for dinner, how they acquired work, how often their cells were searched and what state they were left in, whether property was confiscated, being let out for exercise, movement between spurs on the wing, or requests for changes of wing location. These practices varied by wing, shift, or officer, reflecting the 'moral status' of prisoners in the eyes of staff, and as a result, by other prisoners. The main challenge to prisoners' emotional equilibrium was the use of power: 'Obviously, they've got power over us. We all know that...but you don't want to see it all the time' (Prisoner). Arbitrary power, often in full view of others, and including the tone, loudness, pitch, and content of dialogue, offended prisoners' dignity. Humiliations, sometimes reminiscent of earlier humiliations, could lead to 'feeling traps' in which shame and anger were generated, contained, or redirected toward the self (see Scheff & Retzinger 2001).

Prisoners and staff sometimes engaged in power struggles—using language, relative size, or the rules to win a battle. Scores were settled later. Prison officers almost always had the advantage. There were, however, exceptions. Prisoners were ready to talk about the best examples of their treatment by staff. Even in the unlikeliest of circumstances, being known and treated as human changed a potentially damaging encounter into a 'tragic' but controlled incident in which pride and dignity stayed intact. For example, during a restraint:

> This is going to sound funny but one of them...was lying on top of my back when I was on the floor, and I knew his name...just pretend his name's Mark, I said 'Mark, get off my back, I can't breathe' and he said 'Oh, sorry, [prisoner's nickname]' and got up. [*both laugh*] And...and the woman that was there, she was stroking my head when I was on the floor and she was saying 'Don't worry, everything's going to be all right'. This is what it boils down to. It boils down to communication and how you get on with people. 'Cause if you do get on with someone properly...they know me. They know that it's not, like, nothing to do with them, so obviously as long as I've stopped and I'm all right... (Prisoner).

This interaction, despite involving a restraint procedure, was described as 'fair' by this interviewee. He felt known, 'recognized', and treated accordingly. No more force was used than necessary.

Other prisoners were more concerned about the effects of this maximum-security form of imprisonment on their 'value system and worldviews' (Haney 2009, p. 167), or their character. One prisoner, also interviewed in the first study and, by this stage, elsewhere in the system, reflected with us on our account of the changing temperature and mood in the prison:

> I remember being there...on the edge of a precipice. You lose all hope. Your inner self changes. You start to think, what does anything matter?... It builds up—your efforts to be good are not being recognized. You think, 'I've tried, you're not giving me a chance'. You hit a wall where nothing matters. Suddenly, you are capable of

anything. You'd betray anyone... You lose your moral compass. It's a sort of giving up. You sort of know you can either step back or forward. Intellectually, I knew where I was. My (Catholic) faith said, 'don't do it'. I wouldn't give in to it. I didn't want to become what I could see myself becoming. You see so much nastiness in prison—you have to develop a strategy not to become cynical and bitter and angry' (Former Whitemoor prisoner).

Prisoners described the development of 'bad habits', attitudes and dispositions: the behaviors and value orientations they learned in order to survive. They described new defenses (a tough exterior, assertive use of space, hyper-vigilance, hyper-masculinity, regular use of the gym, the acquisition of goods), and the closing down of emotions ('you can't grieve'). They described the effects of being perceived as wholly dangerous—recounting self-monitoring and a constant anxiety about being 'left alone' with female members of staff because 'the situation is officially prohibited'.

They often lost friends or family members outside to illness, violence, or old age. None of the ordinary processes of honoring the loss or receiving support were available. Prisoners described a 'fake' environment in which all action was strategic and self-protective. When incidents of violence occurred on the wing, others watched blankly, or sought out the day's newspaper, thinking, 'there's going to be a lock down'. They reflected in interviews with us about their reactions to these events, knowing they were damaging. Their observations about these processes of change became a topic of note. The effects of distrust were adverse (see Liebling, with Arnold 2014, p. 243; Haney 2009, p. 216; Dolovich 2012).

Conclusion: challenging the new ecology of cruelty

Prisoners retain the essence of human dignity inherent in all persons. Respect for that dignity animates the Eighth Amendment prohibition against cruel and unusual punishment (*Brown v. Plata*, No 09-1233, Kennedy, J May 23 2011).

The question left to us by *Brown v. Plata* is whether the enhanced status of dignity as an Eighth Amendment value, along with court challenges to a host of mass-incarceration practices, can break up those dense blocks of punitive power, compelling legislators and administrators to revisit and rebalance a system that clearly overimprisons people with little relationship to an individual's moral blameworthiness or a realistic assessment of his future dangerousness (Simon 2014, p. 144).

Jonathan Simon has argued in his analysis of mass incarceration that the qualitative story of mass imprisonment has been missing from policy debates, and critically, from legal arguments about its justification. What goes on in high-security prisons forms an important part of this story and is illustrative of the 'extreme' form imprisonment now takes. Increasing racial disproportion, over-dramatized perceptions of dangerousness, lack of access to meaningful occupation, and damage inflicted on communities are some of the problems of long-term imprisonment. Its form and effects are illegitimate.

The 'problem' in the changing high-security prison is twofold. There is growing distance between 'policy' and prisoners' experiences. This distance—which, once expressed, continues along a power chain to policy implementers, senior managers, and staff—makes fear and 'othering' both possible and likely (see Bauman 1989). There is something profoundly inhuman about the way in which prisoners are thought about, and their regimes devised, in contemporary penal practice. They are 'undeserving' of forgiveness, kindness, humanity, opportunities for redemption, or even fairness (Irwin 2009). Humanity requires intimacy, sympathy, dialogue, and courage, but is extinguished by distance and fear.

The second is the damage being done to civic order by a form of imprisonment that undermines rather than supports 'agentic capacities' and civic virtues or a 'civil disposition' ('attitudes of trust and trustworthiness', Jacobs 2014):

> The combination of eroded agency, worsened character, and deficit of civil disposition is that, upon release, many prisoners have a substantially diminished capability for participating successfully in civil society (Jacobs 2014, p. 202).

'Character' here does not mean simply 'strength of character'. The qualities of good character may require 'fragility', (Harris 1997)—a 'virtue' that can be highly dangerous in the prison environment.

Punishment should be 'morally intelligible' (Jacobs 2014, p. 216). Where punishment 'fails to serve any legitimate penological purpose' it becomes 'unconstitutional cruelty' (Haney 2009, p. xiv). Poor understanding, and underestimations, of the experience or effects of long-term imprisonment make 'facile gestures' in the politics of long-term imprisonment increasingly likely. Lack of access to educational, creative, or life-affirming activities *constitutes* a form of cruelty. The new ecology—a 'bare life' (Agamben 1998)[4]—creates more dangerousness rather than reining it in or bringing about change. As Simon argues, 'human dignity and public safety go together' (Simon 2014, p. 9). Dignity 'requires prison regimes that promote individualization, normalization and the preparation of all prisoners for the possibility of return to the community' (van Zyl Smit & Snacken 2009). The dignity principle places a 'positive duty on the State to assist socially vulnerable groups in their social and personal development' (Lazarus 2006, p. 749). Penal practice is moving away from all four of these principles.

Now and again, humanity 'seeps in' and prisoners become people with potential. One or two specially designed (smaller, modern, purpose built) wings, with a wholly different 'enabling environment' ethos, are being piloted on an experimental basis. In these moments, and places, new and better avenues are created. There are 'cracks in the dam' (Irwin 2009, p. 127; Graham & White 2014). The next project to flow from our return visit to Whitemoor will explore, and seek to grow, these cracks.[5]

Notes

1 Many of the prisoner quotations in this chapter are taken directly from interview transcripts. Published sources from this study include Liebling & Arnold 2012; Liebling 2014; and Liebling, Arnold & Straub in press.

2 Helen Arnold, Christina Straub, and Alison Liebling.

3 The Woolf Report was based on an independent public inquiry into a major series of disturbances at Manchester Prison (Strangeways) and other prisons during April 1990. It was hailed as the most impressive analysis of the English penal system since the Gladstone Report of 1895. Its diagnosis of the main problems of the Prison Service were instability arising from overcrowding; poor conditions and regimes; staff shortages and inadequate staff training; and poor staff attitudes toward prisoners. The report suggested that there was a moral crisis in the penal system, or lack of clarity about purpose, which also contributed to the disturbances (see further Liebling, with Arnold 2004; and Home Office 1991).

4 A life both excluded from and captured or constituted by a political system, marking its boundary; a norm of modern democracies. 'Since bare life is included within democracies as their hidden inner ground...modern politics is about the search for new racialized and gendered forms of exclusion' (Ziarec 2012; see also Rhodes 2009).

5   An ESRC-funded project being conducted by Alison Liebling, Ruth Armstrong, Richard Bramwell, and Ryan Williams: 'Locating and building trust in high-security prisons: religion, moral status, prisoner leadership, and risk in maximum-security prisons'.

References

Agamben, G 1995, *Homo sacer: sovereign power and bare life*, Stanford University Press Stanford, CA.

Bauman, Z 1989, *Modernity and the Holocaust*, Cornell University Press, Ithaca, NY.

Bottoms, A & Tankebe, J 2012, 'Beyond procedural justice: a dialogic approach to legitimacy in criminal justice', *Journal of Criminal Law & Criminology*, vol. 102, pp. 119–70.

Brown v. Plata, No 09-1233, Kennedy, J May 23 2011.

Crawley, E & Sparks, R 2005, 'Older men in prison: survival, coping and identity' in *The Effects of Imprisonment*, eds A Liebling & S Maruna, Cullompton, Willan Publishing, Devon.

Crewe, B 2009, *The prisoner society: power, adaptation and social life in an English prison*, Oxford University Press, Oxford.

Crewe, B, Liebling, A & Hulley, S 2014, 'Heavy/light, absent/present: rethinking the "weight" of imprisonment', *British Journal of Sociology*, vol. 65, no. 3, pp. 387–410.

Dolovich, S 2012, 'Creating the permanent prisoner', in *Life without parole: America's new death penalty*, eds CJ Ogletree & A Sarat, New York University Press, New York.

Fader, JJ 2013, *Falling back: incarceration and transitions to adulthood among urban youth*, Rutgers University Press, New Brunswick, NJ.

Graham, R & White, R 2014, *Innovative justice*, Routledge, London.

Haney, C 2009, *Reforming punishment: psychological limits to the pains of imprisonment*, American Psychological Association, Washington DC.

Haney. C 2008, 'A culture of harm: taming the dynamics of cruelty in supermax prisons', *Criminal Justice and Behaviour*, vol. 35, pp. 956–84.

Harcourt, BE 2007, *Against prediction: profiling, policing and punishing in an actuarial age*, University of Chicago Press, Chicago, IL.

Harris, GW 1997, *Dignity and vulnerability: strength and quality of character*, University of California Press, Berkeley, CA.

HMCIP 2008. *Report on an unannounced full follow-up inspection of HMP Whitemoor, London: HM Inspectorate of Prisons*, HM Inspectorate of Prisons, London.

Home Office 1968, *The regime for long-term prisoners in conditions of maximum security. Report of the Advisory Council on the Penal System* (Radzinowicz Report), HMSO London.

Home Office 1984, *Managing the long-term prison system (the Control Review Committee report)*, HMSO, London.

Home Office 1991, *Prison disturbances April 1990: report of an inquiry by the Rt. Hon. Lord Justice Woolf (Parts I and II) and his Honour Judge Stephen Tumim (Part II)*, HMSO, London.

Irwin, J 2009, *Lifers: seeking redemption in prison*, Routledge, London.

Jacobs, J 2014, 'Punishing society: Incarceration, Coercive Corruption, and the Liberal Polity.', *Criminal Justice Ethics*, vol. 33, no. 3, 200–219.

Lazarus, L 2006, 'Conceptions of liberty deprivation', *The Modern Law Review,* vol. 738, pp. 740–4.

Liebling, A 2002 'A "liberal regime within a secure perimeter"? Dispersal prisons and penal practice in the late twentieth century', in *Ideology, Crime and Justice: A Symposium in Honour of Sir Leon Radzinowicz,* eds M Tonry & AE Bottoms, Cambridge Criminal Justice Series, Institute of Criminology, Cambridge, pp. 97–150.

Liebling, A 2014, 'Moral and philosophical problems of long-term imprisonment', *Studies in Christian Ethics,* vol. 27, no. 3, pp. 258–69.

Liebling, A, with Arnold, H 2004, *Prisons and their moral performance: a study of values, quality and prison life,* Clarendon Studies in Criminology, Oxford University Press, Oxford.

Liebling, A & Arnold, H 2012, 'Social relationships between prisoners in a maximum security prison: violence, faith, and the declining nature of trust', *Journal of Criminal Justice,* vol. 40, no. 5, pp. 413–24.

Liebling, A & Price, D 2001, *The prison officer,* Prison Service (and Waterside Press), Leyhill. 2nd edition completed February 2009.

Liebling, A, Arnold, H & Straub, C 2011, *An exploration of staff-prisoner relationships at HMP Whitemoor: twelve years on,* National Offender Management Service, London.

Liebling, A, Arnold, H & Straub, C 2015 (in press), 'Prisons research beyond the conventional: dialogue, "creating miracles" and staying sane in a maximum security prison', in *International Handbook of Prison Ethnography,* eds D Drake, R Earle & J Sloan, Palgrave Macmillan, Houndmills, Basingstone, UK.

Maruna, S, LeBel, TP, Mitchell, N & Naples, M 2004, 'Pygmalion in the reintegration process: desistance from crime through the looking glass', *Psychology Crime & Law,* vol. 10, no. 3, pp. 271–81.

Padfield, N 2002, *Beyond the tariff: human rights and the release of life sentence prisoners,* Willan Publishing, Devon.

Rhodes, L 2004, *Total confinement: madness and reason in the maximum security prison,* University of California Press, Berkeley, CA.

Rhodes, L 2009, 'Supermax prisons and the trajectory of exception', in *Special Issue New Perspectives on Crime and Criminal Justice (Studies in Law, Politics and Society, Volume 47),* ed A Sarat, Emerald Group Publishing Limited, Bingly, pp. 193–218

Scheff, TJ & Retzinger, SM 2001, *Emotions and violence: shame and rage in destructive conflicts,* iUniverse, Lincoln, NE.

Shalev, S 2009, *Supermax: controlling risk through solitary confinement,* Willan Publishing, Devon.

Shapland JM & Bottoms A 2011, 'Reflections on social values, offending and desistance among young adult recidivists', *Punishment & Society,* vol. 13, no. 3, pp. 256–82.

Simon, J 2001a, 'Entitlement to cruelty': the end of welfare and the punitive mentality in the United States' in *Crime, Risk and Justice: The Politics of Crime Control in Liberal Democracies,* eds K Stenson & RR Sullivan, Willan Publishing, Devon, pp. 125–43.

Simon, J 2001b, 'Fear and loathing in late modernity: reflections on the cultural sources of mass imprisonment in the United States', *Punishment & Society* vol. 3, no. 1, pp. 21–33.

Simon, J 2014, *Mass incarceration on trial: a remarkable court decision and the future of prison in America*, The New Press, New York.

Sparks, R, Bottoms, AE & Hay, W 1996, *Prisons and the problem of order*, Clarendon Press, Oxford.

Van Zyl Smit, D & Snacken, S 2009, *Principles of European prison law and policy: penology and human rights*, Oxford University Press, Oxford.

Ziarec, E 2012, 'Bare life', in *Impasses of the Post-Global: Theory in the Era of Climate Change, Vol. 2*, ed H Sussman, Open Humanities Press.

6

Seclusive Space: Crisis Confinement and Behavior Modification in Canadian Forensic Psychiatric Settings

Stuart J. Murray, Carleton University
Dave Holmes, University of Ottawa

This essay offers a theoretical reflection emerging from the authors' qualitative empirical studies examining ethical practice and mental health care in Canadian forensic psychiatric settings. Forensic psychiatry is a specialized area of psychiatry uniting the fields of mental health, law, and criminology. Forensic psychiatry implies the use of (para)medical psychiatric knowledge or 'opinion' concerning patients who have legal issues. According to the American Academy of Psychiatry and the Law, forensic psychiatry involves 'civil, criminal, correctional, regulatory or legislative matters, and...specialized clinical consultations in areas such as risk assessment or employment' (AAPL 2005). While the AAPL's ethics guidelines acknowledge the 'special hazards' and 'potential for unintended bias' in the practice of forensic psychiatry—particularly in the courtroom—the Academy urges its members to 'minimize such hazards' and to 'strive' to reach an 'objective opinion' (AAPL 2005). Our research focuses on the clinical use of forensic psychiatry within correctional facilities, where it is applied to a captive population of inmates who have been diagnosed with a mental disorder linked, in some respects, to their incarceration.

This research milieu is of particular interest because it represents a hybrid space where psychiatry and corrections are entangled: correctional settings serve both as psychiatric hospitals and, foremost, as prisons where patient-inmates are serving out a criminal sentence. They are both, and yet neither in any straightforward sense. As such, the milieu affords particular insights into the ways that corrections has been psychiatrized, and, conversely, how psychiatry has been informed by correctional or penal techniques, such as behavior modification programs (BMPs). As these settings are both psychiatric and correctional, the ethical collisions of these respective practices and discourses begin to come to light. Thus, our analysis may be germane to a critique of seclusion—especially segregation used as part of a BMP strategy—in both psychiatric hospitals and correctional facilities. Considered independently, the forensic psychiatric settings under study offer a privileged perspective on the manner in which psychiatric and correctional practices and discourses are mutually (albeit selectively) informative. This raises explicit questions about the nature of punishment in these settings: whether it is carried out in the name of corrections, in the name of psychiatric treatment, or at the extremities of each, in an equivocal space that secretes elements of both. It also raises questions about the authority of psychiatric and correctional interventions and the claims to 'knowledge' or 'opinion' upon which they rely.

Our argument focuses on the use of seclusion as an integral dimension of institutional behavior modification programs and part of a patient-inmate's mental health treatment regimen. Because there is little empirical data, it is very difficult to trace the history of the use of the seclusion room as a BMP strategy in the Canadian context; however, it is worth noting that forensic psychiatric hospitals (special hospitals) and psychiatric units in the federal correctional system represent two settings where the use of seclusion was (and still is) linked directly, in many instances, to BMPs. Although the history of such a practice is difficult to establish, these two settings are sites where the practice began in a very systematic manner in the 1970s (Rothman 1975). BMPs were then 'exported' to (regular) psychiatric institutions when patients 'controlled' through these plans were transferred from corrections/special hospitals to regular psychiatric settings. If the former settings held the expertise to develop and implement BMPs, these plans were simply deployed in regular psychiatric settings following a training session with a liaison-nurse, usually offered when a 'difficult' patient is transferred from a highly secure environment to a less secure one. The penetration of these 'special' plans into regular psychiatric settings has had a salient impact on their use. Indeed, regular psychiatric settings have linked the use of seclusion to BMPs, and in many instances this practice has prompted public inquiries from professional colleges. Repeatedly, professional colleges have reaffirmed irrevocably that the use of seclusion for BMP purposes constitutes a breach of professional ethics (e.g., OIIQ-CMQ 2011).

This chapter advances an ethical perspective, arguing that seclusion and the use of BMPs cannot be understood without a nuanced, critical examination of the place of the lived-body and how that body assumes a place, and takes place, as a necessary dimension of human subjectivity and personhood—for it is on this dimension of human subjectivity, we argue, that seclusion and BMPs are brought to bear. This constitutes the extreme nature of such 'treatment', as it occurs in ways that are not necessarily visible or quantifiable as punishment per se. If the lived-body is neither visible nor quantifiable as such, the challenge is to render the invisible visible, much as Pittendrigh (this volume) seeks to do in her analysis of inmates' words, gestures, and symptoms, an agency which only makes sense within the context of the lived-body. We adopt a critical phenomenological perspective (Guenther 2013; Merleau-Ponty 1962; Murray & Holmes 2013, 2014) that understands the experience and the place of the lived-body as crucial to ethical inquiry. Our analysis unfolds in three parts, the first two elaborating a critical theoretical frame for the analysis of forensic psychiatric settings that follows in part three. In the first part, we begin with a discussion of medical 'crisis' (Foucault 2008a) in historical and contemporary contexts. We contend that the rhetoric of crisis offers us some useful terms by which we might better understand the effects of seclusion on lived-bodies. While the original meaning of 'crisis' was abandoned by medicine in the early 19th century, we explore its use in the history of psychiatric discourse. Through a discussion of seclusion, we argue for the value of crisis as a way to grasp the phenomenology of the lived-body and as a way to counter the neoliberal understanding of seclusion, which involves ubiquitous management paradigms and economic 'efficiencies' increasingly in place across forensic psychiatric institutions, including correctional facilities.

In the second part, we draw on Guenther's (2013) chronology of seclusion or solitary confinement in the US prison system—from its early redemptive impetus, to reformative strategies, and then most recently its neoliberal guises. While Guenther does not discuss forensic psychiatric facilities, we argue that her historical periodization of seclusion is relevant here. She claims that the history of seclusion must be understood within the structural context of race and racism, both socially and institutionally. We take up the question of race in the Canadian setting, discussing the ways the secluded lived-body is stigmatized both by mental illness and the legacy of race and racism. Our purpose is to suggest that critical methodological approaches to race and racialization, such as Guenther's, are of value to a critical phenomenological study of forensic psychiatry, BMPs, and the place of seclusion within this nexus.

Finally, in the third part, we use this theoretical frame to return to the place of seclusion and the use of BMPs in the forensic psychiatric setting. We argue that seclusion represents an extreme foreclosure of place, and yet place is nevertheless the necessary condition within which the lived-body takes place, where its subjectivity is made meaningful and personhood and ethics are properly conceived. In the foreclosure of place, then, personhood and ethics become inconceivable. In effect, persons have been disappeared, reduced to objective bodies for the application of liberal law, penalty, and psychiatry. We call for a different understanding of the seclusive spaces in which these powers are exercised—spaces that correctional and psychiatric powers constitute 'objectively' as grids of intelligibility, securitization, and management. We argue that, for those who experience them, these spaces are neither neutral nor objective sites of medical knowledge or correction; they are, rather, intersubjective *places* that are lived, inhabited, and embodied subjectively, by a lived-body.

The phenomenological crisis of the secluded body

> While administrative segregation is seen as an essential tool for crisis management, the Committee learned that CSC [Correctional Services Canada] uses it too often to deal with offenders with mental health issues (Standing Committee on Public Safety and National Security 2010, p. 53).

The rhetorical use of the term 'crisis' gives us a way to think about what it means for a lived-body to occupy space, objectively, and to take up a meaningful place, intersubjectively, in relation to his or her lived environment. 'Crisis' is an ancient term, dating back to the Hippocratic corpus, and yet today it is married, as it is above, with a neoliberal 'management' paradigm, alongside 'seclusion' or 'administrative segregation', which is conceived as an 'essential tool' for 'dealing with' a captive population with mental health 'issues' (note the elision of 'illness' in this report). For more than two millennia, crisis was a pivotal concept for medicine, before the advent of modern pathological anatomy in the early 19th century. Crisis represented the truth of a disease, the turning point in its development, announced in, on, and through the lived-body itself. As Foucault (2008a) writes of this early definition, 'the crisis is quite precisely the moment of combat, the moment of the battle, or even the point at which the battle is decided. The battle between Nature and Evil, the body's struggle against the morbific substance, or, as doctors in the eighteenth century will say, the battle between solids and humors' (p. 242).

The early understanding and use of crisis gradually disappears from medicine beginning in the late 18th century with the birth of statistical medicine, anatomopathology, and physiopathology. However, while medicine abandoned the crisis paradigm, in the 19th century early psychiatry came paradoxically to rely increasingly on medical crisis, provoking and producing crises as a rhetorical justification for psychiatry's own claims to science and truth, for its own institutionalization and self-authorization. Psychiatry needed bodily crisis, Foucault argues, because 'neither the disciplinary regime...nor pathological anatomy, enabled psychiatric knowledge to be founded as truth' (2008a, p. 250). In other words, with no anatomical etiology for most mental illness, psychiatry invented one. With this critique, Foucault seeks to discredit psychiatry as baseless, unscientific, the domain of simulation and mere opinion. No surprise, then, to find early psychiatry allying itself with crime and penalty: crime was cast as a form of madness, and the mad as potential criminals. The prison, with its captive population, was the ideal laboratory. This allegiance was a way, Foucault writes, 'of founding psychiatric power, not in terms of truth, since precisely it is not a question of truth, but in terms of danger' (2008a, p. 250). The crises of mental illness ostensibly posed a danger to civil society, and society had to be protected from mad crimes (here early psychiatry anticipates the rise of neoliberalism and its calls for the efficient management of 'dangerous' offenders). In this manner, psychiatry comes to justify itself on the basis of pseudo-medical and criminological knowledge, observation, and demonstration. Foucault concludes: 'the psychiatric hospital literally invented a new medical crisis. This was no longer that old crisis of truth played out between the forces of the disease and the forces of nature...but a crisis that I will call a crisis of reality, which is played out between the mad person and the power that confines him, the doctor's power-knowledge' (2008a, p. 252). Consequently, the seclusion room becomes a privileged locus for the dramaturgical 'realization' of madness, the space in which madness is made 'real' through a crisis that is induced, in a circular logic, by seclusion itself.

In Foucault's understanding, as we are reading it, crisis is the *effect* of psychiatric seclusion rather than its cause (also see Reiter & Blair this volume). Psychiatry produced crises and then explained them as physiological in origin. But the effect of seclusion is not simply physiological;

it is a 'crisis of reality' for lived-bodies, which are not simply objects distributed spatially among other objects, *partes extra partes*. They are relational subjects confronting the powers that confine them and the power-knowledge and 'objective opinions' of the medical establishment. In other words, the secluded person is subject; he or she inhabits a place, takes place, and lives in and through that place. While the term 'space' might be construed as geometric, Cartesian, and easily mapped in reality, by contrast we propose the term 'place' as experiential, lived, and embodied. Thus, crisis is produced and provoked when the phenomenological *places* of the lived-body are dis-placed by the *spaces* of seclusion. Merleau-Ponty (1962) argues that the lived-body is essentially intersubjective, a subject that exceeds its physical location or biophysiology. And as Guenther (2013) discusses in the context of prisoners subject to solitary confinement, 'the intersubjective basis for their concrete personhood, and for their experience of the world as real and objective, as irreducible to their own personal impressions, is structurally undermined by the prolonged deprivation of a concrete, everyday experience of other people' (p. 35). Seclusive space dismantles the referential and interpersonal place of the lived-body, structurally undermining the conditions for a meaningful experience of the subject's personhood and humanity. Together, lived-body, place, and the intersubjective presence of others permit a mode of subjectivity without which therapeutic relationships and mental health are reduced to lifeless abstractions and (punitive) injunctions. Along with Malpas (2003), our understanding of place concerns 'the making of persons through place and, more particularly, the way in which human persons are determined in their character as persons, or, indeed, as non-persons, through the institutional places in which they are located' (p. 234).

To be clear, we are not arguing for a return to pre-pathological nosology based on the early Hippocratic crisis; nevertheless, we would like to suggest that crisis is a fruitful metaphor to understand the lived-body phenomenologically (Murray 2012). And it may give us a way to describe the place of the lived-body in terms that continue to resonate for those who experience seclusion. The battle between nature and evil, or against a morbific substance, as Foucault (2008a) describes it, is perhaps not so alien to the experience of secluded patient-inmates, particularly those who suffer from a mental illness. This way of speaking might be more appropriate if we hope to understand intersubjective relationships, which necessarily involve embodied fear, vulnerability, trust, interdependence, and uncertainty—elements that have no clear anatomical or biophysiological origins. We are arguing for a sense of crisis that is necessary and intrinsic to relationality, sociality, and embodied history—a bodily exposure and precariousness (Butler 2004) without which there can be no true therapeutic relation, no mental health, and no ethical treatment program.

This existential sense of crisis is undermined by seclusion: seclusive space is no-place, it is what Foucault would call a heterotopia. Heterotopias, he writes, 'are something like counter-sites...outside of all places, even though it may be possible to indicate their location in reality' (Foucault 1984 [1967]). Foucault's brief history of heterotopias sheds light on the crisis of the secluded body: from bodies entering sacred or forbidden places to social bodies 'in a state of crisis: adolescents, menstruating women, pregnant women, the elderly, etc.' (n.p.). He contends that these sites of bodily crisis are disappearing in our society: 'heterotopias of crisis are disappearing today and are being replaced, I believe, by what we might call heterotopias of deviation: those in which individuals whose behavior is deviant in relation to the required mean or norm are placed' (n.p.). Existential and bodily crises (in the ancient sense) have given way to crises of deviance and abnormality—crises that are socially and institutionally manufactured, by psychiatry and by the prison (and Foucault names them both). In other words, we move from the crisis of a body in transition to a crisis of permanent and endemic deviance and abnormality.

The shifting notion of 'crisis' comes to correspond to particular places, and these places, increasingly, are not just sites where bodily crisis is localized, but they produce crisis, and become essential tools or technologies for crisis management, through the social and institutional ascription and then containment of deviance and abnormality. Foucault (1984) characterizes heterotopias through the metaphor of the mirror, a placeless place. 'In the mirror I see myself there where I am not, in an unreal, virtual space that opens up behind the surface; I am over there, there where I am not, a sort of shadow that gives my own visibility to myself, that enables me to see myself there where I am absent' (n.p.). This is a (non)place, then, of self-relation, in which the subject seeks in vain for self-reflection. As Foucault remarks, the mirror is both real and unreal: 'The mirror...makes this place that I occupy at the moment when I look at myself in the glass at once absolutely real, connected with all the space that surrounds it, and absolutely unreal, since in order to be perceived it has to pass through this virtual point which is over there' (n.p.). That unreal virtual point is social, intersubjective, and embodied. I am given back to myself through others, in a relational exchange that cannot wholly be subjected to neoliberal, statistical, or predictive rationalities, to management or efficiency paradigms. To offer a critical articulation of these de-realizing forces, we turn now to a history of seclusion in the prison setting before taking up the specific question of seclusion and BMPs in forensic psychiatry.

Confinement in historical context

> Replacing chains with total institutions was merely a first step in a seemingly endless process of enslavements, culminating in the self-enslavement of today's so-called 'service users', 'voice hearers' and miscellaneous mental patients on the dole demanding free 'professional services' from the very professionals they identify as their victimizers (Szasz 2014, p. 28).

In her recent book on solitary confinement in US prisons, Guenther (2013) offers a history of what she identifies as three waves of solitary confinement since the 19th century (based on Shalev 2009). Guenther's overview of what we are calling the crisis of the secluded body helps to situate our own analysis of seclusion in the forensic psychiatric setting. She characterizes the first wave as a moral and religious reform movement in the 1850s, which 'gave rise to the penitentiary system as a site of redemption through prolonged solitude' (Guenther 2013, p. xvi). While the first wave was organized around the redemption of the prisoner's soul, the second wave in the 1960s and 1970s adapted Cold War studies in counterintelligence interrogation and sensory deprivation to emphasize rehabilitation through BMPs that included seclusion as part of the correctional paradigm. Finally, the third wave began with the rise of neoliberalism in the 1980s 'and was led by prison administrators who sought less to redeem or rehabilitate criminal subjects than to isolate and control prison populations in ways that best suited the needs of wardens, prison staff, legislators, planners, and other stakeholders in the political economy of crime and incarceration' (p. xvii). The US supermax prison is the quintessential embodiment of this third wave of solitary confinement, where seclusion is used to control a 'dangerous' population and to manage risk with the greatest possible efficiency.

Guenther's text is more than an institutional history; she looks toward social, cultural, and political forces at play in the practice of seclusion. And she argues that the long history of solitary confinement in the US prison system cannot be understood apart from the legacy of slavery and the mass incarceration and hyperincarceration of people of color: 'a complex history of slavery, abolition, reconstruction, Jim Crow, and the convict lease system, in which African Americans were both freed from slavery and hypercriminalized in ways that replicated and even intensified the dynamics of slavery' (p. 139). Institutionalized racism thus complicates the historical periodization of solitary confinement, suggesting an ongoing history of discrimination where the politics of 19th-century moral reform and redemption continue to operate implicitly across behavior modification, discourses of rehabilitation, and the efficient 'management' of predominately racialized populations (including purported gang members) deemed to pose some risk to a fantasized neutral, law-abiding population that is white, middle-class, and cast as essentially if not enduringly vulnerable. Solitary confinement in the prison is presented as one available tool to securitize law-abiding citizens and to stave off their moral panic—while discursively reproducing and invoking that panic, perpetually, through the reification of endemic dangerousness. The logic is circular. Within the neoliberal context, the use of statistics, models, and forecasts, involving costing, type of crime (violent, etc.), crime rates and rates of recidivism (by gender, age, race, socioeconomic status, region), and so on, are presented as self-evident 'facts' supporting this pursuit, while they nevertheless veil a social and structural classism and racism that operates as a violent norm and that perpetuates the systemic violence of the prison system itself. We might even say that these 'facts' reify or produce an understanding of race (or class) as real, or even biological, and thus serve to justify racism (or classism) as the consequence, rather than contributing cause, of incarceration. Much in the way that early psychiatry provoked and produced crisis as ostensibly physiological in origin, these sites simultaneously produce and punish what is constituted as intrinsic deviance, abnormality, located in and as the offending body itself.

To be clear, this is not an essay on the vagaries of race and racism in corrections or mental health, whether in the American or Canadian systems. Nor was this the object of our empirical studies. And yet, we would be remiss to ignore how race and racism operate as social and structural fantasies and forces in these contexts, how race and racism operate on the lived-body in ways that are often difficult to see or quantify—one manner, in Pittendrigh's terms (this volume), to make visible the invisible conditions of human suffering and harm. What is most significant for our argument here is the centrality of the lived-body and place— racialized, in one register, psychiatrized in another, and oftentimes both at once. Race and mental illness are the structural effects of social, institutional, and political *processes* that are too often tactically eclipsed by the ostensible neutrality of statistics and 'facts' (also see Metzl 2010).

While the Canadian context differs in many ways from the American one, Canada's prisons are also sites of racialization and hyperincarceration of people of color, notably for Black and Aboriginal populations (Office of the Correctional Investigator 2014). Public Safety Canada (2014) reports in particular that the number of incarcerated Aboriginal (*self-identified* Inuit, Innu, Métis, and North American Indian) persons is disproportionately high: 33.0 percent of incarcerated women, 22.6 percent of men, while Aboriginal adults represent barely 3.0 percent of the Canadian population—an over-representation that far exceeds the per capita over-representation of African Americans in the US prison system. In Canada, Aboriginal persons also serve a higher proportion of their sentences before being released on parole. According to the Office of the Correctional Investigator (2013), 31 percent of offenders in segregation units self-identify as Aboriginal. However, these statistics only represent federal institutions, not provincial ones, and thus they do not include the many institutions that run segregation facilities known euphemistically and variously as 'alternative housing arrangements, secure living environments, special needs units, mental health units, intensive support units or gang ranges'. The government report flippantly refers to these as 'Segregation "Lite"' (government reports are not known for their irony, and in this spirit we are inclined to satirize these policies as 'Racism Lite'). As the report attests, these provincial units operate outside of administrative segregation law, and, therefore, according to the Correctional Investigator (2013), 'do not have [the] appropriate level of procedural safeguards/oversight'.

Thus, race and mental illness variably define the bodies and experiences of those who find themselves incarcerated and in segregation units, for these are lived-bodies that find themselves no-place in society, beyond the vanishing point of the mirror. As Szasz (2014) suggests, race and mental illness are historically interrelated: 'Replacing chains with total institutions was merely a first step in a seemingly endless process of enslavements, culminating in the self-enslavement of today's so-called "service users," "voice hearers" and miscellaneous mental patients on the dole demanding free "professional services" from the very professionals they identify as their victimizers' (p. 28). Szasz's position (for some, controversial) is that neither race nor mental illness are natural categories but are the effects of normalized social, historical, and political institutions. Racialized and pathologized suffering is no less real, of course, but it would be mistaken to see this suffering as emanating from 'race' or 'pathology' as such. He observes the historical continuity from slave plantations, to prisons, to psychiatric total institutions, and finally, to our 'advanced psychiatric society' (Castel, Castel & Lovell 1982), where psychiatric power is normalized, widespread, and informs the ready uptake of neoliberal 'self-help' regimes, whether they are peddled by 'Dr. Phil' or are elaborated and underwritten by statistical 'science'. The statistics tell one kind of story, certainly, but they belie the lived experience, the phenomenology of those bodies that they seek to encompass; nor do statistics permit a real understanding or critique of the social and ideological forces that are propagated and implemented by institutions, turned into technologies and spaces that seize upon the lived-body and reify its place and its experience. In neoliberal terms, we are meant to believe that the patient-inmate confines him- or herself, through the rational, free, and autonomous choices he or she willfully makes, or through the imminent 'nature' of his or her race or pathology.

But it is much more than this if we begin to consider the ways that one's particular embodiment is intersectional and lived across and through the meaningful ways of appearing and being-in-the-world, much as Fanon (1963, 1967) does so eloquently in the context of race, racism, and subjectivity. Borrowing from Merleau-Ponty (1962), Fanon (1967) describes the lived-body in terms of 'bodily schema', which captures the ways our bodies are referential and intersubjective: 'In the white world the man of color encounters difficulties in the development of his bodily schema' (p. 110). 'Then', he continues, 'assailed at various points, the corporeal schema crumble[s], its place taken by a racial epidermal schema' (p. 112). The Black man finds himself no-place, and yet he is fixed in his place, his subjectivity foreclosed, with a meaning that is 'negative', a 'third-person consciousness' that defines the relation between his lived-body and the world as objective, 'epidermal'. The place of the racialized body, as Fanon describes it, helps us to grasp how bodies are displaced in and by particular settings or spaces, diagnoses, or 'opinions'. While the legacy of slavery in the US informs Black subjectivity and the carceral archipelago, in Canada, we must come to terms with the grim legacy of Aboriginal residential schools, the expropriation and exploitation of Native lands, high rates of poverty, HIV infection, suicide, and substance abuse, among many other social realities, the historical and institutional causes of which are multiplex. If Aboriginal youth are more likely to be incarcerated than to finish high school, this statistic must be understood together with the historic crimes committed in and by the residential school system, the crimes of the Church, the history of institutional barriers to resources, systemic racism, a medical system that condoned human experimentation on Aboriginal populations, and the intergenerational trauma of these experiences (see Coulthard 2014).

Admitting the significance of such a legacy, it is clear that the three historical periods of seclusion, as Guenther (2013) describes them—to redeem, to reform, and to implement a neoliberal management paradigm—overlap in subtle and often less subtle ways. Indeed, such a neat periodization (one could hardly call it 'progress') becomes somewhat implausible in the context of forensic psychiatric treatment and its use of seclusion. In our neoliberal present, the 'rhetoric of rehabilitation or spiritual redemption' is not 'gone', as Guenther (2013) at one point suggests of the US prison system; in forensic psychiatry it discreetly continues to inform stigmatizing perceptions of mental illness and treatment. We see, for example, a discourse on moral redemption operating when seclusion, used for behavior modification purposes, is presented as a therapeutic, rather than punitive, intervention, or as part of a behavior 'contract' or so-called 'administrative' segregation, the phenomenological effects of which are neither truly contractarian nor administrative. While moral redemption might strike us as an outmoded concept, it is nevertheless obliquely produced and demanded by neoliberal discourses that are hyper-individualizing and disciplinary, where the will and the interior desires of the subject must be reified and normalized through an entrepreneurial project of self-help and self-management. The normative force of neoliberalism is experienced as a *moral* imperative. It is driven by an onto-logic that turns the subject back toward what is presumed to be an interior reality, the identitarian 'truth' of who he or she is. In the supplicant, solitary interiority of seclusion, the subject is enjoined to find some causal link to an identity, as if his or her behavior emerged from some interior reality.

Meanwhile, what is violently effaced are the subject's history, sociocultural environment, race, embodiment, and relationships—in short, the subject's world, his or her lived-body. Seclusion becomes the perfect metaphor for the neoliberal subject, turned back on the self, in itself, to take stock of his or her own resources, as if the world flowed from the self, and as if the failure to recognize this could justify cruel punishment or 'correction'. In Foucault's (2008b) terms, the neoliberal subject is an 'entrepreneur of himself, being for himself his own capital, being for himself his own producer, being for himself the source of his earning' (p. 226). This subject is 'manageable' and 'governable'; this subject is rational, statistically informed, and 'accepts reality'. 'Rational conduct is any which is sensitive to modifications in the variables of the environment and which responds to this in a non-random way, in a systematic way, and economics can therefore be defined as the science of the systematic nature of responses to environmental variables' (p. 271). Under such a regime, achieving mental health would require the economic analysis of the subject's own resources and rewards—enabling him or her to accept the reality of new 'environmental variables', and to work within them in order to maximize profits and minimize loss.

While Guenther and others (e.g., Davis 2002; Oshinsky 1996) have argued that the legacy of racism complicates the history of solitary confinement in the US prison system, we suggest that the study of mental illness and seclusion in forensic psychiatric settings could benefit from their social critique and how such a critique is modeled and deployed methodologically. While race and mental illness are dissimilar social phenomena, would it be farfetched to suggest that racism and psychiatry are mobilized by similar biopolitical and neoliberal strategies? The point, most emphatically, is not to reduce one to the other, but to complicate both fields of power-knowledge, to locate their intersections, and to attend to the embodied dimensions of these experiences (e.g., see Metzl 2010). If the 'truth' of race is (re)produced through the prison system, and evidenced in part through the history of solitary confinement, to what extent might we say that the 'truth' of mental illness is (re)produced through forensic psychiatry and its use of seclusion? And what might this suggest for a study that turns to a critical account of the place of the secluded body?

Seclusion in/as behavior modification

> [W]e must insist on distinguishing between such diverse and mutually antagonistic goals as custody and rehabilitation. We cannot permit administrators to slip so conveniently from one rationale to another (Rothman 1975, p. 23).

Most behavior modification programs (BMPs) are presented as 'incentivizing', comprising rewards and punishment programs, where 'token economies' are used and subjects are fashioned as the entrepreneurs of their own success or failure. Under such a regime, behavioral infractions can cause patient-inmates to lose 'points' that can be used to 'purchase' various rewards (snacks, or 'life rewards' such as television, social time, or later bedtimes). It matters little whether this is construed as a 'loss' of a potential reward or as a 'punishment', properly speaking. The results are experienced as equivalent. In one setting under study, these behavior modification techniques are administered by nursing staff, which, as we have argued (Holmes & Murray 2011), conflates and confuses the purposes of care and corrections, with potentially devastating effects on the therapeutic relationship between a psychiatric nurse and his or her patient. We have critiqued such practices as neoliberal biopolitical paradigms that extend far beyond particular institutional constraints that might be deemed simply 'repressive' or 'extreme'. But BMPs do not solely consist of rewards-based 'token' economies; compliant behavior is also enforced through the threat of *losing* rewards and privileges, often involving seclusion as a negative reinforcement, a consequence of behavioral deviation in need of 'correction'.

Although the use of seclusion and BMPs in nursing is ethically controversial and has been criticized when employed as part of a patient's treatment plan (Holmes, Kennedy & Perron 2004; Holmes & Murray 2013; Muir-Cochrane 1995; Muir-Cochrane & Holmes 2001; Taxis 2002), the hybridity of the forensic psychiatric space allows these practices to continue unabated, in a gray zone—just one instance where correctional paradigms take priority over, transform, and often undermine, ethical therapeutic practice. At one of the facilities under study, the *Policies and Procedures Manual* (1997/2010) states: 'the [name of institution] is first and foremost a correctional institution. The operation needs of correctional services and the administration of justice in the provincial criminal justice system *will have priority* in the manner in which MCSCS [Ministry of Community Safety and Correctional Services] approaches its relation with [the hospital]' (emphasis added). Notwithstanding Rothman's (1975) early historical overview of behavior modification that warns against the 'convenient' administrative slippage between 'such diverse and mutually antagonistic goals as custody and rehabilitation', the very design of this setting facilitates and institutionalizes such slippage and antagonism.

In some respects, then, the institution becomes the metaphor (Douglas 1986)—from its behavior modification/treatment programs to its architecture—through which the individual comes to relate to him- or herself in neoliberal terms. And these neoliberal modes of (self-)relation are presented as the institutional means by which subjects will achieve their own redemption or salvation, by which they will be (re)habilitated to our new socioeconomic 'reality'. Once again, the use of seclusion to 'transform' behaviors is an apt metaphor for the self-reliant, entrepreneurial subject who is enjoined to claim responsibility for his or her own being, in isolation from—or 'ideally', as an individual in competition with—others. When used in conjunction, seclusion and BMPs seek to (re)habilitate and modify an individual's behavior to conform to a neoliberal socioeconomic system that is not in the least 'social' in any edifying sense. It champions an individualism that is ultimately sociopathic.

Here, a crisis of reality cannot be meaningful because we lose the sense in which the body is intrinsically and irreducibly relational, social, and historical. For mental health can only mean that the individual is not only or solely responsible for him- or herself, but to the commons, for a world that is shared, and for those wider conditions that will ensure that his or her place in that world is valued, meaningful, real.

The counter-therapeutic effects of seclusion are well documented. Grassian (2006) reports specific psychiatric symptoms linked with solitary confinement: (a) hyperresponsivity to external stimuli, (b) perceptual distortions, illusions, and hallucinations, (c) panic attacks, (d) difficulties with thinking, concentration, and memory, (e) intrusive obsessional thoughts, (f) overt paranoia, and (g) problems with impulse control (pp. 335–6). Meehan, Vermeer, and Windsor (2000) observe that patients who had experienced seclusion perceived the practice as punitive rather than therapeutic. Nevertheless, in one facility under study, BMPs constituted a regimen that included seclusion, managing patient-inmates' access to other parts of the unit, controlling how patient-inmates will spend their time, and dispensing or withholding 'rewards' and 'privileges'.

When used in conjunction with BMPs, seclusion is intended to modify or to correct deviant behavior—behavior that breaches what is figured as the 'social contract' in force at the institution. In one institution under study, upon release from 'administrative' segregation, patient-inmates are asked to sign a 'behavior contract' before being reintegrated into the unit. The contract states: 'In exchange for the privilege of spending time in his room out of locked seclusion, _____ will agree to…', which is followed by a bullet point list that includes the following: 'take olanzapine [which treats psychosis and bipolar disorder]…if either he or nursing staff feel he requires it to calm down, or de-escalate'; 'agree to re-enter the special observation room if either he or nursing staff feel he is escalation [*sic*] or losing control'; and 'no unsupervised contact with other [inmates] for 72 hours'. At the end it states: 'If any of the above criteria are not met, you _____ will be transferred to the [number] unit, and into a locked cell'. The contract is to be signed by the patient-inmate and two 'witnesses'. In one respect, these behavior contracts do operate loosely as social contracts intended to maintain order on the unit and to give the subject a sense of agency with respect to his or her actions, with the awareness that there are consequences for behaviors deemed unacceptable.

But this is not a contract in the proper sense of the term. Consent is illusory because the patient-inmate does not enter into this contract freely or as an equal subject under the law; this person has had no hand in designing the contract's terms or penalties, and they remain in some instances vague. He or she accepts from the position of a secluded subject, not a social one; the subject accepts as one whose social privileges have been revoked, who no longer holds the moral authority to enter a binding contract; social reintegration is promised, and purchased, with compliance. The illusion of freedom and agency is the manner by which the subject comes to conform to a set of norms, to modify his or her behavior. Yet, if the nursing relationship involves embodied fear, vulnerability, trust, dependence, and uncertainty, then the therapeutic relation is arguably undermined when intersubjectivity becomes contractarian, when its terms are abstract, and when nursing staff are required to police and punish breaches of contract. This power exceeds, if it does not pervert, the therapeutic relation; the contract figures this power as purposefully arbitrary, based on what the individual nurse 'feels' is best. Finally, we might even say that BMPs and their related discourses seize a subject who is not really there, a phantom subject—in the name of a future subject, a subject, who, ideally, one day, through (re)habilitation and compliance, will become empowered to consent, but who cannot do so here and now. There is an odd temporality at work. At the moment the 'contract' comes into effect, it references a time that is not-yet, for a subject who is out of time. And spatially, it operates through a place that is no-place, for a subject who is nowhere.

Conclusion

> Even in its solitude, the thing, like the thinker, never stands alone (Malpas 2012, p. 231).

There is no way, with empirical certitude, to fully account for the sociocultural history of bodies that live and die within the attenuated atmosphere of race and racism, or with the suffocating stigma of mental illness. This does not mean that we need not respond. We must. But the response must attend to what is at stake. It might be in kind, it may even be symbolic, and it may well acknowledge that it is sure, in some respects, to fail. It is difficult, if not impossible, to locate, to name, the disappeared subject of seclusion—and to imagine a subject, in that place, who could resist such subjugation. There is no subject who resists subjugation anymore than there is a single individual who subjugates him or her within this nexus of historical, social, and institutional forces; the subject is a lived-body, a cipher for a wider set of relations, who takes up a singular place vis-à-vis those others with and through whom he or she is reflected, with and through whom he or she returns from the vanishing point in the mirror. In an ethical vein, we might call this 'responsibility': we are responsible for that which we cannot claim full responsibility, and for that which we cannot fully know (Butler 2005), for institutions and for structures, for those conditions in and through which the lived-body takes place, where its subjectivity is made meaningful, and personhood and ethics are properly conceived. This cannot and must not be reduced to a biopsychiatric, or pharmacological, intervention; care is more than this. It is the relationship between lived-bodies that have complex histories, are culturally situated, and produced as racialized, ill, delinquent, and so forth. Indeed, *refusing* to recognize these intersectional dimensions constitutes a veritable crisis in the phenomenological sense, forcibly misrecognizing the body-in-seclusion as an object of liberal law, penality, and psychiatric power-knowledge.

The lived-body is not simply an object among other objects. It is subject; it stands-with, subject to and subject for, others. It does not live and breathe in cartographic space but inhabits a place and takes place, living in and through that place. As Merleau-Ponty (1962) argues, place 'is not a setting (real or logical) in which things are arranged, but the means whereby the position of things becomes possible' (p. 284). We must be responsible for these means because seclusion undermines the possibility of positioning oneself, and psychiatry often turns seclusion into a treatment program (when used in conjunction with BMPs) that forecloses upon the very thing it is purported to foster. In other words, seclusion is the foreclosure of that place in and through which the person assumes a place, and takes place. Legal and psychiatric rituals of civil death, within prisons or hospitals or increasingly in hybrid spaces, capture what Goffman (1961) terms being *mort au monde*—literally, dead to the world, dead to civil society. The civilly dead person is dead to the law (*civiliter mortuus*) but alive in fact, objectified biological life that is dispossessed of social and civic ties, displaced from the world. For it is the world, in a capacious phenomenological sense, that provides context and meaning for the lived-body and a life lived. It is this shared world that is lost in seclusion, which is no place, a placeless place, the absence of place, heterotopic. We have termed this 'seclusive space', a processual space that serves the double function of both providing and causing existential seclusion. In the first sense, being locked up provides (sometimes welcome) seclusion from others, which is obvious enough. In a second sense, however, isolation extends beyond objective bodily confinement, causing the seclusion of oneself in oneself, civil death.

In this sense, the subject is not just locked up but also locked in on him- or herself, unhinged from those intersubjective anchors that make the world a meaningful place, a condition of human personhood and ethics.

As researchers who live our lives on the outside, it is tempting to qualify—and perhaps dismiss—our intervention as (merely) an external critique. We are guilty, it might be said, of importing our external categories and applying them through righteous indignation. This is no doubt partly true. Fassin (2012) explains: 'For some, the task is to unveil. For others, it is to translate. Those on the outside denounce the social order. Those on the inside offer a grammar of social worlds' (p. 245). Ultimately, inside and outside might represent a false binary. We have denounced, but have attempted to straddle both positions in this chapter. Inasmuch as we have sought to 'translate', to provide a 'grammar of social worlds', this has as much as possible emerged through the crisis of the secluded body and an understanding of the ways that lived-bodies take place in an embodied social world—a world that is made and made meaningful through a human intersubjectivity that we all share. A phenomenological approach bridges—or at least problematizes—our commonsense understanding of inside and outside, interiority and exteriority, just as a critical appraisal of the structural social and historical conditions of human being does, since it references the place of a shared world rather than a movement of some interior ideational 'content' that would be exteriorized as 'truth'. Finally, it points to something real, essential, that resists, in the end, a regime of visibility and quantification.

References

AAPL 2005, *Ethics guidelines for the practice of forensic psychiatry*, American Academy of Psychiatry and the Law. Available from: <http://www.aapl.org/ethics.htm>. [10 January 2015].

Butler, J 2004, *Precarious life: the powers of mourning and violence*, Verso, New York.

Butler, J 2005, *Giving an account of oneself*, Fordham University Press, New York.

Castel, F, Castel, R & Lovell, A 1982, *The psychiatric society*, Columbia University Press, New York.

Coulthard, GS 2014, *Red skin, white masks: rejecting the colonial politics of recognition*, University of Minnesota Press, Minneapolis.

Davis, A 2002, 'From the convict lease system to the super-max prison', In *States of confinement: policing, detention, and prisons*, ed J James, Palgrave Macmillan, New York, pp. 60–74.

Douglas, M 1986, *How institutions think*, Syracuse University Press, Syracuse.

Fanon, F 1963, *The wretched of the earth*, Grove Press, New York.

Fanon, F 1967, *Black skin, white masks*, Grove Press, New York.

Fassin, D 2012, *Humanitarian reason: a moral history of the present*, University of California Press, Berkeley.

Foucault, M 2008a, *Psychiatric power: lectures at the Collège de France, 1973–1974*, Picador, New York.

Foucault, M 2008b, *The birth of biopolitics: lectures at the Collège de France, 1978–1979*, Picador, New York.

Foucault, M 1984 [1967], 'Of other spaces: heterotopias [*Des espaces autres*]', in *Architecture, Mouvement, Continuité 5*, M Foucault, pp. 46–9. Available from: <http://foucault.info/documents/heterotopia/foucault.heterotopia.en.html>. [10 January 2015].

Goffman, E 1961, *Asylums: essays on the social situation of mental patients and other inmates*, Random House, New York.

Guenther, L 2013, *Solitary confinement: social death and its afterlives*, University of Minnesota Press, Minneapolis.

Grassian, S 2006, 'Psychiatric effects of solitary confinement', *Washington University Journal of Law & Policy*, vol. 22, pp. 325–38.

Holmes, D, Kennedy, SL & Perron, A 2004, 'The mentally ill and social exclusion: a critical examination of the use of seclusion from the patient's perspective', *Issues in Mental Health Nursing*, vol. 25, no. 6, pp. 559–78.

Holmes, D & Murray, SJ 2011, 'Civilizing the barbarian: a critical analysis of behaviour modification programmes in forensic psychiatry settings', *Journal of Nursing Management*, vol. 19, pp. 293–301.

Malpas, J 2003, 'Bio-medical topoi—the dominance of space, the recalcitrance of place, and the making of persons', *Social Science and Medicine*, vol. 56, no. 11, pp. 2343–51.

Malpas, J 2012, *Heidegger and the thinking of place: explorations in the topology of being*, MIT Press, Cambridge.

Meehan, T, Vermeer C & Windsor, C 2000, 'Patients' perceptions of seclusion: a qualitative investigation', *Journal of Advanced Nursing*, vol. 31, no. 2, pp. 370–7.

Merleau-Ponty, M 1962, *Phenomenology of perception*, Routledge & Kegan Paul, London.

Metzl, JM 2010, *The protest psychosis: how schizophrenia became a black disease*, Beacon Press, Boston.

Muir-Cochrane, EC 1995, 'An exploration of ethical issues associated with the seclusion of psychiatric patients', *Collegian: Journal of the Royal College of Nursing, Australia*, 2(3), 14–20.

Muir-Cochrane, EC & Holmes, CA 2001, 'Legal and ethical aspects of seclusion: an Australian perspective', *Journal of Psychiatric & Mental Health Nursing*, vol. 8, no. 6, pp. 501–6.

Murray, SJ 2012, 'Phenomenology, ethics, and the crisis of the lived-body', *Nursing Philosophy*, vol. 13, pp. 289–94.

Murray, SJ & Holmes, D 2013, 'Toward a critical ethical reflexivity: phenomenology and language in Maurice Merleau-Ponty', *Bioethics*, vol. 27, no. 6, pp. 341–7.

Murray, SJ & Holmes, D 2014, 'Interpretive phenomenological analysis (IPA) and the ethics of body and place: critical methodological reflections', *Human Studies*, vol. 37, no. 1, pp. 15–30.

Office of the Correctional Investigator 2013, *Segregation in Canadian federal corrections: a prison ombudsman's perspective*, Government of Canada. Available from:

<http://www.oci-bec.gc.ca/cnt/comm/presentations/presentations20130322
-23-eng.aspx>. [10 January 2015].

Office of the Correctional Investigator 2014, *A case study of diversity in corrections: the Black inmate experience in federal penitentiaries final report*, Government of Canada. Available from: <http://www.oci-bec.gc.ca/cnt/rpt/oth-aut/oth-aut 20131126-eng.aspx>. [10 January 2015].

OIIQ-CMQ 2011, *Rapport d'enquête sur la qualité des soins en santé mental au CSSS de St-Jérôme*, Ordre des infirmières et infirmiers du Quebec and Collège des médecins du Québec. Available from: http://www.oiiq.org/sites/default/files/uploads/pdf/ salle_de_presse/rapport-enquete-saint-jerome-20110616-VCA-oiiq-VF.pdf>. [10 January 2015].

Oshinsky, D 1996, *'Worse than slavery': Parchman Farm and the ordeal of Jim Crow justice*, Free Press, New York.

Public Safety Canada 2014, *Corrections and conditional release statistical overview*, Government of Canada. Available from: http://www.publicsafety.gc.ca/cnt/ rsrcs/pblctns /crrctns-cndtnl-rls-2013/index-eng.aspx>. [10 January 2015].

Rothman, DJ 1975, 'A historical overview: behavior modification in total institutions', *Hastings Center Report*, vol. 5, no. 1, pp. 17–24.

Shalev, S 2009, *Supermax: controlling risk through solitary confinement*, Willan, Portland, OR.

Standing Committee on Public Safety and National Security 2010, *Mental health and drug and alcohol addiction in the federal correctional system: report of the Standing Committee on Public Safety and National Security*, Government of Canada. Available from: <http://www.parl.gc.ca/content/hoc/committee/403/secu/reports/rp 4864852/securp04/securp04-e.pdf>. [10 January 2015].

Szasz, T 2014, 'Varieties of psychiatric criticism', in *Power and the psychiatric apparatus*, eds D Holmes, JD Jacob, & A Perron, Ashgate Publishing, Farnham, UK, pp. 25–34.

Taxis, JC 2002, 'Ethics and praxis: alternative strategies to physical restraint and seclusion in a psychiatric setting', *Issues in Mental Health Nursing*, vol. 23, no. 2, pp. 157–70.

7

Normalizing Exceptions: Solitary Confinement and the Micro-politics of Risk/Need in Canada

Kelly Hannah-Moffat, University of Toronto, Mississauga
Amy Klassen, University of Toronto, Mississauga[1]

Extreme forms of prison management including the use of force, restraints, and solitary confinement have become de facto behavior management strategies for prisoners struggling with mental health issues in Canada. This chapter focuses specifically on the use of solitary confinement (segregation) in Canadian female federal prisons to illustrate how extreme forms of penal control are becoming increasingly normalized in Canadian prisons (Zinger 2013), thus exacerbating the overall pains of imprisonment.[2] According to the Office of the Correctional Investigator of Canada's 2013 report, approximately 24.3 percent of the federal prison population has spent some time in segregation. Much of the increase in the prison population being subjected to segregation is limited to certain classes of offenders, especially those with mental health issues.

Despite the critical attention directed at extreme institutional practices including segregation, organizational apathy persists regarding the development of alternatives and the implementation of numerous recommendations stemming from a recent coroner's inquest, OCI annual and special reports, and older task force reports about the use of administrative segregation (TFAS 1997; Arbour 1998). In this chapter, we focus on the case of 19-year-old Ashley Smith, who died from self-inflicted injuries in segregation in one of Canada's gender-responsive federal women's facilities. In this chapter, we explore why, despite the overwhelming evidence that exposure to long-term segregation has devastating mental health outcomes, Correctional Service of Canada (CSC) continues to use segregation routinely as a preventative and punitive tool to manage women who self-injure.

Ashley had a long history of disruptive and challenging behavior before and during her time in youth custody. While in custody in the New Brunswick Youth Centre, Ashley spent much of her time in solitary confinement and accumulated 50 additional criminal charges for interactions with correctional guards, typically over her self-harming behaviors. As a result of her additional charges and her extremely challenging behavior, Ashley was transferred into the federal correctional system in 2006, as soon as she turned 18. From 2006–07, she was involved in 150 security incidents in federal institutions, usually surrounding her use of ligatures. Despite being placed in solitary confinement to reduce her self-injurious behavior, Ashley's level of resistance continued to escalate (Sapers 2008). During her time at Grand Valley Institution, she had no clothing other than a smock, no shoes, no mattress, and no blankets. On 19 October 2007, despite being under 24-hour suicide watch, Ashley used a ligature that ended her life. A formal coroner's inquest was initiated in 2012. In December 2013, the coroner's jury ruled that her death was a homicide (Smith, 2013; CanLII 92762 (ON OCCO)). The designation of her death as a homicide does not imply criminal responsibility. Instead, in Canadian law it means 'that through acts or omissions, a person or persons has or have contributed to Ashley's death' (CSC 2014, p. 1). This case offers many insights into how prisons struggle to manage prisoners in crisis and how punishment and risk-informed logics preclude more humane, evidence-based responses identified in community mental health literatures.

We demonstrate that the use of segregation and more extreme forms of control (e.g., physical, mechanical, and chemical restraints; restraint chairs, straitjackets, four-point bed restraints, 'WRAP'[3] (a cocoon-like device used to immobilize prisoners from the neck down), and antipsychotic medications such as Seroquel[4]) are (or are at risk of becoming) a normalized managerial response to prisoners who engage in chronic self-injury (Borrill et al. 2005; Appelbaum et al. 2001; OCI 2013). The use of these types of control is complicated by narrow organizational understandings of what behaviors reflect mental illness—and the different possible interpretations of behaviors as non-compliant, disruptive, and intentional, versus symptomatic or predictable reactions to the 'conditions of confinement'.

Instead of being understood as in crisis, prisoners like Ashley Smith are framed through correctional use-of-force reports and reports from the correctional officers union as risky, purposefully defiant, and disorderly; such framings problematically legitimate and enable punitive and extreme organizational responses to behaviors that could be seen as symptomatic of mental health issues or normative reactions to their environment. In this chapter, we demonstrate how using segregation to manage disruptive (or symptomatic) behaviors can accelerate non-compliance and defiance, sometimes in the form of self-harm, instead of encouraging docility (Zinger 2013; Rhodes 2004; also see Haney 2003, 2006).

After briefly presenting the details of Ashley Smith's case, we demonstrate that the current use of segregation reveals: 1) a narrow framing and lack of understanding of mental health, specifically self-injury; 2) a formal administrative construction of prisoners who are exceptionally high-need as disorderly, risky, threatening, and/or dangerous; 3) an absence of knowledge about how segregation and its preventative use is itself a risk that can *produce* the disruptive behaviors that initiated this administrative response; and 4) an organizational unwillingness to create alternatives and the construction of segregation as the appropriate measure 'given the circumstances'. Although our discussion focuses on how women who engage in self-injury are generally characterized as a 'management problem', and how segregation is used to manage these women, our analysis is generalizable to the management of prisoners with other forms of mental illness.

This chapter draws on the information contained in public briefs (statements, institutional reports, and videos) and testimony at the coroner's inquest into the death of Ashley Smith as well as on an extensive range of public reviews of this case by the correctional officers union, the Office of the Coroner and the Correctional Service of Canada. Similar to the preceding chapter by Stuart and Holmes, we examine some of the conceptual and pragmatic gaps in forensic mental health care, which in this instance resulted in Ashley Smith being shuffled between prison segregation units and psychiatric hospitals with little consensus on how to understand and treat her ultimately lethal, self-injurious behavior. Using this case, we argue that prisoners who self-injure exist in a highly problematic and ethically vacuous 'hybrid space' between psychiatry and corrections where they are simultaneously characterized as rational and irrational. Like, Reiter and Blair (this volume), we show how solitary confinement is constructed as the most appropriate option for the management of serious mental health concerns and, in this case, chronic self-injury, and how the use of solitary confinement can aggravate and produce the behaviors it is meant to control, thus creating a vicious, self-reinforcing cycle of extreme punishments. We argue that the ambiguity surrounding Ashley's diagnosis and treatment, an organizational denial of the productive power of punitive contexts, and the operational emphasis on the management of risky people and events enabled corrections to legitimate the use of extreme interventions.

Ashley Smith: Micro-politics of the risk subject

The case of Ashley Smith exemplifies how prisoners who display behaviors that could be indicative of mental health issues, but who do not conform to the CSC's official classifications of mental illness, are routinely constituted as security threats that must be contained. Within this conceptualization of threat, various forms of physical control are used to contain threatening conduct, which can actually escalate troublesome conduct and exacerbate underlying conditions.

Consistently, researchers have observed that female offenders are not only more vulnerable to having their behavior medicalized (Shaylor 1998, Bosworth & Carrabine 2001, Pollack 2005), but they are also routinely subjected to more invasive forms of control than men when they violate institutional rules (Shaylor 1998; Auerhahn & Leonard 2000; Pollack 2005; Irwin & Chesney-Lind 2008). Irving and Wichmann (2001) identified a number of contributing factors that can increase the likelihood that female prisoners will be placed in higher levels of security: having an uncooperative attitude, having convictions for serious institutional charges, having little/no motivation to comply, possessing contraband, and having a history of escapes. Additionally, Shaylor (1998) found that women are more likely than men to be placed in solitary confinement for minor infractions, for example to prevent suicide attempts. She also argued that such harsh treatment is used to control women who do not conform to the social standards of femininity: 'the central function of prisons in general is to punish women who fail to subscribe to a model of femininity that historically has been (re) produced in the discourse of white, pure, passive, heterosexuals, and located in motherhood. When women operate outside of this model, even slightly, they are disciplined harshly for doing so' (Shaylor, cited in Arrigo & Bullock 2008, p. 634).

One way that female prisoners fail to conform to the stereotypical attributes of femininity is by displaying behavior that counters common expectations of how women should act in prison. Because Ashley was difficult to manage and acted out both in the juvenile and adult systems, she spent a majority of her sentenced time in segregation throughout her incarceration at Grand Valley Institute for Women (GVI; and in the other regions (Sapers 2008, p. 6)), with very little time in the general population. Her original sentence of 30 days in youth custody was for throwing a crab apple at a postman. She had few opportunities to leave her cell and extremely limited meaningful interpersonal contact. Beyond proscribed levels of surveillance and monitoring by psychologists and staff, Ashley was given no opportunity for programming at GVI and limited access to recreation and showers.

When attempting to negotiate her safety in a self-injurious context, staff would (on most occasions) enter her cell in full riot gear and use force, as required, to remove ligatures. Types of force included the use of OC spray or pepper spray, physical handling, and various types of restraints. Ashley was generally, but not always, compliant with staff during these interventions. Officers were sometimes able to negotiate a resolution, but at times needed to forcefully remove ligatures from her neck, sometimes as many as six or seven times a day, while Ashley would frequently wrestle with, spit on, or bite officers. The self-initiated choking became so severe that her facial blood vessels burst, leaving her face permanently discolored; she also lost sight in one eye and suffered nosebleeds (Union of Canadian Correctional Officers 2008).

Ashley had little control over her living conditions and daily activities, and her challenging behaviors were often geared toward obtaining items with which to harm herself, not others. One officer described her living conditions as follows:

> In reality, this girl was living in a cell in which all the floor tiles were removed, all the light fixtures were gone, and the sprinkler had been covered. They retrofitted the segregation shower so she couldn't get any pieces of metal. She was only ever allowed two pieces of toilet paper at a time. She wasn't allowed a food tray. We had no way of knowing if she was actually taking her medication. We don't even have direct observation rooms. She would lie down on the floor in front of the food slot on the dried tar left from the tile adhesive, right against the door where we couldn't see her well (Union of Canadian Correctional Officers 2008, p. 8).

In less than one year, Ashley was moved 17 times between three federal penitentiaries, two treatment facilities, two external hospitals, and one provincial correctional facility (Sapers 2008). Her segregation clock restarted each time she was moved, meaning the legally mandated seven- and 30-day reviews needed to justify continued segregation never occurred, thus leaving her perpetually in segregation. Additionally, nine of the 17 transfers were between four of the five CSC regions: during these transfers she was sometimes duct-taped to her airplane seat. Each time she entered a new institution, she was placed in segregation with restrictions on her cell effects; at times she was placed directly in physical restraints or subjected to chemical restraints or drugs to keep her calm. It is questionable as to whether she consented to psychiatrically pre-scribed medications. Video evidence presented at her coroner's inquest on a number of occasions showed her being physically restrained to a bed in order to be administered medications.

Most of these institutional transfers were the result of administrative issues such as cell availability, incompatible inmates, and staff fatigue, and had little or nothing to do with Ashley's needs. Each transfer eroded her trust, escalated her acting-out behaviors, and made it increasingly difficult for the CSC to manage her. Although several medical and psy-chological personnel examined her, she was not diagnosed as mentally ill but rather as a 'manipulative and non-compliant' prisoner who used self-injurious behavior to 'get attention' (Sapers 2008). Thus, when Ash-ley complained about her conditions of confinement, and had advo-cates file grievances about her treatment, official responses deemed the grievances as baseless.

According to one official, 'Several officers at Grand Valley Institution went to great lengths to interact with inmate Smith despite a constant threat to their personal safety' (Union of Canadian Correctional Offic-ers 2008). Even though some front-line staff questioned whether her behavior was a function of mental health issues (irrational conduct) or just an attention-seeking attempt at manipulation (rational conduct), correctional staff did seek advice from upper management on how best to deal with her behavior. One of the issues with prisoners like Ash-ley is that correctional officers are given very limited training on how to manage difficult and potentially mentally ill prisoners. The frustra-tion faced by correctional staff often resulted in her being considered 'a manipulative game player out for psychological [and physical] domina-tion' (Drake 2012, p. 66). Being labeled a behavior management prob-lem justified correctional authorities' use of more austere and extreme forms of control.

Because of Ashley's history, senior managers ultimately ordered front-line staff members to not enter her cell unless they had determined that she had stopped breathing as a response to her persistent self-injurious conduct (Sapers 2008). On the day Ashley died, the guards entered her cell too late. Many commentators view her death as a preventable and predictable tragedy that exemplifies a number of structural inadequacies in the prison system: a litany of systemic problems and rights viola-tions associated with the management of women prisoners, especially women characterized by correctional authorities as 'high risk' or 'high need', including the overuse of segregation and physical and chemical restraints. Because Ashley was framed as 'high risk'—as a security threat—her containment in segregation was positioned as a last resort, a protective form of risk management. Nonetheless, she experienced segregation as an extreme form of punishment (Martel 1999). Like all segregated prisoners, she was subjected to constant video surveillance, communication with guards through a food slot, and strictly limited access to 'privileges' (exercise, showers, reading/writing material, and visits) that are afforded prisoners in the general population.

Manipulative, not ill: Self-injury and the production of a 'difficult to manage prisoner'

Over the past eight years Canada has seen a significant increase in the number of self-injury incidents in federal correctional facilities. In 2011–12, there were 912 incidents of self-injury recorded, involving 303 offenders (CSC 2013, p. 1). Although self-injurious behavior largely seen as an issue with female offenders, male offenders also participate in this behavior; but unlike women offenders who often have a pre-prison history of self-harm, 'male offenders who self-harm are more likely to begin this behavior in a federal facility' (CSC 2013, p. 1). Many international scholars have explored the prevalence and nature of self-injurious behavior among incarcerated individuals,[5] estimating that approximately 10–13 percent of female prisoners self-injure during their sentence (Meltzer et al. 2002). Self-injury is a particularly significant problem among women and Aboriginals in Canadian prisons (Shaw 1991; CSC 2013). For example, one study of 26 female inmates admitted to the Intensive Healing Program at the Prairie Regional Psychiatric Centre revealed that 73 percent of these women had engaged in self-injurious behavior prior to their admittance (Presse & Hart, cited in Fillmore & Dell 2000). Researchers have documented a general lack of understanding among staff members about women who harm themselves (Weekes & Morison 1992; Snow 1997): most see self-injurious behavior as a means of acting out, seeking attention, or manipulation, and/or as a potential danger to others. Even though empirical evidence suggests that self-harming is a coping behavior used by women in distress, the reality of how self-harm is managed suggests that it is frequently positioned as a security risk rather than as a coping strategy.

The connection between self-harm and penal security is complicated when we consider whether self-harming behavior may be a product of an underlying mental health concern. Fundamental to our understanding of how Ashley and other women who self-injure come to be understood as 'difficult to manage', disruptive, and defiant, is first, the narrow conceptualization of what constitutes a mental illness in Canadian correctional facilities and, consequently, what is approached as a health concern, and second, the tendency of female offenders to be over-penalized for behavior that goes against institutional expectations.

In the Canadian context, mental health diagnoses are limited to schizophrenia and bipolar conditions (Blanchette & Montuik 1996). Individuals who suffer from major depression, substance abuse, anxiety, and personality disturbances (e.g., borderline personality disorder) are not officially characterized as 'mentally ill'. As discussed in more detail below, female prisoners who do not conform to institutional expectations are often labeled as having borderline personality disorder (BPD) when they engage in self-harm. Boisvert has defined BPD as a 'pervasive pattern of instability in one's relationships, self-image, and impulses that disrupts daily functioning' (2004, p. 47), and has argued that the defining feature of people with BPD is a 'real or imagined abandonment by others, intense relationships marked by idealization and devaluation, impulsivity expressed as substance abuse, suicidal thoughts or behaviors, and outbursts of anger' (Boisvert 2004, p. 47). Importantly, BPD is not officially considered a mental illness that requires specialized health services. Instead, women exhibiting this cluster of symptoms in prison are framed as difficult to manage, not as suffering from mental illness. Unsurprisingly, McDonagh et al. (2002) found that Canadian prisoners diagnosed with BPD are over-represented in secure housing.

The use of catchall categorizations like BPD to frame acts of self-injury facilitates the characterization of self-injury as a security threat rather than as a medical problem (Kilty 2006; Richard 2008). This places a vast majority of potentially challenging prisoners outside the spectrum of penal health services. As a result, behaviors associated with some mental health conditions may become characterized as intentional, manipulative, or antagonistic, and thus best managed using security or force rather than psychiatric or therapeutic best practices by prison staff. Another consequence is that prisoners with personality disorders represent a significant proportion of prisoners housed in higher levels of security and administrative segregation. This finding is consistent with other research about prison mental health, which consistently shows that offenders who struggle with their mental health are generally classified as more 'disruptive' to prison order, incur more disciplinary infractions, have histories of psychiatric inpatient treatment, have more incidents of self-injury, and are often excluded from the types of treatments that may help alleviate their disruptive behavior (Haney 2003; Arrigo & Bullock 2008; Bauer et al. 2011). The general perception that women are weak, powerless, and compliant is disrupted when female offenders violate normative expectations. Such violations are often pathologized by a diagnosis of borderline personality disorder (BPD), which leads to the deployment of various forms of *behavioral* therapies designed to illicit compliance and normative behaviors to manage self-injury (see the chapters by Murray & Holmes and Reiter & Blair in this collection for additional analysis).

In Ashley Smith's case, guards were told to strictly enforce a behavioral agreement created with Ashley and to not engage in discussions that she might initiate regarding self-injury. Instead they were to refocus the conversation and redirect to discussion surrounding TV, radio, her interests, and neutral topics.[6] They were also told to illicit her compliance by allowing privileges (TV or radio—through the meal slot) for limited time periods (i.e., 10 minutes) if she did not self-injure or calmed down. However, concerns about Ashley's so-called defiance also led to additional punitive and preventative measures. Her cell was searched daily, and any items brought into her cell were to be monitored. When Ashley was removed from the cell for showers or recreation, she was to be escorted by three officers and restrained in handcuffs and leg irons. In keeping with the literature described above, there is little evidence that the correctional system ever approached the management of her self-injury through a mental health lens or considered the possibility that such punitive and restrictive conditions of confinement could exacerbate Ashley's already problematic behaviors.

Despite CSC's recommendation that administrative segregation should be used only as a last resort for disruptive prisoners (CSC 2010), as in Ashley's case, segregation is often not only the first option but is used as a prolonged form of punishment for women who self-injure (Kilty 2006; Richard 2008; Sapers 2008). The 'pains of imprisonment' are a major contributing factor to self-harm for incarcerated women. Among these 'pains' are negative relationships with staff and other prisoners, confinement in segregation, stressful living conditions, and rigid and arbitrary rule enforcement. For women who engage in self-injurious behavior, prolonged periods of segregation can elevate crisis situations rather than diffuse them. According to the Canadian Human Rights Commission (2003), women tend to experience segregation as rejection, abandonment, invisibility, and a denial of their existence. More recently, the 2013 report of the Correctional Investigator of Canada reinforces the problems with using segregation for the management of self-injury (OCI 2013). Segregation does not further women's rehabilitation or enable program participation or access to health services, and it often jeopardizes a woman's safety and mental health by increasing her distress.[7]

Fillmore and Dell (2000) interviewed self-harming women offenders and corrections staff members in Canada about self-harm in Canadian prisons. According to the female offenders they interviewed, self-harming can help prisoners cope with a variety of issues including isolation and loneliness and lack of power and control. Interviewees reported engaging in self-harm to deal with isolation and loneliness, as a cry for attention and nurturing, for self-punishment and self-blame, as an opportunity to feel *something*, as a way of distracting and deflecting emotional pain, as a release and cleansing of emotional pain, as an expression of painful life experiences, and to provide a sense of power and control.

Corrections staff members identified similar functions, but their accounts differed from those of offenders in important ways. Staff members tended to minimize the women's need for attention and nurturing, expand the interpretation of control to include women influencing others to take control for them, downplay the role of isolation and loneliness in the women's lives, not recognize self-harm as a means to express painful life experiences, and consider self-harm a form of manipulation (Fillmore & Dell 2000).

The ways in which correctional staff members interpret self-injury affect their responses to it. Constituting self-injury as a threat to prison order that must be mitigated justifies the placement of 'disruptive' prisoners in solitary confinement until those prisoners can demonstrate the capacity to follow institutional rules (Task Force on Administrative Segregation 1997). Additional forms of restraint may be used to immobilize individuals who are unwilling to comply. For example, Ashley was subjected to tasers, pepper spray, and a device euphemistically referred to as the 'wrap', to promote compliance and prevent self-injury. Bernard Richard, the ombudsman of New Brunswick (2008), described the wrap as

> the most severe of restraint methods…very much like a cocoon. She was bound from head to toe, unable to move. The 'wrap' consists of applying restraint belts beginning at the prisoner's feet, all the way up to his or her shoulders, ceasing all possibility of bodily movement. Then a hockey helmet is placed on the head which would prevent one from injuring themselves in the event of a topple over, and also preventing the subject from biting anyone (2008, p. 22).

The use of the wrap is organizationally defended as a form of risk prevention. It allows staff to keep a prisoner 'safe' and to prevent acts of self-injury, and thus is characterized as a legitimate intervention. However, the wrap is an extreme measure not experienced as supportive or even therapeutic. Rather it is a humiliating form of physical and psychological control. As a technique, the wrap enables an uneasy organizational assemblage of care and control that enables and reinforces the normalization of extreme interventions in the name of 'safety' and prevention.

When restraints and attempts at isolation do not make prisoners compliant, they are sometimes transferred to a psychiatric hospital for evaluation. As a consequence of persistent security incidents associated with Ashley's self-injury, correctional officials repeatedly tried to have her assessed for a mental health condition. Ashley was transferred to mental health facilities where her chronic self-injuring was classified as defiant behavior rather than as symptomatic of mental illness (Sapers 2008). Because these psychiatric assessments failed to identify a mental disorder, Ashley was returned to the penitentiary. Prisons that operate under punitive risk-based logics have few meaningful alternatives for managing disruptive behavior other than using preventative restraints and segregation. This vacillation and cycling between segregation and hospitals creates a vicious cycle. Once a prisoner's behavior becomes so troublesome that CSC is unable to effectively manage it, the prisoner is transferred into the forensic psychiatric system: if no mental illness is detected, the prisoner is returned to the penitentiary, where behaviors may escalate if the prisoner is preventatively returned to segregation. Without a mental health diagnosis, symptomatic behaviors and self-injury are defined as defiance and manipulation, enabling the vicious cycle that Reiter and Blair describe in Chapter 9. Documenting Ashley's self-injury effort as 'manipulative' rather than symptomatic becomes the organizational 'justification for dismissing suffering' (see Pittendrigh this volume) and legitimating punitive tactics as 'deserved' or measured responses to resistance and defiance.

In Ashley's case, her personality disturbances and self-destructive behavior led to a total of at least three transfers to psychiatric hospitals, where she was subjected to involuntary medications to manage her actions (Sapers 2008; Beaudry 2010). Each time she returned from the hospital, she was placed in a segregation unit, where she accumulated additional institutional charges and time in solitary confinement. Despite the perception that prisoners are rational subjects capable of making responsible choices, Ashley's case exemplifies the dichotomy between notions of rationality and irrationality when so-called resistant women are uncontrollable within a prison. The consistent attempts of CSC to have her labeled with a psychiatric diagnosis that could be recognized by the prison (i.e., schizophrenia or bipolar disorder) reveal how the actions of women like Ashley are not considered sane reactions to segregation.

Criminogenic and iatrogenic qualities of segregation

The use of segregation operates within an institutional framework that struggles to 'provide safe, supportive correctional environments' for women offenders as well as 'opportunities that empower women to live with dignity and respect, to help rebuild their lives as law-abiding citizens and create safer communities for all' (CSC 2015, n.p.). CSC has instituted many policy initiatives that are designed to protect the rights of federal prisoners, but it also places a neoliberal emphasis on individual responsibility and accountability: prisoners are expected to make responsible choices in how they act. Responsible choices, in essence, are actions that harmonize with prison rules and programs. Prisoners who 'choose' not to follow the rules are subjected to heightened forms of isolation, including solitary confinement. Researchers have consistently shown that federal officials have a limited range of available choices for dealing with prisoners (Hannah-Moffat 2000; Hannah-Moffat 2001) and that decisions about who should remain in segregation tend to overlook how the prison environment may itself produce disruptive conduct.

'Risk' or 'disorder' is a fluid subjectivity that is actively (re)produced through institutional practices. Once a prisoner is designated as high-risk or difficult to manage, he or she is exposed to intensified forms of surveillance, scrutiny, and spatial restrictions. Restrictions on liberty are justified by lack of compliance: any form of acting out (self-injury, outbursts, violations of institutional rules, etc.) reinforces the risk designation and is typically interpreted as resistance, rather than as a survival or coping strategy. For example, in response to Ashley Smith's persistent self-injurious behavior, correctional officials instituted an emergency order not to intervene unless she stopped breathing. Despite obvious concerns about humane treatment, this order was justified as a means of *preventing* her disorderly conduct: her behavior was interpreted as a threat to prison order. Additionally, when Ashley would resist attempts to remove her ligatures, the use of force and harm escalated (Sapers 2008). In this context, her right to treatment and life-saving interventions, which meant staff needed to enter her cell, was recast as a risk that needed to be managed.

The same level of scrutiny and accountability is rarely brought to bear on systems of punishment when they violate the principles of legality that underscore broader judicial and humane expectations of punishment. In this context, rights violations become secondary to the management of disorderly prisoners, and analyses and evaluations of a prisoner's conduct tend to neglect issues related to the custodial experience itself. An offender's problems, and the treatments (or lack of treatments) he or she receives, are no longer situated within a broader penal context. This is an important issue to address, because it affects how penal subjects are characterized and broadens the scope of managerial options.

Institutional practices such as segregation are themselves criminogenic (Haney 2006) and contribute to the rhetoric of risk thinking. Risk is interpreted though a narrow lens of normativity and individuality, but risky subjects are not static and change over time and place. The tendency to essentialize the risky subject neglects the mechanisms underpinning this construction. The prison as place of punishment has difficulty understanding behaviors as symptomatic of disorders or even as iatrogenic—products of confinement. In extreme cases of prolonged segregation, a common pattern is evident. Inquiries and public accounts of segregated prisoners' behaviors and institutional responses reflect a series of events where the prisoner 'acts out' while in 23-hour lockdown by attempting to self-injure, covering cell windows and cameras, throwing bodily fluids, grabbing at staff through meal slots, banging their heads, screaming or shouting profanities, starting fires, destroying property, or acting aggressively when taken out of the cell for brief periods to shower or for recreation (Haney 2003; 2006; 2009). The institutional response to these behaviors typically involves negative reinforcement, and at times force, when entering the prisoner's cell. During this time, the prisoner may resist or engage in physical altercations with staff, who are often armed with restraints (chemical or physical) and riot gear. Immediately the prisoner is restrained and the problematic behavior contained. Repeated attempts to self-injure can be used by corrections to reframe mental health needs as risk and to legitimize the use of such austere forms of control as a justification for perpetuating the heightened state of necessity inherent in the state of exception. In this regard, the use of force functions to legitimize the executive power of prison officials to wield solitary confinement as a necessary tool to maintain order, becoming the institutional foundation for justifying the continued use of solitary confinement (see also the subsequent chapter by Reiter & Blair). In essence, the structure of segregation produces the social space where violence and force become normalized and routine (Reiter 2014).

Organizational apathy: Knowing what else to do

Most correctional staff members have received minimal training on how to manage self-injurious prisoners. Fundamental to changing prison responses to women who self-injure is education and training about why incarcerated women harm themselves and alternative responses that could be used within the prison system, since the use of extreme force and segregation exacerbates women's crises. The common perception of chronic self-harmers as intrinsically difficult or frustrating is integrally linked to the work environment, which is often not equipped to manage this behavior or to support staff members providing services to the self-harming individual (Marzano & Adler 2007). Prisoners who chronically harm themselves through suicidal gestures or attempts or self-mutilation demand considerable attention and resources. If not carefully managed, the potential for staff frustration or burnout is high. Appropriate treatment and management are often made more difficult due to time pressures and the need for intensive staff involvement, which are functions of the frequency, severity, and unpredictability of some self-injurious acts. This lack of resources, knowledge, and training, coupled with restrictive organizational definitions of mental health conditions and the need to maintain security leads to condemnation of the prisoners and an unsurprising reliance on physical and pharmacological restraints, including the continuous use of segregation (Jones 1986; Martel 1999; Kilty 2006; Dell et al. 2009). As discussed above, this can produce a vicious circle, escalating women's self-destructive behaviors and thereby solidifying the need for correctional authorities to restrict prisoners' environments to prevent further self-harm. To reiterate, Ashley Smith's experiences provide ample evidence of these patterns. Within this context, self-harm becomes constituted as an act of resistance, thereby justifying the need to reduce threats to prison order: official narratives construct segregation as intrinsically defensible primarily on security grounds.

Ironically, Canada's official policy suggests that segregation is part of the CSC's overall obligation to provide prisoners and staff with safe, secure, and humane conditions within the institution (CSC 2002). It is only to be used as a last resort for the shortest period of time necessary to improve inmate conduct. According to this logic, the actual use of segregation should be rare, and when it is used the process should be reasonable. However, in response to criticism from advocacy groups and the Correctional Investigator, the CSC has repeatedly defended its use of segregation as a legally viable, necessary, and appropriate form of prisoner management in a range of situations, including the management of mental health issues (Arbour 1998; OCI 2013; Taskforce on Administrative Segregation 1997). Still, the Correctional Investigator recommends that the 'long-term segregation of seriously mentally ill, self-injurious or suicidal inmates...be expressly prohibited' (2013, p. 29).

However, despite calls for the prohibition of segregation for self-injurious prisoners, segregation is positioned as the only viable option available to front-line staff. The CSC cannot risk the appearance of 'doing nothing' about these threats. So faced with high-need prisoners, punitive techniques like segregation and restraint are often used preventatively in anticipation of future events that could threaten the security of the prison or the safety of the prisoner. The increasing normative use of segregation mirrors how maximum-security units operate based on a 'threat mentality' (Drake 2012; see also Ewald 1999). These penal strategies use the language of prevention as the primary justification for using segregation.

Academic research, as well as past inquiries and inquests, have consistently documented the degrading and dehumanizing effects of isolation and segregation. For women with mental health difficulties, and those who engage in self-injurious behavior, prolonged periods of segregation can exacerbate crisis situations rather than diffuse them. Segregation does not further women's rehabilitation, and it often jeopardizes a woman's safety and mental health by exacerbating her distress. According to one female prisoner, 'This [segregation] has affected me greatly as now I see or perceive myself to [sic] being a monster and rejected' (CHRC 2003, p. 45). Many researchers have investigated whether the conditions in which prisoners are confined affect their mental health (e.g., Haney 2003, 2006; Motiuk & Blanchette 2001; Gaes & Camp 2009; Adams 1986; Arrigo & Bullock 2008; Zinger, Wichmann & Andrews 2001; Porporino & Montiuk 1995; Martel 1999). Together, the findings indicate that segregation tends not only to exacerbate prior mental health problems, but can lead to the development of previously undetected mental health problems. Segregation can exacerbate cognitive–behavioral problems among prisoners, such as difficulty solving interpersonal problems, unawareness of the consequences of their actions, an inability to make positive choices, and a tendency to display disregard for others as a result of being socially unaware and impulsive (Montiuk & Blanchette 2001). It also restricts factors that are known to be beneficial to prisoners: environmental stimulation; contact with the broader prison community; and access to personal items, programming, visits, and phone calls (Haney 2009; Wooldredge 1999).

Moreoever, Goebil et al. (2007) found that women who were placed in higher levels of security tended to exhibit more misconduct. They concluded that misconduct by female prisoners is an individual-level problem and not caused by the prison environment. However, this individualized conception of misconduct ignores the vast body of literature demonstrating that the prison environment plays an essential role in determining prisoner behavior and wellbeing (Blanchette & Montiuk 1996; Haney 2003; Kupers 2006; Kruttschnitt & Vuolo 2007; Richard 2008; Sapers 2008). The ability of prisoners to adjust to prison may be a direct reflection of the dynamics of the prison environment, so a sole focus on individual-level pathways ignores the important mediating role of the prison environment. Considering Ashley Smith's well-known history of self-harm and disruptive behavior, the conditions of her confinement may have played a role in the continuation of her self-harming behaviors and ultimately her death.

Recognizing the potential mental health effects of Ashley's long-term segregation, the jury in her coroner's inquest recommended that segregation should be eliminated for self-harming women and that the use of segregation for mentally ill offenders should be abolished. Interestingly, despite the jury's findings about the negative impact segregation had on Ashley's self-harming behavior, CSC refuses to eliminate the use of segregation. It took over a year for the Service to respond to the jury's recommendations. Even though they publicly state that segregation should be used as a last resort and should be used for the least amount of time, the Service continues to argue that segregation is a valuable security and behavior modification tool that it will not eliminate (CSC 2014).

Conclusions

The preceding discussion has demonstrated the destabilization of perceived normalcy, the need for contextualization, and the problematic use of restraints and segregation for prisoners in crisis. Trauma-related mental health models need to consider how environmental factors influence mental health and, although complicated, devise multi-disciplinary therapeutic approaches that recognize self-harm as a coping mechanism and incorporate non-punitive approaches to manage self-harm. Segregation can result in a vicious cycle where a prisoner's extreme behavior and 'acting out' leads to increases in physical altercations with staff members, raising the levels of frustration for both prisoners and staff. Additionally, by framing the resistant prisoner as 'risky' rather than 'needy' and thus less entitled to protections, the institution theoretically justifies a suspension of human rights.

Providing treatment within an institution mandated to punish implicates a number of inherent contradictions. Prison mental health staff members work primarily for the correctional service, not the prisoner. This structurally-bounded relationship creates a conflict that requires skilled management. Additionally, the punitive nature of the prison environment, especially segregation, inevitably makes any addition of programs and services vulnerable to being co-opted by security and risk concerns. Correctional mental health professionals need to be mindful of the environments in which they practice and how they interpret the behaviors of prisoners, and prisoners' possible lack of willingness to participate in programs, disclose personal information, or foster relations of trust. For example, the CSC could reserve beds in secure mental health facilities for high-need women. In this kind of setting, individuals like Ashley Smith would be more likely to be treated as having a mental health problem rather than as a security risk. This would require a broader consideration of what is and is not considered a mental health problem in the first place. In addition, this sort of setting would provide a high level of security along with better access to specialized psychiatric care. However, implementation of this recommendation should not replace the additional need to improve access to psychologists, social workers, and health-care professionals in prisons.

Notes

1 Authors listed in alphabetical order.
2 Zinger's data source is The Correctional Service of Canada Data Warehouse. 2013-01-21.
3 The 'wrap' is used within Canadian correctional settings as a preventative strategy for persistently self-harming individuals and for those who display aggressive behaviors toward themselves and others. See Richard 2008 for more details on this form of physical restraint.
4 See Kilty 2012 and Kilty 2008 for more detail on the use of anti-psychotic medications.
5 See Fagan et al. 2009 for a comprehensive literature review.
6 See evidence document: Inmate management plans by Acting Warden August 31–October 15, 2007 at GVI, September 7, 2007.
7 See Sapers 2008; Beaudry 2010 for more details on her case.

References

Adams, K 1986, 'The disciplinary experience of mentally disordered inmates', *Criminal Justice and Behavior*, vol. 13, pp. 297–316.

Arbour, L 1998, *Report of the Commission of Inquiry into certain events at the Prison for Women in Kingston*, Pubic Works and Government Services Canada, Ottawa.

Appelbaum, KL, Hickey, JM & Packer, I 2001, 'The role of correctional officers in multidisciplinary mental health care in prisons', *Psychiatric Services*, vol. 52, pp. 1343–1347.

Arrigo, BA & Bullock, JL 2008, 'The psychological effects of solitary confinement on prisoners in supermax units: reviewing what we know and recommending what should change', *International Journal of Offender Therapy and Comparative Criminology*, vol. 52, no. 6, pp. 622–640.

Auerhahn, K & Leonard, ED 2000, 'Docile bodies? Chemical restraints and the female prisoner', *The Journal of Criminal Law and Criminology*, vol. 90, no. 2, pp. 599–634.

Bauer, RL, Morgan, RD, & Mandracchia, JT 2011, 'Offenders with severe and persistent mental illness', in *Correctional mental health: from theory to best practice*, eds TJ Fagan & RK Ax, Sage Publications, Thousand Oaks, CA, pp. 189–212.

Beaudry, P 2010, 'Ms. Ashley Smith: psychiatric opinion based on record review'. Available from: <http://www.falconers.ca/documents/CorrectionalInvestigators PyschiatristsReviewofForcedInjectionsApril192010.pdf>. [20 January 2015].

Blanchette, K & Montiuk, LL 1996, *Female offenders with and without major mental health problems: a comparative investigation*, Research Branch of Correctional Service of Canada, Ottawa.

Borrill, J, Snow, L, Medlicott, D, Teers, R & Paton, J 2005, 'Learning from "near misses": interviews with women who survived an incident of severe self-harm in prison', *The Howard Journal*, vol. 44, no. 1, pp. 57–69.

Boisvert, JA 2004, *An integrated and women-centered approach to treating borderline personality disorder*, Correctional Service of Canada. Available from: <www.csc -scc.gc.ca>. [1 February 2011].

Bosworth, M & Carrabine, E 2001, 'Reassessing resistance: race, gender and sexuality in prison', *Punishment & Society*, vol. 31, no. 4, pp. 501–515.

Canadian Human Rights Commission 2003, *Protecting their rights: a systemic review of human rights in correctional services for federally sentenced women*, Canadian Human Rights Commission. Available from: <http://www.chrc-ccdp.ca/ sites/default/files/fswen.pdf>. [20 January 2015].

Correctional Service of Canada (CSC) 2002, *Commissioners directive 001: mission statement*, Correctional Service of Canada. Available from: <http://www.csc-scc .gc.ca/text/prgrm/fsw/fsw-eng.shtml>. [20 January 2015].

Correctional Service of Canada (CSC) 2010, *Updated progress report on the August 14, 2009 Correctional Service of Canada (CSC) Response to the Office of the Correctional Investigator's death in custody study, the correctional investigator's report: A preventable death and the CSC National Board of Investigation into the death of an offender at Grand Valley Institution for women*, Correctional Service of Canada. Available from: <http://www.csc-scc.gc.ca/publications/rocidcs/grid4-eng.shtml>. [20 January 2015].

Correctional Service of Canda (CSC) 2013, *39th Annual report to Parliament: summary of issues and challenges in the management of prison self-injury,* Office of the Correctional Investigator. Available from: <http://www.oci-bec.gc.ca/cnt/comm/presentations/ presentationsAR-RA1112Info-eng.aspx>. [18 January 2015].

Correctional Service of Canada (CSC) 2014, *Response to the coroner's inquest touching the death of Ashley Smith.* Available from: <http://www.csc-scc.gc.ca/publications/005007-9011-eng.shtml>. [18 January 2015].

Correctional Service of Canada (CSC) 2015, *Women's Corrections.* Available from: <http://www.csc-scc.gc.ca/women/index-eng.shtml>. [25 January 2015].

Dell, CA, Fillmore, C & Kilty, J 2009, 'Looking back 10 years after the Arbour inquiry: ideology, policy, practice and the federal female prisoner', *Prison Journal,* vol. 89, pp. 286–308.

Drake, D 2012, *Prisons, punishment and the pursuit of security,* Palgrave Macmillan, London.

Fillmore, C & Dell, CA 2000, *Prairie women, violence and self-harm,* Elizabeth Fry Society of Manitoba, Manitoba.

Gaes, GG & Camp, SD 2009, 'Unintended consequences: experimental evidence for the criminogenic effect of prison security level placement on post-release recidivism', *Journal of Experimental Criminology,* vol. 5, pp. 139–162.

Hannah-Moffat, K 2000, 'Prisons that empower: neo-liberal governance in Canadian women's prisons', *British Journal of Criminology,* vol. 40, pp. 510–531.

Hannah-Moffat, K 2001, *Punishment in disguise,* University of Toronto Press, Toronto.

Haney, C 2003, 'Mental health issues in long-term solitary and "supermax" confinement', *Crime & Delinquency,* vol. 49, pp. 124–156.

Haney, C 2006, *Reforming punishment: psychological limits to the pains of imprisonment.* American Psychological Association, Washington, DC.

Haney, C 2009, 'The social psychology of isolation: why solitary confinement is psychologically harmful', *Prison Service Journal,* vol. 181, pp. 12–20.

Irwin, K & Chesney-Lind, M 2008, 'Girls' violence: beyond dangerous masculinity', *Sociology Compass,* vol. 2, no. 3, pp. 837–855.

Irving, J., & Wichmann, C. (2001). An investigation into the factors leading to increased security classification of women offenders. Ottawa: Correctional Service of Canada.

Jones, A. (1986). 'Self-mutilation in prison. A comparison of mutilations and nonmutilators'. *Criminal Justice and Behavior,* vol. 13, no. 3, pp. 286–296.

Kilty, J 2012, '"It's like they don't want you to get better": psy control of women in the carceral context', *Feminism & Psychology,* vol. 22, no. 2, pp. 162–182.

Kilty, J 2008, 'Governance through psychiatrization: Seroquel and the new prison order', *Radical Psychology,* vol. 7, no. 2, pp. 1–22.

Kilty, J 2006, 'Under the barred umbrella: is there room for a women-centred self-injury policy in Canadian corrections?', *Criminology & Public Policy,* vol. 5, no. 1, pp. 161–182.

Kruttschnitt, C & Vuolo, M 2007, 'The cultural context of women prisoners' mental health: a comparison of two prison systems', *Punishment & Society,* vol. 9, pp. 115–150.

Kupers, TA 2006, 'How to create madness in prison', in *Humane Prisons,* ed D Jones, Radcliffe Publishing, Oxford, pp. 47–58.

Martel, J 1999, *Solitude & Cold Storage*. Women's Journeys of Endurance and Segregation. Alberta: Elizabeth Fry Society of Edmonton.

Marzano, L & Adler, JR 2007, 'Supporting staff working with prisoners who self-harm: a survey of support services for staff dealing with self-harm in prisons in England and Wales', *International Journal of Prisoner Health*, vol. 3, no. 4, pp. 268–282.

McDonagh, D, Noel, C & Wichmann, C 2002, Mental health needs of women offenders: needs analysis for the development of the intensive intervention strategy. Ottawa: Correctional Service of Canada. Available from: <www.csc-scc.gc.ca>. [1 February 2011].

Meltzer H, Lader D, Corbin T 2002, *Non-fatal suicidal behaviour among adults aged 16 to 74 in Great Britain, 2000*, Office of National Statistics, Great Britain. Available from:<http://www.ons.gov.uk/ons/rel/psychiatric-morbidity/non-fatal-suicidal-behaviour-among-adults/aged-16-74-in-great-britain/index.html>. [20 January 2015].

Montiuk, LL & Blanchette, K 2001, 'Characteristics of administratively segregated offenders in federal corrections', *Canadian Journal of Criminology*, vol. 43, pp. 131–143.

Office of the Chief Coroner of Ontario. (2013). Verdict: Ashley Smith Inquest. Toronto: Ontario. CanLII 92762 (ON OCCO). Available from: <http://canlii.ca/t/g7cqv>. [16 December 2014].

Office of the Correctional Investigator 2013, *Risky Business: An investigation of the treatment and management of chronic self-injury among federally sentenced women*, Office of the Correctional Investigator of Canada.

Office of the Correctional Investigator of Canada 2014, *A three-year review of federal inmate suicides*, Office of the Correctional Investigator of Canada.

Pollack, S 2005, 'Taming the shrew: regulating prisoners through women-centered mental health programming', *Critical Criminology*, vol. 13, pp. 71–87.

Porporino, FJ & Motiuk, LL 1995, 'The prison careers of mentally disordered offenders', *International Journal of Law and Psychiatry*, vol. 18, no. 1, pp. 29–44.

Reiter, K 2014, 'The supermax prison: a blunt means of control, or a subtle form of violence', *Radical Philosophical Review*, vol. 17, no. 4, pp. 457–475.

Rhodes, L 2004, *Total confinement: Madness and reason in the maximum security prison*, University of California Press, Berkley.

Richard, B 2008, *The Ashley Smith Report: A report of the New Brunswick ombudsman and child and youth advocate on the service provided to a youth involved in the youth criminal justice system*, Office of the Ombudsman & Child and Youth Advocate. Available from: <https://www.gnb.ca/0073/PDF/AshleySmith-e.pdf>. [20 January 2015].

Sapers, H 2008, *A preventable death*, Office of the Correctional Investigator. Available from: <http://www.oci-bec.gc.ca/cnt/rpt/pdf/oth-aut/oth-aut20080620-eng.pdf>. [20 January 2015].

Shalyor, C 1998, '"It's like living in a black hole": women of color and solitary confinement in the prison complex', *New England Journal of Criminal and Civil Confinement*, vol. 24, no. 2, pp. 385–416.

Shaw, M 1991, 'Women in prison: a literature review', *FORUM on Corrections Research*, vol. 6, no. 1. Available from: <http://www.csc-scc.gc.ca/research/forum/e061/e061d-eng.shtml>. [20 January 2015].

Snow, L 1997, 'A pilot study of self-injury amongst women prisoners' in *Suicide and Self-Injury in Prisons,* ed GF Towl, British Psychological Society for the Division of the Criminological and Legal Psychology, Leicester, pp. 50–59.

Task Force on Administrative Segregation 1997, *Task Force on Administrative Segregation: Commitment to legal compliance, fair decisions and effective results,* Government of Canada, Ottawa.

Union of Canadian Correctional Officers. (2008). A rush to judgement: A report on the death in custody of Ashley Smith, a prisoner at Grand Valley Institution for Women. Available from: <http://www.uccosacc.csn.qc.ca/ScriptorWeb/scripto.asp?resultat=261990>. [10 January 2011).

Weekes, JR & Morison, SJ 1992, 'Self-directed violence: differentiating between suicidal, malingering and self-mutilating behaviours', *FORUM on Corrections Research,* vol. 4, no. 3. Available from:< http://www.csc-scc.gc.ca/research/forum/e043/e043h-eng.shtml>. [20 January 2015].

Wooldredge, J 1999, "Inmate experiences and psychological well-being", *Criminal Justice and Behavior,* vol. 26, pp. 235–250.

Zinger, I 2013, 'Segregation in Canadian Federal Corrections: a prison ombudsman's perspective'. Paper presented at *Ending Isolation: An International Conference on Human Rights and Solitary Confinement,* Winnipeg, Manitoba, Canada.

Zinger, I, Wichmann, C & Andrews, DA 2001, 'The psychological effects of 60 days in administrative segregation', *Canadian Journal of Criminology,* vol. 43, no. 1, pp. 47–83.

8

Making Visible Invisible Suffering: Non-deliberative Agency and the Bodily Rhetoric of Tamms Supermax Prisoners

Nadya Pittendrigh, University of Illinois at Chicago

Brian Nelson speaks fast, and his Chicago 'dees' and 'dats' promise to spare his audience some of the usual fluff; he evokes sympathy in his audience while handling his own outrage or recalling tough memories. In the spring of 2010, Brian was released from Tamms Closed Maximum Security prison (CMAX), the Illinois supermax, after spending 12 years in solitary confinement. Opened in 1998 and closed in 2013, Tamms was originally meant to function as temporary added punishment for prisoners already serving time in other state prisons. Yet many prisoners, including Brian, wound up being held in isolation at Tamms for many years—some for the duration of its operation. During Brian's incarceration at Tamms, he suffered severe depression, became a central figure in litigation over the treatment of Tamms prisoners with mental illness, and organized a prisoner-written newsletter and hunger strike for improved conditions. Since his release, he has been a vocal activist, attempting to persuade members of the public that the conditions of extreme punishment in US supermax prisons inflict invisible but lasting psychological harm. Like the other former supermax prisoners who provide the impetus for this chapter Brian possesses considerable personal and political agency. Yet when he speaks about Tamms, he becomes visibly upset, often choking back tears and shrugging as though he has momentarily given up trying to explain his experience.

This chapter focuses on the non-verbal communications of former supermax prisoners, exploring how bodily expressions of suffering function as effective political rhetoric, despite never having been intended

156

as such. I argue that the non-deliberative bodily rhetoric supermax prisoners manifest functions as effective political rhetoric precisely insofar as 1) audiences perceive the prisoners' bodily rhetoric as unintentional, and 2) advocates outside the prison (who are in a position to do so) can deliberately harness the prisoners' rhetoric, publicize their suffering, and call for change.

This chapter makes two points, meant to refine our understanding of prisoners' agency and the political rhetoric involved in advocacy. First, the chapter points out what might otherwise be imperceptible, namely, the non-deliberative political agency of prisoners' bodies and the involuntary actions taken by these bodies. In the case of the grassroots activism that mobilized against Tamms, these actions ranged from former prisoners tearing up while making a speech all the way to self-mutilation among those still inside Tamms. I argue that these unwilled, unplanned, targetless actions actually had important effects—and were often more impactful than spoken text—when they happened in public or were made public by activists. Furthermore, in pointing out the role of the bodily, non-deliberative, rhetorical agency of former Tamms prisoners, the chapter also highlights the importantly *cooperative* activist effort between prisoners who expressed their suffering, often unintentionally, and activists outside the prison, who took action to make the suffering of supermax prisoners widely known.[1]

In keeping with the typical tenor of rhetorical scholarship, which seeks and emphasizes rhetorical *effectiveness* in discussions of 'agency', and in keeping with the rhetoric of advocates, who celebrate the dignity, will, and potency of prisoners' political actions, the following analysis focuses on the surprising effectiveness of unintentional demonstrations of bodily suffering by current and former Tamms prisoners. Yet in zeroing in on these affective, non-verbal appeals of prisoners, this argument also challenges a habitually distorted view of agency, which tends to privilege prisoners' political will as well as effective, repeatable rhetorical strategy, but risks concealing both the non-deliberative and cooperative dimensions involved in the movement to close Tamms prison.[2] In seeking to broaden our view of political agency to include non-deliberative acts, I focus on the non-verbal appeals of prisoners with mental illness, demonstrating how mentally ill supermax prisoners provide a particularly clear view into 1) the credibility problem that supermax prisoners face, namely, how to signal psychological harm without being dismissed as manipulative malingerers, and 2) the question of whether volition plays an essential role in what we refer to as the 'agency' of supermax prisoners, whose disturbed behaviors—whether intended or not—communicate extreme anguish.

In an important sense, the argument presented here represents a rescue mission on behalf of the notion of agency. For the same reason that no stable, universal definition of 'justice' can be firmly established, rhetorical scholars cannot quite settle upon a satisfactory definition of the word 'agency', and yet we preserve the term 'agency' because it is a placeholder for something we want to describe. The term 'agency' actually refers to whatever causes social change, and our attempts to understand what causes social change prompts us to come up with new definitions, precisely because the causes of social change are dynamic, dependent on complex circumstances, and difficult to pin down. Such discussions seek to identify the strategy that the agent ought to adopt in order to be effective—a question that inherently guides our attention toward the *deliberative*. Given that emphasis, this chapters seeks to draw attention to one aspect of 'agency' that is easy to overlook because assumptions about what causes social change are so heavily tilted toward deliberative acts.

This chapter's critique of what we call political 'agency', through analysis of Tamms prisoners' bodily rhetoric, emerges from my own participation with and observation of the Tamms Year Ten campaign. The Tamms Year Ten campaign formed in 2008 with the goal of bringing public accountability to Tamms on the ten-year anniversary of its opening. Led by Laurie Jo Reynolds, who organized with family members of Tamms prisoners, former prisoners, artists, educators, lawyers, and other advocates, the group began corresponding with Tamms prisoners in 2006, documenting and publicizing the prisoners' letter-based testimony of what it was like to be incarcerated there. Between 2008 and 2013, that project expanded and became a public campaign. We sought to inform voters, legislators, and the press about conditions at Tamms, lobbying initially for reform legislation and eventually for Tamms' closure.

The rhetorical focus of this chapter's argument arises from my own experiences and observations of the pressing need for activists to prove that the damage of long-term solitary confinement should be taken seriously by members of the public. The testimony of current and former Tamms prisoners played a central role in mobilizing support for the campaign. The testimony also raised questions for the organizers about how to demonstrate the psychological damage Tamms prisoners suffered.

Two former Tamms prisoners (I will call them Hakeem and Ronnie) became active spokespeople for Tamms Year Ten, not only because they could describe firsthand what it was like to be incarcerated at Tamms, but because their charming personalities challenged the stereotypes associated with supermax prisoners. Yet at the same time, their self-possession and charisma seemed to contradict claims that Tamms does permanent damage to prisoners' mental health. In that context, one moment during a meeting early on in the Tamms Year Ten effort proved not only moving, but pivotal from an organizing perspective: Ronnie arrived at the meeting and announced that he had brought a friend, recently released from Tamms, but that he was having trouble coaxing the friend to come in. Ronnie returned to his car to try again, just as another former prisoner arrived at the meeting and was asked to speak. This new former prisoner's name was Ray, and he was asked if he could describe what the experience of isolation was really like. Ray recollected some of the facts of his physical existence there, but eventually began to weep, saying 'I really don't know how to explain what happened to me at Tamms.' In response, the 25 or so people at the meeting held their breath or choked up, and one mother of a current Tamms prisoner cried openly. When Ronnie came back with his friend from the car, the friend barely looked up from the floor, then turned on his heel and left, and Ronnie commented, 'That's just what Tamms does to you'.

Moments like these were important for organizing early on, even for the family members of Tamms prisoners, because the people who were involved in the campaign knew relatively little about Tamms at the time and stood in need of some affective bond to the prisoners themselves, through witnessing their suffering. When Ray's eyes welled up and he said that he didn't know how to provide proof and indicated that words or the explanation were beside the point, the bodies of others in the room simply responded. Many other similar scenes were repeated at public meetings helping to build the campaign's support base during Tamms Year Ten's efforts to reform and eventually close Tamms. Having observed the persuasive power of these non-verbal appeals, I seek to make the case for the surprising rhetorical effectiveness of such inter-corporeal communication—as non-deliberative persuasion.

In the following pages, I first provide an overview of Tamms itself and then describe the protest rhetoric that has dogged the prison since its inception. This provides the context for the chapter's analysis of the extreme rhetorics of the body, created in the context of supermax confinement. In that extreme context, prisoners experience prolonged social and sensory deprivation, similar to that of foreign detainees in Guantánamo, and frequently also desperation, rage, and social and psychological disintegration (see Koenig this volume; Reiter & Blair this volume). The following analysis explores the special rhetorical constraints inherent in such a context, in which rhetorical manipulation, or deliberative agency, works against prisoners who express their own suffering. In detailing not only supermax prioners' lived experience of punishment, but also the special rhetorical problems faced by those prisoners, the chapter extends discussions in this volume by Murray and Holmes, as well as Reiter and Blair, who scrutinize a pattern of placing mentally ill prisoners in solitary confinement for ostensibly non-punitive reasons.

Tamms

Tamms Closed Maximum Security prison (also referred to as the Illinois supermax) opened in 1998, officially for the purpose of short-term isolation of the state's so-called 'worst of the worst' prisoners. The original theory was that it would work as a temporary coolout zone (for one to two years) for the state's most dangerous prisoners and serve as a potent deterrent against serious misbehavior. Tamms was meant to be the prison that one would go to from prison. Yet given the breadth of the language in the Illinois Department of Corrections (IDOC) Administrative Code governing which prisoners or behaviors would qualify for transfer to Tamms, many were sent under an 'administrative detention' designation, meaning that they were sent without the pretext of having committed any specific disciplinary infractions. (The Illinois Department of Corrections' 'Ten Point Plan', published in 2009, reports 162 prisoners housed in Tamms under the administrative detention designation, compared to 83 who were, at the time, placed in Tamms under disciplinary segregation, for having been charged with violating some specific rule or law within the state prison system.) Furthermore, the Illinois Administrative Code leaves open the possibility of sending prisoners with mental illness to the supermax, and in fact, many prisoners with mental illness wound up being sent to Tamms.[3] (For an extended account of the mutually reinforcing relationship between mental illness and solitary confinement in US prisons see Reiter & Blair this volume.) The pervasive lack of evidence-based safeguards or due process protections against illegitimate transfer into the prison also meant that there was no system for earning one's way out. The result was that a significant number of prisoners wound up staying at the prison for over a decade. As the IDOC repeatedly estimated at hearings and public meetings between 2008 and 2013, one-third of the population during that period had been held in Tamms since it opened in 2008.[4]

Extreme isolation characterized the conditions for prisoners housed in Tamms. Prisoners spent 23 to 24 hours per day in their cells, with no group activity; no educational, religious, or rehabilitative programs; no phone calls; and no 'contact' visits. Instead, visitation took place through bulletproof glass, and, since the prison was a six-hour drive from Chicago (where most prisoners came from), many received no visits at all.[5] In this context of social and sensory scarcity, some of the prisoners who had never experienced mental illness prior to being placed in Tamms developed symptoms while they were there, and many displayed increasingly desperate acts of self-harm.

Activism outside of Tamms

In January of 2013, the then-governor of Illinois, Pat Quinn, closed Tamms. He cited the state's severe fiscal strain as justification. But he also closed Tamms in the wake of a long-standing protest against the prison. Various groups organized in opposition to the supermax as early as 1993, before Tamms even opened. Some later joined with family members of Tamms prisoners and called themselves the Tamms Committee. Two lawsuits were filed shortly after Tamms opened, exerting pressure on officials and publicly challenging the prison's lack of mental health treatment and due process. In *Rasho v. Snyder,* attorney Jean Maclean Snyder sought relief on behalf of prisoners with serious mental illness. Representing Ashoor Rasho and three other plaintiffs, Snyder argued that for prisoners with mental illness, conditions at Tamms amounted to cruel and unusual punishment. Though the case was denied status as a class action, and eventually settled, it exerted pressure on the administration, which later modified some aspects of prison policy related to mental health treatment at Tamms.[6] In *Westefer v. Snyder,* Alan Mills successfully represented Robert Westefer and 31 other prisoners, arguing that some prisoners were sent to Tamms as retaliation for filing lawsuits against the administration, and that prisoners ought to be provided with due process before being sent to the prison. Later, in 2008, Laurie Jo Reynolds (an artist and activist in Chicago) organized the Tamms Year Ten campaign, whose multiple activist tactics included legislative lobbying and artistic, cultural, and educational events—all of which presented testimony by current and former Tamms prisoners and their family members to the public.

This chapter's argument about the affective, non-deliberative agency and bodily rhetoric of Tamms prisoners speaks to an ongoing conversation among prison activists, in which prison abolitionists, including

Angela Davis (2003), challenge prison reformers, like the above-described Tamms activists, to imagine and work for the abolition of prisons instead of merely making them more humane.[7] As part of a larger response to Davis's critique of prison reform, which suggests that small acts can help to create conditions that are ripe for closing prisons, this chapter demonstrates that small, apparently non-agentive expressions by prisoners can, given the right circumstances, contribute to more significant changes. By calling Tamms' legitimacy into question over the course of years, reformers may have contributed to the conditions of possibility in which the Governor of Illinois closed Tamms. Prisoners' non-volitional expressions of suffering had important effects in that effort, by making visible their otherwise invisible suffering. In fact, we can glimpse and appreciate the role of the rhetoric of activists, whose call for Tamms reform helped pave the way for the prison's closure, through an analysis of the non-volitional bodily rhetoric of Tamms prisoners. Like the reformist rhetoric of Tamms activists that played a role in making Tamms' closure possible, the unintentional bodily rhetoric of prisoners operates somewhat out of the spotlight, yet can also effectively contribute to processes that lead to more substantial change.

* * *

One of the first Tamms Year Ten meetings, in February of 2008, established a pattern repeated at later meetings, with former Tamms prisoners and family members seeking to inform others about the experience of confinement at Tamms. Jim Chapman, an early organizer of the Tamms Committee, also spoke at that meeting about the resilience of former Tamms prisoners, and cautioned those who were present against an overly pathetic image of prisoners. Yes, there are many who deteriorate psychologically in solitary, he argued, but '[t]hese are strong guys, and the strong survive'. In siding with redemption, and delineating between 'the strong' versus the psychologically vulnerable, Chapman voiced a narrative that not only figures importantly in discourse about supermax prisoners, but also mirrors the pattern of rhetorical scholarship critiqued here, which habitually figures 'agency' as efficacy or potency, and emphasizes 'strength'.

Employing that same narrative of 'the strong' versus the vulnerable in 'Changing the Subject: Conversation in Supermax', Lorna Rhodes asks readers not to forget those assumed to be strong. Given successful recent interventions on behalf of mentally ill supermax prisoners, she suggests that 'those left behind are, by definition, not the "vulnerable"', but their relative strength should not justify their confinement in the supermax (2005, p. 404). Like Chapman, she emphasizes the strength and agency of the supermax prisoners, even among those whose sociality is most constrained, and in doing so, she rejects the abject vocabulary of Giorgio Agamben.

In *Homo Sacer,* Giorgio Agamben (1995) theorizes Western political structures as dominating over and then abandoning what he calls bare life—or life that has been left naked of legal protections. Rhodes counters that even supermax prisoners, ostensibly stripped, not only of the protections of due process but of sociality and therefore political agency, are not really 'bare' in Agamben's sense. As she sees it, the supermax attempts prisoners' total isolation but never fully achieves the bare life Agamben theorizes. In documenting conversations between supermax prisoners, she argues that they continue to participate in an admittedly constrained, but still real, outpost of the public sphere.

Like many other skeptics of Agamben (e.g., Hauser 2012; Laclau 2007), Rhodes rejects Agamben's vocabulary of 'bare life' if it means a lack of agency. Rhodes and others defend the idea that prisoners have agency, because of the assumption that unless they have access to agency, or some means of intentional striving toward improvements, then their situations are without hope. While I agree that the most abjectly mentally ill prisoners are not bereft of agency, I argue that part of their rhetoric lies outside of intentional or deliberative agency. Furthermore, even though supermax prisoners do retain a sense of agency, any insistence upon that agency risks inflecting it for heroism and implies a misplaced demand for transcendence of circumstance— a particularly neoliberal conception of agency, critiqued elsewhere in this volume by Murray and Holmes. Thus, despite the considerable personal and political agency of supermax prisoners, I highlight their narrowed rhetorical palette. What they assert about themselves, or what they say using logic (logos) or personal credibility (ethos), faces many obstacles.

Yet within that constrained rhetorical context, I also argue, there are many things about one's body, and perhaps even one's neurological being, that can be made apparent for rhetorical purposes. The result for the political rhetoric on the Tamms Year Ten campaign was that the bodily rhetoric of Tamms prisoners was susceptible to intentional harnessing by activists, who exposed prisoners' suffering to public audiences. In that sense, political agency was a collaboration between prisoners suffering on the inside and activists who were in a position to make use of that suffering in public. Given Jim Chapman's emphasis upon strength described above, I provisionally label deliberative agency as 'strong agency'. Without denying that the intentional acts of activists play an invaluable political role, this analysis simply includes less visibly forceful rhetoric as part of what can function forcefully within rhetoric.

'Malingering' and the difficulty of proving invisible harm

In 2009, artist activist Laurie Jo Reynolds, Tamms Year Ten's organizer, lead a discussion at the Mess Hall community space in Chicago, posing a key rhetorical challenge for opponents of supermax confinement: How to make the invisible psychological harm caused by indefinite social isolation visible to the public so that it might be taken seriously?

That rhetorical problem hinges on the ethos, or credibility, of the person making the case that they have been harmed. This presents a challenge for prisoners generally, who may well manipulate and/or be seen as manipulating their surroundings in order to provoke attention, but for whom evidence of such 'manipulation' often negates claims of legitimate psychological distress. Beyond the antagonism that one might expect between prisoners and staff over whether prisoners were being manipulative or were truly mentally ill, between 1999 and 2000, the IDOC (2009) developed and codified an institutional directive that incentivized and institutionalized that skepticism. The directive conceded that Tamms should not house prisoners with mental illness. Yet as Brian Nelson reports, as a consequence, Tamms mental health staff persistently resisted diagnosing prisoners with 'serious mental illness', claiming that prisoners faked mental illness in order to be transferred to Dixon psychiatric correctional facility. In such a context, the smallest sign of rationality or planning became sufficient pretext to dismiss signals of mental illness as 'malingering'. Thus, the rhetorical situation in the supermax was characterized not only by extreme deprivation, but also by a demand for proof of either psychological damage caused by those conditions, or pre-existing mental illness, which might have prevented prisoners from being housed in those conditions in the first place. Yet the demand for proof of psychological suffering is inherently difficult to satisfy, not only because psychological suffering is invisible, but also because, for supermax prisoners, any offered proof risks being dismissed as fake.

In the case of Tamms, that dynamic contributed to escalating rhetorics of suffering, embodied particularly vividly in the behavior of mentally ill supermax prisoners. These conditions placed extra weight upon the apparently unwilled rhetoric of prisoners' bodies, and in that sense, the bodies of prisoners became central in the political rhetoric that paved the way for change at Tamms. Below, I provide evidence of the special rhetorical challenges of supermax prisoners, resulting in extra rhetorical weight being placed on their bodily expressions, based on the record of *Rasho v. Snyder* and *Westefer v. Snyder,* as well as investigative reporting, which exposed the prison's harsh conditions.

G. Patrick Murphy's 'Findings of Fact' in the *Westefer v. Snyder* lawsuit helped make a credible public case that conditions at Tamms did inflict psychological damage by producing the evidence of prisoners' bodies, as presented to him by prisoners who testified in the case.[8] In 2010, the US District Judge ruled that conditions at Tamms prison represented exceptional conditions of confinement, and therefore prisoners sent to Tamms should be given due process hearings prior to being sent there. The extensive quotation in Murphy's 'Findings' from Tamms prisoners reads like a response to the rhetorical question posed above: How can invisible psychological harm be made visible? How can the real, deleterious effects of social isolation be proven? In Murphy's findings, he maintained that, given the extreme conditions at Tamms, being transferred there from another prison in the state did in fact present 'atypical and significant hardship'. Insofar as his findings reproduce the evidence that persuaded him, they suggest that he found the physiological change reported by prisoners the most persuasive:

Q: Have you noticed any changes in yourself since you were at Tamms?

A: Whew, yeah.

Q: Tell us about that.

A: Well, I—I'm going to have to say being in isolation is kind of a trip. If you are not pretty strong then you might become a bug. I mean, have mental issues.

Q: But how about you personally? Did you notice any change once you got out of Tamms as compared when you were back at Menard before you went to Tamms?

A: Yeah, I don't like being around crowds too much. Being around people. [I]t was a trip having a celly, being in isolation for so long, to have to live with another man, you know? But...being in isolation is kind of hard (*Westefer v. Snyder* 2010, p. 21).

Murphy's text includes multiple similar accounts of prisoners' deteriorating social ease, as well as descriptions of diminished mental health. As one prisoner testifies:

> For some reason I became paranoid after leaving Tamms—as I've stated before, I've been around hundreds of men, fox holes, and, I mean, in the military and out of the military and welding schools, and never experience any form of paranoid before in my life that I ever known of until I was released from Tamms (*Westefer v. Snyder* 2010, p. 22).

The sheer volume of quotations from prisoners describing psychological decline has substantiating power and makes the harm of long-term isolation visible. Unlike many state officials before him, Murphy accepted this testimony from prisoners as credible evidence of sensory deprivation at Tamms, and his citing of the above passages in his findings lends them evidentiary force.[9]

Beginning in 2009, *The Belleville News Democrat* published a pivotal investigation of Tamms, exposing the above-described, ongoing, dysfunctional pattern between prisoners exhibiting extreme, disturbed behavior, and Tamms staff discounting that behavior, or responding with escalated punitive sanctions. In their profile of Tamms prisoner Faygie Fields, for instance, reporters George Pawlaczyk and Beth Hundsdorfer (2009) write: 'Fields smeared excrement in his cell so often that maintenance men painted it with an easier to clean coating. He [also] swallowed glass'. Fields' attorney, Jean Snyder, documented similar behavior by Fields years earlier in her complaint for *Rasho v. Snyder*. She described Fields' claims that staff at Tamms were poisoning his food, and his belief 'that Tamms was built on a burial site where spirits are resting. He believes that the spirits visit him; but they are not friendly', and she added that he resisted leaving his cell to meet her for fear that another inmate would somehow kill him (*Rasho v. Snyder* 2000, p. 23). Yet, as *The Belleville News Democrat* series demonstrated, Fields' sense of reality remained intact enough that he worried in a letter (written in an idiosyncratic style) about his own sanity: 'Please know that Tamms is driving ME CRAZY all of them keep saying none of us can leave here. But keeps all here? + in a Eternal Twilight Zone that has no ending?' (Pawlaczyk & Hundsdorfer 2009a). Similar indications of self-awareness, however slight, have prompted authorities to label certain Tamms prisoners as malingerers, a belief that has, in turn, justified punitive responses to prisoners' extreme behaviors. For instance, Pawlazyk and Hundsdorfer (2009a) report that Tamms staff charged Fields '$5.30 for tearing up a state-owned sheet to make a noose to kill himself.' When prison officials respond to such disturbed behaviors with punitive sanctions, they proceed, at least officially, as though they believe they are participating in a rational negotiation.

The *Belleview News Democrat* series reported a similarly punitive response to the behavior of Anthony Gay. Gay's story is particularly striking given the triviality of the offense that originally sent him to prison—he was caught stealing a hat and a dollar bill. Yet, based on 'angry outbursts that involved throwing bodily wastes and struggling with guards', decades were added to his prison sentence, setting back his parole date to 2093 (Pawlaczyk & Hundsdorfer 2009b).[10] Like Fields, Anthony Gay habitually mutilated himself at Tamms. Pawlazyk and Hundsdorfer (2009b) described Gay's right arm as being so scarred that 'it was difficult to discern areas of skin that had not been sliced'. Gay's most shocking act of self-mutilation involved him severely mutilating his own genitals. According to the doctor at Tamms who found him, Gay 'was standing at the cell door with some scrotal part of him, possibly a testicle, tied to the sliding door' (Pawlaczyk & Hundsdorfer 2011). Staff responded to the incident by sending Gay to a 'strip cell'. In another *Belleville News Democrat* piece covering Gay's lawsuit, a judge familiar with Gay described him as articulate and competent when acting as his own attorney (Pawlaczyk & Hundsdorfer 2009b). That observation of Gay's verbal competence speaks to the misunderstanding at the center of this analysis: the assertions of his legal adversaries suggest that since he behaved as a rational actor in some settings, his relatively disturbed behaviors in other settings should be understood as conscious manipulation, not as evidence of mental illness. Consistent with the neoliberal 'rationality' described by Murray and Holmes in this volume, when prison officials framed Gay's cutting as manipulation, they applied the logic of rational self-interest. That same logic also drives officials' punitive response to the 'rationality' they see in Gay's self-mutilation.

Perhaps prison officials rightly identify a kind of 'rationality' in Gay's self-mutilation, since his cutting did indeed serve some purposes. As Kupers et al. (2009) explain in their discussion of the prevalence of self-mutilation among supermax prisoners, one purpose that cutting serves for prisoners in the supermax is 'some momentary relief from anxiety immediately after the act' (p. 9). These observations do suggest rationality, insofar as cutting represents a kind of coping, while at the same time demonstrating an empathetic alternative to escalating punitive incentives. Furthermore, the mutually reinforcing cycle evident in the above stories of Fields and Gay, of extreme behavior met with extreme punishment, suggests that officials' punitive responses may well contribute to the problem that officials are supposedly disincentivizing. Yet if some relatively sympathetic observers respond to the apparent 'rationality' of prisoners' desperate acts with calls for treatment and an end to long-term solitary confinement, what preempts an empathetic response in other observers?

Less sympathetic observers simply refuse the self-mutilating prisoner's incitement to empathy as a manipulation that must be negated; it looks too much like trickery. Breaking his admitted silence on the Tamms issue, for instance, Rich Miller, who runs the influential *Capital Fax Blog*, covering news from the Illinois state capital in Springfield, commented: 'One of the reasons that I've been so hesitant to go into detail of *The Belleville News Democrat*'s series on Tamms is that prisoners are known to say just about anything' (Miller 2009). Such observations exhibit an understandable aversion to being lied to. Though, from the perspective of clinicians and advocates, it need not matter if Anthony Gay was being manipulative, if he clearly needed both human attention and mental health treatment. Even so, certain observers side with the intuition that if the prisoner is deliberately trying to elicit human attention or some other privilege, that prisoner must not be granted that privilege; the prisoner should not be rewarded for his trickery. Yet, as I argue below, the assumption that we must choose between empathy and invulnerability to being 'conned' depends upon a simplified view of prisoners' agency, which overestimates the significance of deliberation and planning.

That common misunderstanding about both agency and the significance of deliberation emerges in particularly absurd relief in the testimony of those who find themselves professionally obliged to defend Tamms in the news coverage of Anthony Gay's lawsuit. Gay and his lawyers litigated for his transfer out of Tamms on the grounds that conditions there were exacerbating his mental illness. Terry Kupers, for instance, testified that someone who is 'so bizarre and extreme in his emotional disturbance that he cuts his testicles, is clearly extremely self-harming and functionally impaired...and should never be consigned to supermax isolation' (Pawlaczyk & Hundsdorfer 2011). Yet predictably, prison staff again simply maintained that Gay was 'a manipulator who cuts himself to get what he wants' (Pawlaczyk & Hundsdorfer 2011). The state's attorney appellate prosecutor asserted, as evidence of Gay's incorrigible manipulation, that while Gay was at Pontiac, another maximum-security prison in Illinois, he threw bodily waste at officers in order to intentionally 'force a transfer back to [Tamms] to be with the female psychologist with whom he was in love' ('Inmate Wants Opportunity'). Here, Tamms' defenders assumed that if Gay had a plan, there was rational manipulation involved, and he should not be rewarded with legitimate attention. Yet their evidence was that he at one point had a plan to get back to Tamms to be with a staff member that he had fixated on as a love object. In other words, regardless of the irrational content of the plan, regardless of the nurse's non-participation in his fantasy of a romantic relationship, the fact that Gay had a plan at all, according to prison officials, outweighed the competing claim of mental illness. To serve their purposes, defenders of prison policy figured Gay as a person of sound mind because he was able to make plans, despite the fact that those plans were based on a delusion.

Ironically, however, prison officials are not the only ones who emphasize the rational planning of prisoners. Sympathetic advocates for Tamms prisoners also tend to interpret the disturbed behavior of mentally ill prisoners as intentional, but in the latter case, in order to grant it dignity. Like Kupers et al. (2009), who describe cutting as a form of coping, a 2012 report by the John Howard Association (JHA) described the self-mutilation of Tamms prisoners as serving as 'a morbid but effective form of self-help that brings inmates temporary relief from intense feelings of depersonalization, disassociation, rage, or fear brought on by extreme isolation' (p. 19). Though the JHA stresses that self-mutilation often indicates 'deep psychiatric illness and trauma', the report also argues:

> [A]cts of self harm can also be perversely rational because it is often only through such risky, extreme behaviors that inmates can credibly signal they have urgent, unmet needs, where 'cheap' signals like crying or verbal requests for help are routinely discounted or ignored (p. 19).

Here, the JHA grants the extreme behaviors of supermax prisoners maximum dignity by framing them within the terms of professional doctoring. According to the report, the Tamms prisoner intentionally applies a form of self-medication, an interpretation that proceeds from the author's intuition that whoever has no dignity has no rights. The JHA report does not dare presume that the public would be willing to help these men if they do not have the dignity associated with deliberative agency. In other words, the JHA frames the prisoners' self-harm as intentional self-help based on the assumption that deliberative agency has a monopoly on agency, and that only a person who has that precious form of agency will be granted the sympathy and help that a human being deserves. Yet that commonly held and seldom questioned assumption, that only a person who has the dignity associated with deliberative agency deserves sympathy and rights, is as if calculated to exclude people like the Tamms prisoners, because the rhetorical conditions of being a prisoner in Tamms are such that deliberation looks, to unsympathetic observers, like manipulation.

Like other relatively sympathetic observers of prisoners' rights and prisoners' agency, rhetorical theorist Gerard Hauser (2012) highlights intentionality in his study of passive resistance among political prisoners as central to prisoners' dignity:

> The moral vernacular of bodily pain becomes a potent form of resistance insofar as the body in pain can acquire voice and rhetorical agency. When the prisoner of conscience (POC) uses it by design, it functions as a rhetorical mechanism, as an instantiation of passive aggression.... Passive aggression, in the context of this discussion, refers to the prisoner's use of the body to establish physical relationships that accentuate the power differential with the penal institution (p. 123).

Here, Hauser helps us to see prisoners' bodies as rhetorical, and insofar as prisoners employ rhetoric through their bodies as intentional self-help, I agree with him that bodily expression functions importantly, and sometimes potently, within prisoners' rhetoric. Yet Hauser's view also provides the jumping-off point for the argument in this chapter that, insofar as the rhetoric of prisoners' bodies is also sometimes not a matter of either individual or deliberative agency, it is also very potent.

I now turn to the final leg of my analysis, which focuses on the bodily rhetoric of prisoners, which I claim operates differently than either agency or rhetoric that is targeted or deliberative. In a context which not only imposes extreme deprivation on supermax prisoners, but which continually poses the special rhetorical problem of corroborating invisible suffering, the content of what prisoners say is often regarded as suspect. Because the psychological harm that prisoners claim is invisible, they wind up telegraphing suffering through physical affects of the body. In such a context, in which direct claims of harm can be dismissed, laughed away, or taunted as malingering, what supermax prisoners do unintentionally, such as tearing up, does important rhetorical work on public audiences.

The supermax elicits extra-textual rhetorics of the body

Certainly, words and explanations do political work, especially on those already in a position to sympathize with supermax prisoners. Yet because physical demonstrations, or bodily performances of authentic suffering, are not addressed to the minds of audiences, they bypass ratiocination and are less vulnerable to being explicitly rejected. The tears of others simply receive a processing echo, if they work on audiences at all, whereas reasons can be consciously affirmed or rejected; we do not choose to respond or not to someone else's tears. Precisely because we do not choose such inter-corporeal responsiveness, we see the body as the natural medium for involuntary expressions, whereas we see language as a realm in which we can manipulate and control what we telegraph to the world. Therefore, when it comes to the speech of prisoners who have a hard time being heard over the noise of having been convicted of a crime, intentionally seeking sympathy is often not to the purpose. In other words, it is precisely the lack of volition on the part of the prisoner that makes the prisoners' bodily rhetoric effective; the rhetoric of tears in talking about Tamms depends on the tears not having been intended.

Analysis that attends to the materiality of rhetoric investigates meanings that have social force in the world, even when those meanings were not intended by anyone. The John Howard Association's (2012) final report on the Tamms prison provides instances of such rhetoric, which communicates suffering, yet gains its force outside of the text of the prisoners' explicit utterance. Here, the account of conversations with Tamms prisoners allows 'the text beyond the text' to speak for itself:

> An inmate in one of C-Max's elevated security wings presented with white bandages wrapped around his legs and arms. He pressed on the bandages during the interview causing blood to soak through them. The inmate displayed deep scars all over his arms and legs from self-mutilation. He described going through cycles of dark depression where cutting himself was the only relief. The inmate indicated that he received medical treatment when he cut himself, but that mental health conditions were 'bad' in that staff looked for reasons not to provide inmates with mental health treatment. The inmate explained that staff sometimes mocked him and goaded him when he cut himself, telling him that he did not cut deeply enough. During the interview, the inmate's affect verged on frantic at times, and he tended to repeat himself and lose track of his thoughts. When JHA staff explained they had to move on to speak to other inmates, the inmate became very anxious and pleaded that JHA staff stay longer (p. 20).

The text beyond the text here is the blood, evidence of long-term scarring, the prisoner's frantic affect, and his pleading with JHA not to leave. It doesn't matter whether the prisoner knew that JHA was there to gather information for a report that would later be publicized, or if the prisoner had a plan to display his suffering as hyperbolically as possible. The blood soaking through the bandages and the prisoner's manifestation of loneliness and desperation trumps any question of the prisoner 'milking it'. Even if this prisoner is 'milking it' for the benefit of a visitor, the blood, bandages, and scars are far from neutral in their affective power.

Similarly, another prisoner with a diagnosis of schizophrenia, who 'had a history of smearing feces and urine over his cell', told the JHA that he believed he had been moved out of the Special Treatment Unit 'because they "don't like me here"'. The report explains:

> During the interview, the inmate began giving a disjointed paranoid account of how he was being poisoned and produced a small piece of rolled-up paper from his mouth as evidence of this. He said that he felt better since leaving the STU [Special Treatment Unit] because one of the police departments he had written to about his poisoning was finally 'on the case'. The theme returned to over and over by the inmate was extreme loneliness. During the interview, he became dejected and repeatedly stated, 'I'm just so lonely. I'm so lonely all the time' (p. 22).

Whether the prisoner is deliberately trying to garner sympathy, to provoke or annoy guards, or is simply deeply mentally ill and has no clear communicative intent, neither his agency, nor the text of what he says, dominates the narrative. What he is saying about the rolled-up piece of paper in his mouth is nonsense, yet what is proven—not intended—by the prisoner, is that he is mentally ill. The meaning being communicated, beyond the text of what he is saying, is that the system is tormenting a desperately lonely, fragmented, and vulnerable person.

Though I have called attention to the affective, non-verbal, unintended text of some prisoners' bodily rhetoric, I want to make clear that many of the former Tamms prisoners who were involved in the campaign to reform or close Tamms are skilled arguers, and sometimes their self-possession and legal savvy offers its own rhetorical advantage. During high-stakes meetings with the Tamms Year Ten campaign, IDOC employees, and legislators to evaluate Tamms policy, for instance, former prisoners often emerged as especially qualified to spot logical inconsistencies or hypocrisy in what the administration was saying, and many of them embodied triumphant stories of personal agency and overcoming, of having emerged from Tamms into citizenship. Thus, to be clear, I am not saying that the extra-textual bodily rhetoric enacts the only rhetoric that ever works for current and former supermax prisoners. I have simply argued that such logical skill frequently falls on deaf ears, and their credibility is hobbled in a way that those who are not incarcerated do not have to deal with. As a result, their bodily rhetoric, particularly regarding suffering, bears more of the burden of visual and physical demonstration. Also, the involuntary aspects of this bodily rhetoric are easy to overlook, precisely because we value deliberative, intentional, targeted agency so highly.

Conclusion

Gerard Hauser's (2012) *Prisoners of Conscience: Moral Vernaculars of Political Agency* speaks to many of this chapter's observations in his discussion of prisoners' rhetorical uses of their bodies. Hauser describes the bodily vernacular of political prisoners in terms that also accurately register with that of the supermax prisoner, as being 'bodied forth' as physical 'performance', in part because language is suspect. Yet the obvious difference between the political prisoner and the supermax prisoner is that, even if the political prisoner is stigmatized by his or her government, the political prisoner enjoys the moral authority of being criminalized solely for the use of his or her democratic voice. The supermax prisoner operates from a more thoroughly stigmatized position, and therefore has even less access to democratic, deliberative authority than political prisoners. In that sense, supermax prisoners' non-deliberative, extra-linguistic, and embodied performances of pain become a social life-line— a reliable and immediate means of accomplishing human connection. As Hauser (2012) puts it, 'Grasping another's pain takes effort; it has to be translated into language, which can only offer a pale representation' (p. 122). Partly, Hauser registers the frustrating social reality that understanding the pain of other bodies is not a natural default, and that we cannot count on others to understand our pain. Certainly, there are many barriers that stand in the way of such sympathy. However, when a prisoner moves an audience with demonstrations of pain, there is a sense that she or he has superseded the myriad social stigmas or political obstacles that stood in the way of establishing a shared, subjective sense of pain.

What is bodied forth when sympathy does take hold is some kind of corporeal common denominator, a shared baseline between bodies, which is understood as capable of sensation. It is a baseline of corporeal affectivity or ready sympathy commonly shared with animals and which we are typically helpless to resist. Perhaps such mutual receptivity might be operative between people all the time, except for the many social obstacles that interfere. In the case of the Tamms Year Ten campaign, the unwilled expressions of prisoners' bodies spoke to members of the public, who then became motivated to help publicize the prisoners' suffering.

I have sought to bring attention to something that is easy to overlook, a significant contributing factor to social change in the case of Tamms, and very possibly to social change generally—namely, affective, non-deliberative acts, which have the potential to be harnessed as part of a larger movement. Foreclosed opportunities and misconceptions arise from the assumption that planning and will are all that count. The respect and attention that we grant to intentional acts conduces to overlooking things that also turn out to be powerful in activism, such as the affective appeals of prisoners, which, within the Tamms Year Ten campaign, wound up making an invaluable impact on efforts to finally close Tamms.

Notes

1 This chapter's emphasis on the cooperative nature of the activist rhetoric against Tamms registers the repeated insistence of former prisoners involved in Tamms Year Ten, as well as that of the group's organizer, Laurie Jo Reynolds. Former Tamms prisoners said repeatedly in organizing meetings that prisoners inside of Tamms needed the help, resources, and voices of activists, and that former prisoners and family members of Tamms prisoners could not do it by themselves. Laurie Jo Reynolds continuously emphasized that point throughout the Tamms Year Ten campaign, arguing that 'concerned citizens', not just those most directly effected by Tamms, were responsible for the prison and for working to close it. In a personal interview I conducted with Brian Nelson in 2013, he also described the activism that helped to close Tamms as a cooperative effort between prisoners inside and many advocate groups on the outside.

2 Much discussion of 'agency' in rhetorical theory followed postmodernism's challenge to humanist conceptions of the freely choosing subject. A brief survey of such discussions demonstrates the centrality of deliberation, strategy, and freedom of choice in accepted uses of the term (Blair & Cooper 1987; Cooper 2001; Geisler 2004; Greene 2004; Palti 2004; Shaw 2001).

3 According to Section 505.40 of the Administrative Code, as codified by the Illinois legislature, 'Placement in the Tamms Correctional Center shall be based upon the following considerations, including but not limited to: 1) The safety and security of the facility, the public, or any person; 2) The offender's disciplinary and behavioral history; 3) Reports and recommendations concerning the offender; 4) The feasibility of a transfer to another facility; 5) Medical concerns; and 6) Mental health concerns'. The code also stipulates that '[a]mong other matters, an offender who the Department has determined

has engaged in the following activities or who may be planning to engage in these activities may be referred for placement in the Tamms Correctional Center: 1) Escaping or attempting to escape; 2) Assaulting staff, offenders or other persons, resulting in death or serious bodily injury; 3) Engaging in dangerous disturbances; 4) Having influence in activities of a gang or other unauthorized organization; 5) Engaging in non-consensual sexual conduct; or 6) Possessing weapons'. Critics of the code point out that if gang membership qualifies a prisoner for transfer to the supermax, a majority of prisoners would be eligible. See the Joint Committee on Administrative Rules: http://www.ilga.gov/commission/jcar/admincode/020/020005050000400R.html.

4 The estimate of one-third of the current Tamms prison population was consistently given by Illinois Department of Corrections officials at legislative hearings between 2008–13. The 2009 'Ten Point Plan' asserts that 47 prisoners had, to date, spent 11 or more years incarcerated at Tamms.

5 In 2010, as part of reforms outlined in the Illinois Department of Corrections' 'Ten Point Plan', certain Tamms prisoners were granted phone calls.

6 Jean Snyder explains that when Tamms opened, the prison employed no full-time psychiatrists. Instead, medical doctors provided the mental health treatment. Following *Rasho v. Snyder,* the administration employed more mental health staff; opened a Special Treatment Unit for a small number of prisoners deemed by staff to have serious mental illness but not slated for transfer out of Tamms; and issued an institutional directive which said that prisoners with 'serious mental illness' should not be sent to Tamms in the first place. Yet, she adds, 'There is such an overlap between serious mental illness and serious destructive behavior in a prison' that the injunction not to send 'seriously mentally ill' prisoners to Tamms was not strictly enforced.

7 Angela Davis treats the importance of imagining a world without prisons at length in her book *Are Prisons Obsolete?* (2003).

8 The *Westefer v. Snyder* case established that prisoners had a significant liberty interest in not being sent to Tamms from any other prison in the Illinois system. Where such a liberty interest exists, certain minimal due process protections are constitutionally required.

9 Murphy writes: 'In an earlier decision in this case the United States Court of Appeals for the Seventh Circuit observed that, if Plaintiffs' allegations are true, 'being confined to Tamms is to be subjected to virtual sensory deprivation, with prisoners forced to spend most days doing literally nothing but staring at the four blank walls of their cells. Westefer v. Snyder, 422 F.3d 570, 589 (7th Cir. 2005). The record shows that this is indeed the case' (24).

10 Anthony Gay's lengthy sentences were overturned in 2014. His new projected release date is August of 2018.

References

Agamben, G 1995, *Homo sacer,* Stanford University Press, Redwood City, CA.

Blair, C & Cooper, M 1987, 'The humanist turn in Foucault's rhetoric of inquiry', *Quarterly Journal of Speech,* vol. 73, pp. 151–71.

Cooper, MM 2001, 'Rhetorical agency as emergent and enacted', *College Composition and Communication,* vol. 62.3, pp. 420–49.

Davis, A 2003, *Are Prisons Obsolete?* Seven Stories Press, New York, NY.

Geisler, C 2004, 'How ought we to understand the concept of rhetorical agency? Report from the ARS', *Rhetoric Society Quarterly*, vol. 34.3, pp. 9–17.

Greene, RM 2004, 'Rhetoric and capitalism: rhetorical agency as communicative labor', *Philosophy and Rhetoric*, vol. 37, p. 3.

Hauser, G 2012, *Prisoners of conscience: moral vernaculars of political agency*, University of South Carolina Press, Columbia, SC.

Illinois Department of Corrections 2009, *Tamms closed maximum security unit: overview and Ten-Point Plan*, Illinois Department of Corrections.

Illinois Department of Corrections 2012, *Tamms Correctional Center: Institutional Directive, Document 05.12.110*, Illinois Department of Corrections.

John Howard Association 2012, *A price Illinois cannot afford: Tamms and the costs of long long-term isolation*, John Howard Association. Available from: <http:// thejha.org /sites/default/ files/TammsReport.pdf>.

Kupers, TA et al. 2012, 'Beyond supermax administrative segregation: Mississippi's experience rethinking prison classification and creating alternative mental health programs', *Criminal Justice and Behavior*, vol. 36, no. 10, pp. 1037–50.

Laclau, E 2007, 'Bare life or social indeterminacy?' in *Sovereignty & life*, eds M Calarco & S DeCaroli, Stanford University Press, Redwood City, CA.

Miller, R 2009, *Capital fax blog* 18 September 18. Available from: <http://capitolfax .com/ ?p= 9505&wpmp_switcher=desktop>.

Palti, E 2004, 'The "return of the subject" as a historico-intellectual problem', *History and Theory*, vol. 43.1, pp. 57–82.

Pawlawczyk, G & Hundsdorfer, B 2009a, 'Trapped in Tamms: supermax confines inmates to cells 23 hours a day', *Belleville News Democrat* 21 August. Available from: <http://www.bnd.com/2012/08/21/2292279/trapped-in-tamms-supermax -prison.html>.

Pawlawczyk, G & Hundsdorfer, B 2009b, 'Tamms psychiatrist: inmate is a "manipulator"', *Belleville News Democrat* 16 September. Available from: <http://www .bnd.com>.

Pawlawczyk, G & Hundsdorfer, B 2011, 'Inmate wants opportunity to get out of Tamms', *Belleville News Democrat* 11 September. Available from: <http://www .bnd.com>.

Rhodes, LA 2005, 'Changing the subject: conversation in a supermax', *Cultural Anthropology*, vol. 20.3, pp. 388–411.

Rasho v. Snyder 1999, The United States District Court for the Southern District of Illinois, East St. Louis Division.

Shaw, DG 2001, 'Happy in our chains? Agency and language in the postmodern age', *History and Theory*, vol. 40.4, pp. 1–9.

Westefer v. Snyder 2010, Document 540. 1–94. The United States District Court for the Southern District of Illinois.

9

Punishing Mental Illness: Trans-institutionalization and Solitary Confinement in the United States

Keramet Reiter, University of California, Irvine
Thomas Blair, University of California, Los Angeles

Bradley Ballard died of sepsis in May 2014 after he tied a rubber band around his genitals, smeared his body with feces, and passed out in his Rikers Island, New York City jail cell. Ballard had been arrested for assault and public lewdness in 2013; he had previously served six years in New York state prisons for assault charges. Ballard was known to be severely mentally ill; he had spent 38 days in a prison psychiatric hospital in the weeks before he died. In the last week of his life, he made a lewd gesture at a female officer and was subsequently placed in total solitary confinement. For several days, he was not allowed to leave his cell, nor was he given medications. Because he intentionally stopped up his toilet, the water line supplying his cell was shut off (Pearson 2014).

Joseph Duran died in a California prison cell in September 2013 after he was doused in 'pepper spray'[1] and left in the cell with the toxic aerosol burning in his tracheal tube—Duran's only means of breathing. Duran reportedly pulled the tracheal tube out of his neck, in an apparent attempt to clean it of the burning irritant, but then proceeded to place other objects through the tracheostomy hole and into his neck cavity, leading to his death. He had been held in a 'mental health crisis bed' isolation cell at Mule Creek State Prison for three days. At first, the California Department of Corrections and Rehabilitation ruled his death a suicide. Duran's parents were not notified until January 2014, four months after their son died (Stanton & Walsh 2014). (A federal judge later questioned whether the death had been a suicide, and Duran's parents have filed a wrongful death suit.) In California, a federal court recently found that state correctional officials had engaged in a recurring practice of pepper-spraying mentally ill inmates; the judge ordered stricter limits on the use of force against the mentally ill, and more restrictions on how long mentally ill prisoners could be held in solitary confinement (Thompson 2014; *Coleman v. Brown* 2014).

Evan Ebel died in a shootout with police in March 2013. A few days earlier, he had killed a pizza deliveryman; stolen his uniform; driven to the home of Tom Clements, then director of the Colorado Department of Corrections; knocked on Clements's door; and shot him dead (Banda 2013). A month earlier, Ebel had been released directly from one of Colorado's administrative segregation units, where he had been in isolation for more than five years. He had been in isolation for 'safety and security' reasons—to manage his risky behavior, not to punish him for a specific action (Ford 2013). Ebel had been treated for symptoms of mental illness during his years in isolation (Gurman 2014; Greene 2013).

Each of these three cases reveals challenges of managing mental illness in a punitive setting. Different as their stories are, Ballard, Duran, and Ebel share one important factor: solitary confinement. Each of these men spent extended periods of time—from a few days to a few years—in total isolation. The underlying reasons for their isolation were ambiguous. In Ballard's case, a criminal act (indecent exposure) justified punitive isolation. Yet Ballard's history of severe mental illness suggests his actions were manifestations of mental illness, more deserving of treatment than punishment. In Duran's case, mental health problems justified his isolation, nominally for treatment purposes. In Ebel's case, a correctional assessment that he was likely to engage in risky behavior justified administrative isolation, but that isolation, in turn, may have contributed to mental health problems. While the purpose of the solitary confinement was different in each case, each involved the use of solitary confinement on a person with mental illness, and each produced a disastrous outcome.

This chapter describes the perverse symbiosis of solitary confinement and mental illness in the United States. We analyze a variety of sources in order to elucidate the lived, punitive experience of being mentally ill and held in isolation in US prisons. We begin with a background discussion of the co-arising and mutual perpetuation of the use of solitary confinement and the incarceration of mentally ill people. Next, we present original data from interviews with six psychologists working in California's long-term solitary confinement units and examine how individuals working with the mentally ill in solitary confinement attempt to differentiate between care and punishment—a theme also addressed by Murray and Holmes and Hannah-Moffat and Klassen in this volume. We then use examples from recent litigation challenging the treatment of the mentally ill in solitary confinement, especially in California and Pennsylvania, to examine how courts attempt to distinguish care from punishment. As in many of the chapters in this anthology (see particularly Arbel and Murray & Holmes), we argue that *non-punitive* isolation, frequently used to manage or even 'care for' the mentally ill, is experienced as *highly punitive* and characteristically entails destructive rather than therapeutic outcomes.

Our central argument is that solitary confinement is an indispensable tool and, in many cases, a tool of first resort in US prison systems for managing an expanding mentally ill population. Although prison administrators often characterize solitary confinement as an 'administrative' management device (as in Ebel's case), the extreme conditions limit the privileges of mentally ill prisoners, exacerbate health problems, and perpetuate cycles of infractions as increasingly restrictive environments lower the threshold for rule violations. Through examination of such cycles of infraction and confinement, we argue that the management of the mentally ill in solitary confinement serves, itself, as a justification for continued use of solitary confinement—particularly with mentally ill prisoners.

Finally, we attempt to account for a new trend: over the past several years, the US federal government, along with many individual state governments, has increased restrictions on the placement of the mentally ill in solitary confinement. But these legal attempts to disentangle the practice of isolation from the status of mental illness—and attempts to reconcile agendas of punishment with agendas of care—remain preliminary and theoretical, at best. As judicial and public disgust with practices perceived as inhumane or unconstitutional begins to produce changes in policy and practice, conscientious critics must remain vigilant—not only to see injustice rectified, but also to assure that new practices are more humane and not less so.

Solitary confinement: The linchpin of trans-institutionalization

Over the last four decades, the United States has drastically decreased inpatient psychiatric populations and concomitantly increased incarceration—including incarceration of mentally ill individuals and expanding uses of solitary confinement. This process began well before 1963, when President

Kennedy signed the Community Mental Health Act (CMHA) into law, but that legislation was a turning point (Grob 1987). The CMHA authorized $3 billion in federal funds to establish community mental health centers (CMHCs) as an alternative to locked-down psychiatric hospitals, which had been criticized as abusive and unnecessary (National Council for Behavioral Health 2014; Simon 2014, p. 79). Between 1960 and 1980, the population institutionalized in state mental hospitals fell from over 500,000 to under 100,000 (Earley 2006).

However, the US government never fully funded CMHCs or any of the other resources that proponents of deinstitutionalization had imagined to replace mental hospitals. Many of the 'deinstitutionalized', and many who might have been hospitalized a few decades earlier, soon landed in a different kind of institution: jails and prisons (Gilligan 2001). James Gilligan, among others, has explained the relationship between mental illness and imprisonment as a process of 'trans-institutionalization', which took place most drastically between the 1960s and 1990s in the United States (see also Harcourt 2011). Today, America's largest jails—the municipal jails for Chicago, Los Angeles, and New York—are also the country's largest psychiatric hospitals (Torrey 1990; Earley 2006). Rates of mental illness among incarcerated people across the United States are estimated at 50 percent or higher (James & Glaze 2006). According to one analysis—complicated by the difficulties of tracking either beds or people in two sprawling, turbulent institutional systems—there are three times as many people with serious mental illness in prisons and jails as in psychiatric hospitals in the United States today (Torrey et al. 2010).

This process of trans-institutionalization of mentally ill people occurred as a component of mass incarceration. In 1973, as psychiatric deinstitutionalization proceeded, the US prison population began its steady growth. US incarceration rates quintupled between 1972 and 2007; by 2014, the United States had more than two million people in prison, more than any other country in the world (Zimring 2010, p. 1228; International Center for Prison Studies 2014). Although deinstitutionalization and mass incarceration are correlated, mentally ill prisoners are only one of many sub-populations contributing to the growth of imprisonment in the United States (Harcourt 2011). Recent studies suggest that the deinstitutionalization of mentally ill people accounted for only 4 to 7 percent of incarceration growth between 1980 and 2000. And deinstitutionalization accounted for none of the earlier increases in incarceration (Raphael & Stoll 2013).

Our research on the origins and uses of solitary confinement suggests a much stronger relationship between trans-institutionalization and solitary confinement, however, than these numbers first suggest. The use of solitary confinement expanded as part of mass incarceration, and rates of mental health problems in solitary confinement are significantly higher than in general prison populations. As prison populations grew in the 1980s, and states built dozens of new prisons, nearly every state, along with the federal government, built a supermax, a high-tech prison designed for long-term solitary confinement (Naday, Freilich & Mellow 2008; Riveland 1999). Arizona opened the first of these supermaxes in 1986 (Lynch 2009), and California opened two of the biggest in 1988 and 1989 (Reiter 2012). Today, an estimated 80,000 people in the United States are imprisoned in some form of isolation, including shorter-term administrative segregation (usually 30 days to a few months) and longer-term supermaximum security confinement (months to years) (Gibbons & Katzenbach 2006). Less than one-quarter of general population prisoners have serious mental illnesses; by contrast, between one-third to one-half of the 80,000 prisoners isolated on a given day in the United States are seriously mentally ill (Correctional Association 2008). At any given time, 5 to 10 percent of a state's prison population is in solitary confinement, but 50 percent or more of prison suicides take place in solitary (Kupers 2008; Mears 2006). Whether suicide in solitary confinement represents the outcome of previous mental illness or self-destructive behavior induced by the environment—in many cases, both factors apply—this outcome demonstrates the profoundly destructive effects of such confinement (see also the chapters by Hannah-Moffat & Klassen and Murray & Holmes in this volume). The high rates of mental illness and suicide in solitary confinement, relative to the rates of mental illness and suicide in general prison populations, suggest that prisoners with mental illness are overrepresented in solitary.

This overrepresentation of mental illness in solitary happens via two mechanisms. First, mental illness is a risk factor for assignment to solitary. Sometimes, as in Joseph Duran's case, mentally ill prisoners are assigned to solitary for 'treatment'. At other times, as in Bradley Ballard's case, mentally ill prisoners have difficulty following prison rules and end up in solitary for nominally 'punitive' reasons. Second, placement in solitary confinement is itself a risk factor for exacerbation or onset of mental illness. In 1997, Haney and Lynch published the definitive overview of what was then known about the relationship between solitary confinement and mental health. They argued that solitary confinement inflicts intense 'psychological trauma' and that the courts had failed to recognize and regulate 'the nature and magnitude' of this trauma (p. 481). Nearly two decades later, evidence of the psychological trauma of solitary confinement continues to grow—including, for instance, violent rampages by people like Evan Ebel, who was released directly from isolation (Gurman 2014; see also Schulte 2014 describing a similar case in Nebraska). Psychiatrists, psychologists, and criminologists have rigorously documented the detrimental psychological impacts of long-term isolation (Grassian 2006; Haney 2003; King 2007; Kupers 1999). Only one recent study has failed to find evidence of psychological deterioration among prisoners in isolation, but that study has been criticized for having flawed experimental design and biased implementation, including reliance on prisoner-subjects' self-reported assessments of their mood and mental health (O'Keefe et al. 2011; Grassian 2010), an inherently limited approach to clinical research, even in non-institutional settings.

The risk of being placed in solitary confinement as a mentally ill prisoner, and the risk of becoming mentally ill while in solitary confinement, creates a vicious cycle. As a prisoner's mental health deteriorates, he or she often disobeys protocols, breaking prison rules against attempting suicide, yelling, exposing him or herself, or throwing excrement (all behaviors in which ostensibly non-ill prisoners also engage), incurring multiple disciplinary infractions and thereby extending their time in solitary confinement (see especially Rhodes 2004; Lovell 2008; Naday, Freilich & Mellow 2008, p. 87). This vicious cycle makes solitary confinement appear all the more necessary. As prisoners in isolation continually violate rules, they reaffirm prison officials' assessments that they are dangerous and unmanageable.

This perversely symbiotic relationship between mental illness and solitary confinement suggests an overlooked connection between trans-institutionalization and the most extreme practices of mass incarceration. While quantitative analyses have been used to argue that deinstitutionalization of people with mental illness accounts for only a small percentage of the increased rate of imprisonment in the United States in the late 20th century, available evidence suggests that deinstitutionalization might account for a much larger percentage of the increased use of solitary confinement over the same period, since mentally ill prisoners appear to evoke usage of solitary confinement, as a tool of both management and punishment, at disproportionately high rates. More research, and better data, would be needed to tease out the potentially causal nature of this relationship. But close examination of day-to-day practices for handling mentally ill people in solitary confinement and pertinent judicial opinions, presented in the next sections, demonstrates an important mechanism that has facilitated trans-institutionalization:

isolating the mentally ill legitimizes, and re-legitimizes, the policy and practice of maintaining prisoners in long-term solitary confinement.

Darkness under fluorescent lights: Six psychologists' perspectives

In an effort to understand solitary confinement of mentally ill prisoners from the standpoint of those tasked with providing mental health care in such settings, one of us (KR) conducted interviews in 2010 with seven psychologists who practice among the many solitary confinement units scattered throughout the California Department of Corrections and Rehabilitation (CDCR). Six of them gave permission to be quoted. Here, we emphasize three emergent themes from those interviews: clinical ambivalence, administrative ignorance, and self-perpetuation of restrictive confinement of the mentally ill. While these themes reflect case data from a small sample of subjects, they also illustrate the broad institutional patterns already discussed.

Life as a psychologist for people in solitary confinement is characterized by ambivalence, from diagnostic uncertainty to fundamental doubts about the therapeutic validity of the practice environment itself. In these interviews, diagnostic uncertainty manifested in both euphemism and frank acknowledgment of unknowns. Therapy itself, for instance, takes place with prisoners inside phone-booth-sized, steel-grated 'therapeutic treatment modules'—which only one of the six psychologists interviewed was willing to call 'cages'. Such ostensibly therapeutic practices extend to clinical formulations themselves, particularly regarding the distinction between significant illness and mere misbehavior. For instance, one clinician referred to a prisoner who 'was not mentally ill' but 'had some kind of fetish stuff that went on' and '[a history of] severe and extreme abuse and no socialization in his life' (CDCR Psychologist 6). Another commented that 'some of the guys in our PSUs and SHUs have very severe behavioral disorders' (CDCR Psychologist 5) but simultaneously asserted that people with severe mental illness are excluded from SHUs (segregated housing units). Despite working with people isolated for terms of months to years, another psychologist contended that 'we do not have time or the full set of tools...to diagnose whether it is bipolar or schizophrenia' (CDCR Psychologist 1) when a prisoner appears to have severe mental illness. This claim calls into question any attempt to distinguish everyday behavioral dysregulation from manifestations of 'real' mental illness. If thorough clinical diagnostics are not, for whatever reasons, feasible to perform, the possibility of confirming 'real' mental illness—itself a questionable distinction in this environment—disappears. (See also Murray & Holmes in this volume, discussing the co-construction of mental illness and criminality in such forensic settings.)

Such futility is perpetuated by the inaccessibility of prisoner-patients. One psychologist commented that 'a lot of them don't come out [of their cell for treatment] because they say they are too busy, quote unquote' (CDCR Psychologist 1); another observed that 'it's not that somebody comes to the door and says "hey, I'm developing a mental illness"' (CDCR Psychologist 6). Depression and schizophrenia, both typically characterized by social withdrawal, would predispose the most ill to be most avoidant of clinical attention. Attempts at care, too, are infrequent. Minimum SHU stays for the prisoners these clinicians treat are 'at least 90 days, and probably 120', according to one (CDCR Psychologist 4); within this context, psychological evaluation is mandated 'every 30 days, or more often if you can' (CDCR Psychologist 2). In the psychological services units (PSUs, where prisoners are in solitary confinement) and administrative segregation, prisoners are seen weekly (CDCR Psychologist 3).

Although such units are supposed to serve different functions—administrative, punitive, and therapeutic emphases characterizing administrative segregation, SHUs, and PSUs, respectively—these distinctions are frequently only theoretical to the clinicians working in them. As one clinician reported, 'there are inmates who are in Correctional Clinical Case Management System (CCCMS, or CCC) level of care in a SHU. There are inmates at EOP who are in a SHU, but it's called PSU' (CDCR Psychologist 3). This clinician was distinguishing between the Correctional Clinical Case Management System (CCCMS, or CCC), which includes prisoners who need some mental health care but are not so ill as to be precluded from placement in SHUs, and the Enhanced Outpatient Program (EOP), which includes prisoners who are so seriously mentally ill that they are precluded from SHU placement. Another clinician added that 'mental health workers in the rest of the prison...are not quite sure what an EOP person looks like' (CDCR Psychologist 4)—in other words, even dedicated mental health staff are unsure who should be directed to confinement with a relatively therapeutic orientation. Even if such distinctions were made, confinement itself leads regularly, but unpredictably, to mental deterioration: 'we don't know exactly who is going to be vulnerable to that isolation and the problems with it' (CDCR Psychologist 5).

All of these considerations inform basic ambivalence about the validity of the practice environment itself. One psychologist reflected that solitary confinement units, broadly, are 'not really set up to treat people'. For instance, antipsychotic medications frequently lead to impaired temperature regulation, and especially heat intolerance, leading to significant discomfort, at best. At worst, this side effect causes heat stroke, a consequence of taking medications in an environment that deprioritizes, or even flouts, ambient temperature control (see Morain & Hurst 1991). While prisoners 'have to know how to do in-cell time without coming to pieces', which 'requires a certain level of maturity', those who are already overtly ill 'tend to rack up 115s [disciplinary reports] for something or other—whether it's holding a food tray, [or] mouthing off to a custody officer', according to another psychologist (CDCR Psychologist 3). Despite clinicians' individual therapeutic intentions and the theoretical possibility of diversion to a unit dedicated to treating mental illness, the institutional context militates against any therapeutic agenda.

Clinicians' ambivalence nests within a broad context of institutional ignorance; despite theoretically total control, the system is simply not set up to track individuals or patterns of behavior. One clinician recalled working in the SHU early in the process of trans-institutionalization, when 'the whole mental health program was developing. We didn't have standardized forms or standardized requirements for treatment' (CDCR Psychologist 6). Years later, commenting on lack of data and a recent attempt to gather statistics, another lamented that 'in part, we don't have the clinical tracking systems to do it. Our clinical tracking system was archaic...we didn't have it networked... every institution had a separate program...sometimes not even the same version.' Issues such as self-injury and suicide are simply not monitored: 'our monitoring of suicides is done based on completed suicides. Our monitoring is based on 25–30 suicide incidents a year rather than thousands of incidents of self-harm [or] suicide attempts' (CDCR Psychologist 5).

Solitary confinement includes 24-hour-a-day illumination but remains an area of darkness. One psychologist commented that she didn't 'know the outcome measures on whether the SHU works' in preventing adverse outcomes in the prison. There may be *outcomes*, but the phrase 'outcome measures' implies a degree of before-and-after assessment that is foreign to the system and demonstrates unfounded trust, on that psychologist's part, that the context in which she attempts to help prisoners is somehow informed by clinical evidence. Another clinician, who investigated extant research on sensory deprivation, found that 'some of the best information...was done by NASA, who've done research on what it's like to keep people in space travel for long periods of time in small spaces... and the Navy, on submarines' (CDCR Psychologist 5).

Such ignorance helps to facilitate the cycle of mental illness and solitary confinement; without documentation of outcomes, the system is permitted to perpetuate itself. While one psychologist asserted that 'we don't allow the most seriously mentally ill or functionally impaired people in the SHU', he referred moments later to that very practice, speaking of 'very good treatment in some of those programs for some of our most behaviorally disordered...I wish they weren't in the SHU'. Another reflected on 'people who are brain injured. They don't have emotional control. You want them to grow up, but they're not going to grow up' (CDCR Psychologist 2). Asked about the extent to which prisoners develop the 'SHU syndrome' (a pattern of psychological and behavioral decompensation, including social withdrawal and inability to care for oneself, described in Grassian 2006), one stated that 'it's definitely less than half that deteriorate in that setting' (CDCR Psychologist 6). The same clinician, referring to the known role of isolation in causing psychological decompensation, observed that 'the concern with mentally ill people is there is sensory deprivation' (CDCR Psychologist 6). Asked what she tells people who ask how she works in such an environment, another psychologist—who, like her colleagues, expressed empathy toward her prisoner-patients, and an apparently heartfelt desire to help them—named a grounding technique that she uses for herself but which is unavailable in solitary: 'I say that I have to verify that the sun is shining outside' (CDCR Psychologist 2). No such light shines into the units.

Between care and punishment

The history of 'supermaximum security' conditions in California illustrates both the institutional migrations these psychologists have experienced and the judicial frontiers in relating to mental illness and solitary confinement. In 1989, California opened one of the first and biggest supermaxes: Pelican Bay State Prison. The institution was equipped with 1,056 cells designed for total, long-term solitary confinement (Reiter 2012). As of 2011, more than 500 prisoners had spent more than ten years in isolation at Pelican Bay State Prison (Small 2011). Within one year of the prison opening, prisoners and their advocates had filed a class-action lawsuit, *Madrid v. Gomez* (1995), challenging the conditions of confinement at Pelican Bay. Although no US court (either federal or state) has ever found that long-term solitary confinement in supermaxes (even for periods of 10 or 20 years) is, per se, unconstitutional, and although functionally identical conditions of confinement exist at other institutions in California, the *Madrid* court forbade the housing of prisoners with serious mental illnesses in solitary confinement at Pelican Bay. The court explained that where 'the conditions of segregation being challenged… inflict a serious mental illness, greatly exacerbate mental illness, or deprive inmates of their sanity, then defendants have deprived inmates of a basic necessity of human existence' (*Madrid*, 1264). However, the court only forbade such conditions of segregation where the risks of psychological trauma were of 'sufficiently serious magnitude'. For those prisoners with pre-incarceration mental illnesses, 'placing them in the SHU is the mental equivalent of putting an asthmatic in a place with little air to breathe'—incurring a 'plainly "unreasonable"' risk of psychological trauma (*Madrid* at 1265). Precluding placement of the seriously mentally ill in the SHU in the first place averts this risk. In other states, throughout the 1990s and early 2000s, courts reached similar conclusions about the unconstitutionality of housing prisoners with pre-existing mental illnesses in long-term solitary confinement in supermax-style facilities (Arrigo, Bersot & Sellers 2011, pp. 71–2).

Yet almost 25 years after the *Madrid* decision, mentally ill prisoners across the United States continue to spend months, years, or even decades at a time in solitary confinement. (This is true even in the Pelican Bay SHU, because the *Madrid* case only protects prisoners with pre-existing mental illnesses, not those who develop mental illness while in isolation.) California remains an unfortunate trendsetter in this regard. While *Madrid* ostensibly prohibited the housing of serious mentally ill prisoners at Pelican Bay, California prison officials have continued to house mentally ill prisoners in other, functionally identical segregation facilities throughout the state, and prisoners and their advocates have continued to challenge these policies. In 2013, lawyers for the California Department of Corrections and Rehabilitation sought to terminate court oversight of mental health treatment throughout the state prison system (*Coleman v. Brown* Order 2013). This motion backfired, inspiring an extended investigation into the state's treatment of mentally ill prisoners. The court's findings repeatedly made front-page news in the Los Angeles *Times* and other papers: mentally ill prisoners in California, the court found, were disproportionately isolated; significantly more likely to commit suicide in isolation; and, like Joseph Duran, described in our introduction, were regularly sprayed with tear gas in small and poorly ventilated spaces. In August 2014, the state prison system agreed to sweeping changes in the treatment of the mentally ill, including building new units to impose less restrictive conditions of isolation (St. John 2014). California is not alone in facing such criticism. For instance, in 2013, the US Department of Justice issued a report condemning the state of Pennsylvania's practice of placing seriously mentally ill prisoners in solitary confinement based solely on their mental illness status. The Department of Justice ordered substantial reforms to these practices and pledged ongoing oversight (Perez & Hickton 2013).

Interpretations of these interventions have varied. Arrigo, Bersot, and Sellers argue that courts considering the placement of mentally ill prisoners in solitary confinement have focused primarily on 'order-maintenance' and have largely ignored the empirical evidence about the disturbing relationship between 'inmate mental health, solitary confinement, and the potentially cruel and unusual condition of long-term punitive isolation' (2011, pp. 92, 89). But the most recent orders in California's *Coleman* case finally demonstrate careful judicial attention to this empirical evidence. The court weighed testimony from a prisoner plaintiffs' expert about 'the harmful effects of segregated housing on certain mentally ill inmates' against testimony from a prison defendants' expert that 'segregation does not cause the type and severity of psychological harm previously described in descriptive studies'. The court dismissed the claims of the prison defendants' expert as unpersuasive (*Coleman v. Brown* Order 2014, p. 41). In analyzing the California litigation in particular, Simon has argued that courts have been careful to disassociate mental illness from criminality, defining mentally ill prisoners as 'patients...persons at risk, not threats to others' (2014, p. 81).

Simon may be correct that courts, especially in California, have attempted to disassociate mental illness from criminality, but the persistent correctional practice of confining mentally ill prisoners in isolation demonstrates that these judicial efforts have largely failed to translate from a theoretical valence to a practical one. Instead, prison officials have repeatedly justified expanded uses of solitary confinement with reference to the unmanageability and criminality of mentally ill prisoners. Even the most recent decisions in California and Pennsylvania reveal how consistently, and persistently, corrections officials associate mental illness with criminality (see also Lovell 2008, p. 991). Both the litigation and the day-to-day work of managing mentally ill prisoners in segregation has perpetually reassociated mental illness with criminality, which, in turn, legitimizes the ongoing isolation of mentally ill prisoners, and, by extension, grounds the practice of solitary confinement. This process specifically occurs through the implementation of punitive policies in response to the actions of the mentally ill, and symbolically through the use of therapeutic language to describe functionally punitive practices.

First, prison officials routinely isolate mentally ill prisoners because of their mental health status. While these isolative conditions are often labelled 'administrative' or 'non-disciplinary', the conditions are functionally indistinguishable from those in 'punitive' or 'disciplinary segregation': severely curtailed privileges, no contact with family or other visitors, and out-of-cell time limited to one hour per day, at most (*Coleman v. Brown* 2014, pp. 49, 53; Perez & Hickton 2013, pp. 14–16). Second, prison officials routinely punish mentally ill prisoners for engaging in self-harm or attempting suicide. Often, such punishment involves not just longer periods in isolation but the application of excessive force, such as repeated spraying with tear gas in confined spaces or placement in physical restraints for extended periods of time (Stanton & Walsh 2014; Perez & Hickton 2013, p. 18). In such cases, the actions of a mentally ill prisoner are evaluated and punished as though they were deliberate and criminal rather than manifestations of severe depression, mania, or psychosis. Third, prison officials conflate mental illness and criminality when they blame mentally ill prisoners for the violent actions of prison staff. Joseph Duran's death, described in our introduction, illustrates this phenomenon. Prison officials 'pepper-sprayed' Duran without apparent regard for the interaction of tear gas and a breathing tube in a small, poorly ventilated space; Duran's subsequent removal of the tube and placement of food directly into his tracheostomy hole occurred in reaction to this spraying. But Duran's death certificate labelled his death a suicide, thereby redefining the prison officials' violent actions as manifestations of the victim's mental illness (Stanton & Walsh 2014). This relabelling justified correctional attempts at controlling Mr. Duran by moving the locus of infraction from staff to prisoner.

Prison officials also persistently mask these punitive practices by relabelling them in therapeutic terms. Again, litigation in both California and Pennsylvania offers numerous examples of this technique. Perhaps the most egregious is the use of the term 'therapeutic treatment modules' in California—a term used freely by the psychologists we interviewed, as already discussed—to describe the telephone-booth-sized steel cages in which segregated, mentally ill prisoners are locked for 'group therapy' sessions. Jeffrey Metzner, who was appointed in the early 1990s to oversee mental health care in the Pelican Bay supermax as part of the *Madrid* litigation, designed the therapeutic treatment modules for California prisons. According to Metzner, 'the enclosures offer better security and more freedom of movement than alternatives used in most states, which include handcuffing patients to their chairs or shackling an ankle to the floor. Once the inmates are inside the cage, their handcuffs are removed' (Dolan 2010). And Metzner highlighted the importance of the (euphemistic) name: 'The name is important, because if you call them cages, people inside might feel like animals and respond accordingly' (Dolan 2010). Still, in a recent order requiring less restrictive conditions of confinement for mentally ill prisoners, the *Coleman* court described the modules as 'treatment cages'—explicitly acknowledging their appearance and function in plain English and implicitly acknowledging their punitive effect (*Coleman v. Brown* 2014, p. 51).

Such wallpapering of the punitive with therapeutic language is pervasive. Therapeutic labels are also used to identify various forms of segregation specifically designed for mentally ill prisoners. Again, the *Coleman* case reveals the proliferation of terms, detailing the differences between security housing units (SHUs), administrative segregation units (ASUs), and psychiatric services units (PSUs); California designates each kind of unit for a different combination of mental health and security needs. For instance, SHUs, which include the solitary confinement cells at Pelican Bay, must exclude the most seriously mentally ill prisoners. If those prisoners require segregation, they go to PSUs (*Coleman v. Brown* 2014, pp. 60–1). But the *Coleman* court described how seriously mentally ill prisoners can remain in ASUs (designed to be for shorter-term isolation), awaiting placement in PSUs. And even the PSUs are almost indistinguishable from the SHUs; in California, PSUs are at least required to have windows. As one prison psychologist has noted, 'PSU' is as much of a euphemism as 'therapeutic treatment module': 'Some of us in mental health call them punishment units' (CDCR Psychologist 5).

In response to the *Coleman* litigation, the California Department of Corrections and Rehabilitation has proposed two more labels for new isolation units designed for mentally ill prisoners: short-term restricted housing units (STRHUs) and long-term restricted housing units (LTRHUs). 'These units change conditions of confinement in segregated units for this population by allowing inmates increased programming, increased mental health contacts, and increased structured mental health treatment, lessening the risk of decompensation while also allowing CDCR to maintain the safety and security of the institution' (*Coleman v. Brown*, Report on Compliance 2014, p. 2). More concretely, California prison officials propose that mentally ill prisoners be concentrated in specially designated ASUs and provided 15–20 hours (as opposed to five to ten hours) out of their cells per week (*Coleman v. Brown*, Report on Compliance 2014, pp. 5–6). In practice, this plan means that prisoners in the newly labelled STRHUs and LTRHUs will still spend 20 or more hours of every day locked in isolation cells, which now happen to be called by different names. The new units continue to blur the line between 'mental health treatment' and institutional 'safety and security', both euphemisms for relative isolation within an institutional framework that is primarily punitive, despite attempts at therapeutic framing.

The creative application of new labels to old forms of solitary confinement is not unique to California. According to the Department of Justice investigation of the Cresson prison, Pennsylvania also has deployed a proliferation of labels to differentiate between various kinds of segregation associated with varying degrees of mental illness: restrictive housing units (RHUs), psychiatric observation cells (POCs), and secure special needs units (SSNUs). The RHUs seem most similar to California's SHUs, the most restrictive isolation units. The POCs and SSNUs are special isolation units for the mentally ill. Apparently in response to the Department of Justice investigation and critiques, the Pennsylvania Department of Corrections, like the California prison system, has relabelled some of these units. Pennsylvania officials 'eliminated ... SSNUs' and replaced them with a new kind of restrictive housing: secure residential treatment units (SRTUs), which will 'not...use solitary confinement'. However, the report does not detail how restrictive the new SRTUs will be (Perez & Hickton 2013, p. 5).

Our readers' inevitable dizziness amid these infelicitous abbreviations reflects the system's own obfuscation of which category of confinement mentally ill prisoners are experiencing: administrative, punitive, and/or supposedly therapeutic. In both California and Pennsylvania, a relatively straightforward system of solitary confinement (SHUs and RHUs) has become an alphabet soup of ASUs, PSUs, STRHUs, LTRHUs, SSNUs, POCs, and SRTUs—all in the service of segregating and isolating certain categories of mentally ill prisoners in conditions that are highly restrictive and therefore punitive in lived experience, if not in professed administrative intent. Each new unit constitutes a new justification not only for isolating mentally ill prisoners, but also for incarcerating people whose allegedly criminal behavior is driven by psychosis or mania.

Evaluating reform

As of 2008, nine states, along with the federal government, had court-ordered limitations in place to protect the mentally ill from extended solitary confinement (Correctional Association of New York 2008). But these limits are narrowly drawn, providing for more out-of-cell time and additional treatment opportunities but rarely excluding mentally ill prisoners from isolation completely. In the early 2010s, growing momentum against solitary confinement focused increasingly on moving vulnerable populations—such as juveniles, pregnant women, and the seriously mentally ill—out of such confinement. These efforts have resulted in legislation or proposed legislation in at least 11 states (American Civil Liberties Union 2014). In addition, the US Department of Justice, a federal agency that investigates prison-based abuses, has issued a number of reports, such as the Pennsylvania report previously discussed, condemning the abuse of the mentally ill in solitary confinement.

This trend toward attempted reform might suggest hope for the eventual disentanglement of mental illness and solitary confinement. Perhaps, as a first step toward humane systems of justice and care, courts and legislators are finally figuring out how to distinguish between the criminal and the mentally ill (Simon 2014). This chapter illustrates how the opposite trend prevails: criminalization of mental illness is crucial to the design, justification, and continued operation of long-term solitary confinement. Deinstitutionalization of patients from American state mental hospitals in the latter half of the 20th century and concomitant fruition of the prison-industrial complex have led to a system in which mentally ill people who break the law are socially managed as criminals, in institutions designed to punish aberrant behavior with brute force, social isolation, and sensory deprivation, and in which mental health care is a functional afterthought, despite some clinicians' humanistic intentions.

We have argued that solitary confinement itself has become an engine of trans-institutionalization, wherein such confinement is used, administratively and punitively, to manage the very people most likely to suffer the worst of its detrimental effects. In this context, the current wave of attempted reform proposes a new phase of deinstitutionalization, potentially foreshadowing one California prison psychologist's fantasy for the SHU: 'jackhammers'.

Recent history and contemporary practice clearly show that when law-breakers with serious mental illness are treated first as criminals and second as patients, institutional abuses are rampant, and demonstrable therapeutic benefit is negligible. Ongoing litigation in California and Pennsylvania reveals how new systems of response to deviance among persons with serious mental illness fail to relate to offenders primarily in terms of mental health needs, and, in fact, apply practices that make symptoms worse. As reforms take root, however, the history of punishing mental illness demands that we ask whether there are adequate alternatives in place to resist the new and unimagined forms of punishment that might develop in the next round of trans-institutionalization.

Note

1   Pepper spray is a 'lachrymatory agent', or tear gas, specifically designed to burn the eyes and cause temporary blindness. The name 'pepper spray' helps to cloak abuses of authority by making tear gas sound like a condiment. Its widespread use in confined spaces and on people who, like Joseph Duran, rely on tracheal tubes to breathe, is the subject of increasing scrutiny.

References

American Civil Liberties Union 2014, *Stop solitary—state-specific resources*, American Civil Liberties Union. Available from: <https://www.aclu.org/prisoners-rights/stop-solitary-state-specific-resources>. [11 Jaunary 2015].

Arrigo, BA, Bersot, HY & Sellers, BG 2011, 'Inmate mental health, solitary confinement, and cruel and unusual punishment', in *The ethics of total confinement: a critique of madness, citizenship, and social justice*, Oxford University Press, New York, pp. 60–92.

Banda, SP 2013, 'Tom Clements dead: Colorado Department of Corrections chief shot at home, gunman on the road', *Huffington Post* 20 March. Available from: <http://www.huffingtonpost.com/2013/03/20/tom-clements-dead-colorado_n_2914314.html>. [11 January 2015].

California Department of Corrections and Rehabilitation (CDCR) Psychologist 1. Interviewed by Reiter, K. 19 May 2010. Notes on file with KR.

CDCR Psychologist 2. Interviewed by Reiter, K. 27 Jul. 2010. Notes on file with KR.

CDCR Psychologist 3. Interviewed by Reiter, K. 9 Aug. 2010. Notes on file with KR.

CDCR Psychologist 4. Interviewed by Reiter, K. 19 Aug. 2010. Notes on file with KR.

CDCR Psychologist 5. Interviewed by Reiter, K. 29 Aug. 2010. Notes on file with KR.

CDCR Psychologist 6. Interviewed by Reiter, K. 3 Sept. 2010. Notes on file with KR.

Coleman v. Brown 2013, No. NO. CIV. S-90-520 LKK/JFM (PC) (E.D. Cal., Judge Lawrence Karlton). Order, 15 April.

Coleman v. Brown 2014, Order, 10 April.

Coleman v. Brown 2014, California Department of Corrections and Rehabilitation Report on Compliance with Sections 2(b) and 2(e) of the Court's April 10, 2014 Order, 29 August.

Correctional Association of New York 2008, *States that provide mental health alternatives to solitary confinement*, Correctional Association of New York. Available from: <http://www.correctionalassociation.org/wpcontent/uploads/2012/05/Out_of_State_Models.pdf>. [11 January 2015].

Dolan, J 2010, 'California prisons' use of cages questioned', *Los Angeles Times*, Dec. 29.

Earley, P 2006, *Crazy: a father's search through America's mental health madness*, G.P. Putnam Sons, New York.

Ford, D 2013, 'Colorado Governor: shooting suspect Evan Ebel had bad streak', *CNN*, 27 March. Available from: <http://www.cnn.com/2013/03/26/us/evan-ebel-profile/>. [11 January 2015].

Gibbons, JJ & Katzenbach, ND 2006, 'Confronting confinement: a report of the Commission on Safety and Abuse in America's prisons', *Washington University Journal of Law and Policy*, vol. 22, pp. 385–562.

Gilligan, J 2001, 'The last mental hospital', *Psychiatric Quarterly*, vol. 72.1, pp. 45–61.

Glidden, B & Rovner, L 2013, 'Requiring the state to justify supermax confinement for mentally ill prisoners: a disability discrimination approach', *Denver University Law Review*, vol. 90, pp. 55–75.

Grassian S 2006, 'Psychiatric effects of solitary confinement', *Washington Journal of Law & Social Policy*, vol. 22, pp. 325–383.

Grassian S 2010. "'Fatal flaws' in the Colorado Solitary Confinement Study." *Solitary Watch: News from a nation in lockdown*, 15 November. Available at: <http://solitarywatch.com/ 2010/11/15/fatal-flaws-in-the-colorado-solitary-confinement -study/>. [11 January 2015].

Greene, S 2013, 'Evan Ebel suicide note shows parolee was 'ruined' by solitary, bent on revenge: Troy Anderson, friend of Ebel', *Huffington Post* (originally *The Colorado Independent*), 11 April. Available from: <http://www.huffingtonpost .com/2013/04/11/ evan-ebel-friend-suicide-_n_3062371.html>. [11 January 2015].

Grob, GN 1987, 'The forging of mental health policy in America: World War II to new Frontier', *The Journal of the History of Medicine and Allied Sciences*, vol. 42, pp. 410–46.

Gurman, S 2014, 'Evan Ebel forced pizza driver to make recording before his murder', *Denver Post* Feb. 10. Available at: http://www.denverpost.com/news/ ci_25106855/evan-ebel-forced-pizza-driver-make-recording-before [25 June 2015].

Hafemeister, TL & George, J 2012, 'The ninth circle of hell: an eighth amendment analysis of imposing prolonged supermax solitary confinement on inmates with a mental illness', *Denver University Law Review*, vol. 90.1, pp. 1–54.

Haney, C 2003, 'Mental health issues in long-term solitary and "supermax" confinement', *Crime and Delinquency*, vol. 49.1, pp. 124–156.

Haney, C & Lynch, M 1997, 'Regulating prisons of the future: a psychological analysis of supermax and solitary confinement', *New York University Review of Law and Social Change*, vol. 23.4, pp. 477–570.

Harcourt, BE 2011, 'Reducing mass incarceration: lessons from the deinstitutionalization of mental hospitals in the 1960s', *Ohio State Journal of Criminal Law*, vol. 9, pp. 53–88.

International Centre for Prison Studies 2014, *Highest to lowest prison population total* (updated monthly), International Centre for Prison Studies. Available from: <http://www.prisonstudies.org/highest-to-lowest/prison-population-total?field _region_taxonomy_tid=All>. [11 January 2015].

James, DJ & Glaze LE 2006, *Mental health problems of prison and jail inmates* (NCJ 213600), US Department of Justice, Office of Justice Programs, Bureau of Justice Statistics. Available from: <http://www.bjs.gov/content/pub/pdf/mhppji.pdf>. [11 January 2015].

King, RD 2007, 'The effects of supermax custody', in *The effects of imprisonment*, eds A Liebling & S Maruna, Willan Publishing, London, pp. 118–142.

Kupers, T 1999, *Prison madness: the mental health crisis behind bars and what we must do about it*, Jossey-Bass, San Francisco.

Kupers, T 2008, 'What to do with survivors? Coping with the long term effects of isolate confinement', *Criminal Justice and Behavior*, vol. 35.8, pp. 1005–16.

Lovell, D 2008, 'Patterns of disturbed behavior in a supermax population', *Criminal Justice and Behavior*, vol. 35.8, pp. 985–1004.

Madrid v. Gomez, 889 F. Supp. 1146 (N.D. Cal. 1995).

Mears, DP 2006, *Evaluating the effectiveness of supermax prisons*, US Department of Justice. Washington, DC.

Morain, D & Hurst, J 1991, 'Officials seek answers in heat-wave deaths of 3 prison inmates: medication: the men were all using mind-altering drugs known to raise body temperatures', *Los Angeles Times*, 6 July. Available from: <http://articles .latimes.com/ 1991-07-06/news/mn-1565_1_heat-waves>. [11 January 2015].

Naday, A, Freilich, JD & Mellow, J 2008, 'The elusive data on supermax confinement', *The Prison Journal*, vol. 88.1, pp. 69–92.

National Alliance on Mental Illness 2014, *Solitary confinement fact sheet*, National Alliance on Mental Illness. Available from: <http://www.nami.org/Template .cfm?Section=Issue_Spotlights&Template=/ContentManagement/ContentDisplay .cfm&ContentID=147299>. [11 January 2015].

National Council for Behavioral Health 2014, *Community mental health act*, National Council for Behavioral Health. Available at: <http://www.thenational council.org/about/national-mental-health-association/overview/community -mental-health-act/>. [11 January 2015].

O'Keefe, ML, Klebe, KJ, Stucker, A, Sturm, K & Leggett, W 2011, *One year longitudinal study of the psychological effects of administrative segregation* (Document No. 232973). Available from: <www.ncjrs.gov/pdffiles1/nij/grants/232973.pdf>. [11 January 2015].

Pearson, J 2014, 'AP exclusive: inmate died after 7 days in NYC cell', *The Big Story* 22 May. Available from: <http://bigstory.ap.org/article/ap-exclusive-inmate-died -after-7-days-nyc-cell>. [11 January 2015].

Perez, TE (Assistant Attorney General) & Hickton, DJ (United States Attorney) 2013. *Letter to Governor Tom Corbett re: investigation of the State Correctional Institution at Cresson and notice of expanded investigation*, US Department of Justice 31 May.

Raphael, S & Stoll, MA 2013, 'Assessing the Contribution of the Deinstitutionalization of the Mentally Ill to Growth in the U.S. Incarceration Rate', *The Journal of Legal Studies*, vol 42.1, pp. 187–222.

Reiter, K 2012, 'Parole, snitch or die: California's supermax prisons and prisoners, 1997–2007', *Punishment & Society*, vol. 14.5, pp. 530–63.

Rhodes, LA 2004, *Total confinement: madness and reason in the maximum security prison*, University of California Press, Berkeley.

Riveland, C 1999, *Supermax prisons: overview and general considerations*, US Department of Justice, National Institute of Corrections. Available at: <http://www .nicic.org/pubs/1999/ 014937.pdf>. [11 January 2015].

Schulte, G 2014, 'Jenkins case prompts review of Nebraska prisons', *The Kansas City Star* 16 May. Available from: <http://www.kansascity.com/2014/05/16/5028828/ jenkins-case-prompts-review-of.html>. [11 January 2015].

Simon, J 2014, *Mass incarceration on trial: a remarkable court decision and the future of prisons in America*, The New Press, New York.

Small, J 2011, 'Under scrutiny, Pelican Bay prison officials say they target only gang leaders', *89.3 KPCC Southern California Public Radio* 23 August.

St. John, P 2014, 'California proposes isolation units for mentally ill inmates', *Los Angeles Times* 29 Aug. Available from: <http://www.latimes.com/local/political/

la-me-ff-california-prison-system-creates-isolation-cells-for-the-mentally-ill
-20140829-story.html>. [11 January 2015].

Stanton, S & Walsh, D 2014, 'Was it suicide? Questions abound in death of pepper-
sprayed inmate', *Sacramento Bee* 21 January (modified 11 April). Available from:
<http://www.sacbee.com/2014/01/21/6090955/was-it-suicide-questions-abound
.html>. [11 January 2015].

Thompson, D 2014, 'California's mentally ill inmates are treated unconstitution-
ally, judge rules', *Huffington Post* 10 April. Available from: <http://www.huffing
tonpost.com/2014/04/10/california-mentally-ill-inmates_n_5129376.html>.
[11 January 2015].

Torrey, EF 1990, *Care of the seriously mentally ill: a rating of state programs*. Public
City Health Research Group, Washington, DC.

Torrey, EF, Kennard, AD, Eslinger, D, Lamb, R & Pavle, J 2010, *More mentally ill
persons are in jails and prisons than hospitals: a survey of the states*, Treatment
Advocacy Center & National Sheriff's Association. Available at: <http://www
.treatmentadvocacycenter.org/ storage/documents/final_jails_v_hospitals_study
.pdf>. [11 January 2015].

Zimring, F 2010, 'The scale of imprisonment in the United States: twentieth century patterns and twenty-first century prospects', *British Journal of Criminology*,
vol. 100.3, pp. 1225–1245.

10
Between Protection and Punishment: The Irregular Arrival Regime in Canadian Refugee Law

Efrat Arbel, University of British Columbia

The Stanstead border crossing dividing Québec from Vermont is not a typical border crossing point. One would expect to find a wall, a fence, or a checkpoint station to mark the international boundary line. Instead, a simple white line is painted on the concrete bearing the inscription 'Canada' and 'United States' on either side. A row of flowerpots sits atop that white line, dividing one country from another. East of the white line is the Stanstead library, constructed deliberately astride the border, with the front door located in the United States and the collection in Canada. One floor above, the Haskell Opera House stages productions that traverse the border: the cast performs on Canadian soil while the audience sits in the United States. Described by the *New York Times* as a 'symbol of cross-border friendship' (Austen 2007), the Stanstead border crossing presents the Canadian border as many imagine it: open, welcoming, and lined with flowers. This ideal is not simply imagined, but also finds expression in law. For example, in the landmark 1985 decision *Singh v. Canada,* the Supreme Court of Canada ruled that every person who is physically present at or within Canada's borders, including refugee claimants, is legally entitled to basic constitutional protection under section 7 of the *Canadian Charter of Rights and Freedoms*. With this decision, the Court effectively enacted the Canadian border as a site of limited, but nonetheless meaningful, rights protection for refugee claimants.[1]

While this ruling remains intact, the legal and symbolic landscape of the Canadian border has shifted in recent years. With the steady movement toward the securitization of borders in the aftermath of the 11 September 2001 attacks, and the concurrent expansion of Canada's anti-refugee agenda, the Canadian border has been re-charted, re-enacted, and re-constituted as a 'smart' border: a border that is asserted differently 'in relation to different groups of border crossers' (Weber 2006, p. 23). The flowerpots and apparent openness of the Canadian border belie the reality that, for many refugee claimants, the Canadian border is no longer enacted as a site of rights protection, but is increasingly becoming a site of restriction, exclusion, and punishment. This chapter questions the Canadian border's reconstitution as a site of punishment for refugee claimants by examining the Designated Foreign National (DFN) regime, a highly criticized mechanism that permits the Canadian government to discipline foreign nationals for suspected violations of Canadian border laws. Implemented as an anti-smuggling mechanism, the DFN regime empowers the Minister of Public Safety to designate groups of foreign nationals as 'irregular' based on vague and discretionary criteria, including a mere suspicion—not concrete proof—that they were involved in human smuggling activities (Public Safety Canada 2012b). On being deemed 'irregular', designated persons are subject to penalties that are formally classified as administrative but amount to de facto punishment. These include mandatory arrest and detention as well as compulsory reporting and ongoing document inspection. Since implementing the DFN regime in 2012, the Canadian government has directed its application toward 85 refugee claimants, all of whom were suspected of having been smuggled into Canada at Stanstead (CBSA 2014b; Cohen 2012).

When the DFN regime was first introduced, then Minister of Citizenship and Immigration Jason Kenney explained that it was designed as a deterrence mechanism implemented, in part, to address the asserted ineffectiveness of the Canada-US *Safe Third Country Agreement* (STCA), a bilateral agreement between Canada and the United States that restricts asylum flows across the Canada–US border.[2] In this chapter, I analyze the DFN regime in relation to STCA to explore the links between these two measures in detail. My analysis revisits data collected for *Bordering on Failure: Canada–US Border Policy and the Politics of Refugee Exclusion*, a report I co-authored with Alletta Brenner, published by the Harvard Immigration and Refugee Law Clinical Program in 2013. For this report, we examined a series of Canadian and US border measures and analyzed their impact upon refugees, focusing specifically on the STCA. We conducted fact-finding investigations at four ports of entry along the Canada–US border: Buffalo, New York–Fort Erie, Ontario; Champlain, New York–Lacolle, Québec; Detroit, Michigan–Windsor, Ontario; and Blaine, Washington–White Rock, British Columbia. We met with refugee shelters, non-governmental organizations, attorneys, and faith group workers on both sides of the Canada–US border and collected data about the STCA and its application. We requested interviews with various Canadian government officials, including representatives from the Canada Border Services Agency and Citizenship and Immigration Canada. Both agencies declined to participate in an interview.

Our study concluded that, through the STCA and other associated border measures, Canada systematically closes its borders to refugee claimants. We further concluded that since the STCA only applies to refugee claimants at the land border (STCA Art. 4), but does not bar claimants who cross the border clandestinely, it creates clear incentives for irregular entries and has in fact triggered a rise in irregular border crossings and human smuggling into Canada (Arbel & Brenner 2013). In so doing, the STCA contributes to what Audrey Macklin has termed the 'discursive disappearance of the refugee'—the broader process through which legal measures and popular conjectures recast refugees not as legitimate entrants in search of protection but as 'illegals', irregular arrivals, and criminal transgressors (2005). Building on Macklin's claim, I argue the STCA not only closes the Canadian border to refugee claimants, as we concluded in *Bordering on Failure*, it also reconstitutes those claimants through discourses of criminality and illegality, and thus plays a key role in producing the very 'irregularity' that the DFN regime is designed to punish. Proceeding from this claim, I argue that the DFN regime is premised on a legal and conceptual flaw: it presumes 'irregularity' to be an essential subject position that reflects a transgression of Canadian border laws when, in fact, it is a constitutive subject position produced by the laws. By punishing refugee claimants for being deemed irregular the DFN regime does more than enhance Canada's ability to subject refugee claimants to punitive measures like arrest and detention. The regime introduces a far more extreme form of punishment into Canadian refugee law: it effectively empowers the government to punish refugee claimants for trying to avail themselves of the right to seek asylum in Canada.

This chapter begins with an overview of the DFN regime. While the regime applies broadly to all foreign nationals, I focus only on its application to refugee claimants, guided by Catherine Dauvergne's insight that the 'criminalization' of migration 'bite[s] most sharply at the asylum end of the immigration continuum' and thus deserves specific attention (2013a, p. 78). I then proceed to examine the DFN regime against the law and practice of Canadian border enforcement, directing my attention specifically to the STCA. Reviewing the data collected for *Bordering on Failure,* I analyze the STCA by focusing on the discretionary practices of front-line officials tasked with its application. This analysis is guided by Alison Mountz's observation that a state's migration policies are best understood by examining the practices of those who 'produce its borders daily' (2010, p. xix). By focusing on these daily practices, I seek to 'pry open the black box of the border' (Pratt 2005, p. 11), to examine the administrative operation of the STCA and to tease out the links between the STCA and the DFN regime. After analyzing these links in detail, I conclude by highlighting the coercive effects of scripting 'irregularity' as a constitutive subject position into Canadian law, and by explaining what the DFN reveals about the changing role—and location—of punishment in Canada's refugee system.

Legislating irregularity

The Designated Foreign National regime was one of several reform initiatives ushered in by the Canadian government in 2012 through omnibus legislation known as the *Protecting Canada's Immigration System Act.* Introduced after the high-profile arrival of two asylum boats carrying 575 refugee claimants in 2009 and 2010—incidents depicted as revealing Canada's porous borders and its vulnerability to human smuggling[3]—the DFN regime was ostensibly intended to serve as an anti-smuggling strategy. Implemented as a public safety measure, the regime was devised to send 'a clear message to criminal organizations contemplating human smuggling ventures that Canada will take strong, targeted action to prevent abuse of our generous immigration and asylum systems' (Public Safety Canada 2012b), and to deliver 'the message around the world that Canada will no longer be the world's doormat' (Kenney 2011).

As noted briefly above, the DFN regime empowers the Minister of Public Safety to 'designate as irregular arrival' groups of foreign nationals whose identity cannot be verified or who are suspected of having been smuggled into Canada (Immigration and Refugee Protection Act [IRPA], s. 20.1(1)).[4] Importing criminal law tactics, practices, and rhetoric into migration law (Stumpf 2006; Dauvergne 2008; Bosworth & Kaufman 2011; see also Lynch in this volume), the regime mandates that all designated persons aged 16 and over be arrested and detained, with no right of appeal (IRPA, ss. 55(3.1); s.57.1). Those under the age of 16 can elect between two de facto forms of punishment: be held in detention or be separated from their parents and placed under the care of the state (House of Commons Debates 2012, pp. 1100, 1540, 1605;

Bond 2014, pp. 17–18).[5] The regime requires that all designated persons be detained for a minimum period of two weeks but empowers the minister to extend detention orders by six-month increments (IRPA, s. 57.1(2)). Since the IRPA does not impose clear legislative maximums on detention orders, designated persons may in theory be detained indefinitely (IRPA, s. 56(2)).[6] The regime allows designated persons to make refugee claims while detained; however, with limited access to legal assistance and community support, the prospects of advancing successful refugee claims from detention are significantly diminished. Claimants who are denied refugee status cannot appeal negative decisions and are subject to immediate removal (IRPA, s. 110(2)(a)).

While the DFN laws are formally classified as administrative, they enforce a punitive regime of de facto punishment. Upon their arrest, designated persons are typically held in dedicated detention facilities with razor wire fences, surveillance cameras, and guards. They may also be held in provincial jails with the criminal population. A recent Canadian Red Cross (2012–13) report pointing to serious shortcomings in immigration detention practices—including overcrowding and triple-bunked cells, frequent use of restraints, co-mingling with criminal populations, inadequate mental health care, inadequate access to counsel, family separation, barriers to outside family contact, and lack of support for detained children—raises concerns about the conditions designated persons could be forced to endure. The punitive nature of the DFN regime does not end with detention. Rather, the regime imposes restrictions on designated persons for five additional years after they are granted refugee status. During this time, they cannot apply for permanent residency, temporary residency, or stay in Canada on humanitarian and compassionate grounds (IRPA, s.11(1.1), 24(5), 25(1.01)). They also cannot obtain travel documents, leave the state, or sponsor family, and for these purposes are deemed not to be 'lawfully present in Canada' (IRPA, s.31.1), a legal status marked by a specter of illegality and transgression. Designated individuals may also be subject to ongoing reporting obligations and document inspection during this time (IRPA, s. 98.1). In sum, even absent a principled justification, designated persons are subject to significant restriction for five years after securing refugee status: their irregularity remains with them notwithstanding that they have 'regularized' their status as required by Canadian law.

The DFN regime also borrows heavily from the language of criminality and crime control. The regime does not require proof of criminal wrongdoing, but, in 'both legal approaches and public imagination' (Dauvergne 2004, p. 601), it depicts designated persons as dangerous subjects to be feared and contained. On its website, for example, Citizenship and Immigration Canada (CIC) outlines an overview of the DFN regime under the heading 'Protecting Our Streets and Communities from Criminal and National Security Threats' (CIC 2012). The website explains that the DFN regime is targeted at 'possible human smugglers and traffickers, terrorists, or individuals who have committed crimes against humanity', and does not mention its application to refugee claimants (CIC 2012). Blurring lines between smuggler, smuggled, trafficker, and terrorist, CIC casts designated persons as criminal wrongdoers determined to 'abuse our generosity and take advantage of our country' (CIC 2012). Deploying the rhetoric of threat and risk, the website further explains that releasing designated persons into Canadian communities would pose an 'unacceptable risk' to the public (CIC 2012). As a result, CIC continues, it is 'essential that government authorities have the ability to detain, to impose conditions of release, and to remove those who are inadmissible to Canada' (CIC 2012). By raising the specter of danger and implied vulnerability, such depictions engender popular hostility toward designated persons. Akin to the freelance immigration-enforcement process Mona Lynch (this volume) identifies in Maricopa Country, Arizona, these representations imbue designated persons with criminal risk by virtue of their status and deem them as criminal without requiring proof of criminal activity. Also writing of the US context, Brett Story calls these practices de facto criminalization, defined as the 'cumulative effect not just of a political discourse devoted to the amalgamation of migration, illegality, and criminality, but of practices of immigration and asylum authorities, law enforcement officials, and state legislators' (2005, p. 3). Such statements encourage the perception that designated persons 'occupy the same societal role of essentialized threat as "criminals"' (Story 2005, p. 3).

The DFN regime grants the minister unprecedented power to designate any group of foreign nationals as 'irregular' based on elusive and arbitrary criteria like administrative convenience or a reasonable suspicion of human smuggling (IRPA s. 20.1). The legislation's broad language also permits designation by association and fails to differentiate between those who orchestrate, and those who are the subject of, human smuggling operations or other criminal enterprises (IRPA s. 20.1). Moreover, since the legislative scheme already contains provisions that make it an offence to knowingly or recklessly organize, induce, aid, or abet human smuggling operations (IRPA s. 117(1)), the DFN regime does little to enhance the government's ability to target global human smuggling syndicates, or 'protect the safety and security of the Canadian public', as its ministers proclaim (Public Safety Canada 2012a). Instead, the regime functions more as a tool of enhanced border control, expanding the government's authority not only to penalize smugglers, but also to contain and discipline the smuggled. Like other mechanisms surveyed in this volume, the DFN regime operates as 'one among an arsenal of strategies of border control that draw on familiar penal technologies, imaginaries, and practices' (Bosworth & Turnbull in this volume) to restrict access to Canadian rights protection. To the extent that it functions as a tool of border control, the DFN regime is best analyzed against the law and practice of Canadian border enforcement.

Producing irregularity

Canada manages its borders through a complex matrix of territorial and extraterritorial instruments and measures. Underpinning these measures is the Multiple Borders Strategy, devised by the Canada Border Services Agency (CBSA) to rechart the Canadian border for the purposes of enhanced enforcement. The strategy's stated goal is to 'push the border out'—outside the geographic boundaries of the state—to allow Canada to 'identify and intercept illegal and undesirable travellers as far away from North America as possible' (CBSA 2009; CIC 2003a). To advance this goal, the strategy redefines the border as 'any point at which the identity of the traveler can be verified' (CIC 2003a, p. 8). It also deterritorializes the border, viewing it 'not as a geo-political line but rather a continuum of checkpoints along a route of travel from the country of origin to Canada or the United States' (CIC 2003b). The CBSA charts the Multiple Borders Strategy through a series of eight concentric circles. Each circle marks a different borderline, extending from the land border outward to various offshore locations in the high seas and outside state soil. These borderlines include the land border, airport/seaport arrival areas, points of final embarkation, transit areas, points of initial embarkation, airline check-in points, visa screen points, and countries of origin (CBSA 2009b). The Multiple Borders Strategy thus (re)imagines and enacts the Canadian border as multiple, moving lines that can be selectively positioned in various locations at once.

Through the Multiple Border Strategy, Canada shifts its border outward to prevent improperly documented migrants, including refugee claimants, from reaching Canada's territorial frontiers. As Ayelet Shachar explains, by shifting the border of immigration regulation in this way, states transform their borders into 'something more malleable and movable, which can be placed and replaced—by the words of law—in whatever location that best suits the goals of restricting access' (Shachar 2009; see also Mountz 2010). These legal and geographic manipulations are very significant for refugee claimants, whose eligibility for rights protection in Canada is determined in part by reference to their physical location in relation to the territorial border. By shifting and deterritorializing the border, Canada makes it difficult for many refugee claimants to reach its territorial frontiers and claim the rights protections promised in *Singh*.

At each of these borderlines, Canada has intensified and expanded its use of interdiction measures and other enforcement technologies. Many of these measures are targeted specifically at refugee claimants. For example, Canada positions liaison officers in strategic refugee-producing states around the world and tasks them with blocking improperly documented persons from traveling to Canada, including refugee claimants. This program has proven an effective obstruction mechanism: between 2001 and 2012, for example, liaison officers intercepted over 73,000 persons offshore, many of whom were likely refugees (Arbel & Brenner 2013, p. 34). Offshore interdiction works in tandem with carrier sanctions and visa restrictions to 'den[y] most refugees the opportunity for legal migration' (Morrison & Crossland 2001, p. 28; see also Hathaway 2005). As critics have long recognized, these measures work together to close Canada's borders to refugee claimants such that 'vast numbers of bona fide refugees are being caught up in the web of immigration control with devastating results' (Aiken 1999, p. 6; see also Brouwer & Kumin 2003; Crépeau & Nakache 2006).

Offshore interdiction measures, visa restrictions, and carrier sanctions all 'push the border out' in similar ways: they relocate the site of Canadian border enforcement offshore to broaden Canada's discretionary powers in its treatment of refugee claimants and make it easier for Canada to circumvent its legal duties and refugee protection obligations under domestic and international law. As Macklin explains, 'Since asylum seekers' entitlement to claim refugee status is triggered by reaching the frontier of the asylum state, if the border is no longer the border, the state can deny responsibility for entertaining the refugee claim' (2005, p. 369). Reminiscent of other post-9/11 measures that move the physical bodies of detainees offshore to permit states greater leeway in circumventing domestic or international law, these measures instead move the Canadian border offshore, but to achieve the same end (see Koenig in this volume). With the expansion and intensification of these measures, more and more refugee claimants are blocked from reaching Canada by water or air.

Refugee claimants who enter Canada by land face additional barriers to securing legal entry. Those who make a refugee claim at the land border are subject to the Safe Third Country Agreement (STCA), discussed briefly above. The STCA blocks refugee claimants who are in the United States, or traveling through the United States, from making refugee claims at the Canadian border (and vice versa) subject to certain exceptions (STCA, art. 4(1)). While the STCA was not implemented under the rubric of the Multiple Borders Strategy, it follows a similar logic: it determines an asylum seeker's eligibility to enter Canada when she first sets foot on US soil, long before she presents at or even approaches the Canadian border (Arbel 2013). Unless she fits within one of the STCA's exceptions, the fact that she first entered the United States fixes her migration status and disallows her from lawfully making a refugee claim at the Canadian land border. Notwithstanding that the STCA is applied *at* Canada's geographic border, it nonetheless 'pushes the border out' by relocating the site of border enforcement outside Canada's territorial frontiers. Like offshore interdiction, visa restrictions, and carrier sanctions, the STCA enacts the Canadian border as a moving, malleable barrier that can be selectively positioned both within and outside state soil to restrict access to asylum.

The goal of restricting access to asylum was forefront in Canada's mind when implementing the STCA, though this was not initially acknowledged or disclosed. Several years after the STCA, Canada and the United States acknowledged that '[w]hile the primary focus for the United States was security, Canada sought to limit the significant irregular northbound movement of people from the United States who wished to access the Canadian refugee determination system' (US Customs and Border Patrol et al. 2010).[7] Indeed, the STCA ushered in what one US advocate described as a 'crisis on the border' (Vermont Immigration and Asylum Advocates [VIAA] 2012, interview, 10 August), triggering a precipitous drop in the number of refugee claims lodged at the Canadian border, as noted in Table 10.1.

As the figures in Table 10.1 show, the STCA prompted a steady decline in numbers, save 2007–09, when its 'moratorium country' exception was still in effect. This exception permitted entry to refugee claimants from countries on which Canada had imposed a temporary suspension of removals, on the rationale that refugee claims from these countries are often both compelling and urgent. This exception was repealed in July 2009, in part to 'reduce pressures on, and costs to, the refugee protection system' (Canada Gazette 2009, p. 1471).

Table 10.1 Refugee Claims at Canadian Border Before and After Safe Third Country Agreement*

| | Pre-STCA Refugee Claims | | Post-STCA Refugee Claims |
Year	Made at the Border	Year	Made at the Border
1995	7,545	2005	4,041
1996	6,792	2006	4,478
1997	6,000	2007	8,191
1998	6,224	2008	10,802
1999	9,556	2009	6,295
2000	13,270	2010	4,642
2001	14,007	2011	2,563
2002	10,856	2012	3,989
2003	10,938	2013	2,986
2004	8,904	2014	3,636

*Statistics from 2014 cited in CBSA 2015, and are current to 22 December 2014. Statistics from 2012–13 cited in CBSA 2014a. Statistics from 2001–12 cited in CBSA 2012. Statistics from 1997–2001 cited in Canadian Council for Refugees 2005.

The government's decision to remove the moratorium country exception from the STCA was acutely felt. Describing the effect of this change, one US attorney general interviewed for this study remarked:

> Before they got rid of [the moratorium country exception] for example, July 2008, we had 72 people, Freedom House had 72 people cross the border into Canada. And a lot of those people were from those countries. More recently since they got rid of the exception and now basically you are required to have a relative living in Canada, so far we've had 8 people cross the border. So the numbers we are seeing are significantly different given that change (Freedom House 2012, interview, 27 July).

A Canadian refugee-shelter worker explained:

> The number [of refugee claimants received] declined quite sharply when the moratorium country ruling came in... [W]e went from like 400 a month to like 200 a month almost right away. It was a solid 50 percent reduction in volume (Fort Erie Multicultural Centre [Fort Erie] 2012, interview, 25 July).

Pointing to a similar drop in numbers, a Canadian faith worker observed: 'When [refugee claimants] were just free to make an asylum case because they needed protection, definitely, there were many more people coming through' (Casa El Norte (El Norte) 2012, interview, 03 August).

As this statement suggests, the STCA not only blocks refugee claimants at the border, it also marks a shift in Canada's policy toward refugee claimants. With the STCA, claimants are no longer 'just free to make an asylum case because they need protection'. Their eligibility for asylum is instead governed by the exceptions outlined in the agreement.

Since STCA exceptions are the primary means by which refugee claimants can seek asylum at the Canadian border, understanding how these exceptions are evaluated is crucial for a broader understanding of the STCA. The STCA recognizes four exceptions, permitting entry to refugee claimants who have a family member in Canada, have the requisite documentation, enter as unaccompanied minors, or can demonstrate that their admission into Canada is in the public interest (STCA, art. 4(2)(a)-(d), art.6).[8] The family member exception is the most frequently used (Arbel & Brenner 2013, p. 91). The exception requires a claimant to demonstrate that he or she has a spouse or common-law partner, child, parent, legal guardian, sibling, grandparent, grandchild, aunt, uncle, niece, or nephew in Canada (STCA, 4(2)(a)-(b); 1(b)).[9] The burden of proof is on the claimant, though Canadian border officers are instructed to make reasonable efforts to confirm family relationships and to accept credible testimony and sworn statements from relatives where documentary evidence or computer records are not available (CIC 2002, p. 63; Canadian Council for Refugees & Sojourn House 2010, p. 25). Moreover, when the STCA was first implemented, Canadian officials stated they would take a generous and liberal approach to the family member exception and would not insist on documents to prove family relationships (Canadian Council for Refugees & Sojourn House 2010, p. 25).

Interview data collected along the border suggests that despite commitments to the contrary, front-line officials are generally inflexible and inconsistent in assessing family relationships (Vive La Casa (Vive) 2012, interview, 27 July; Freedom House 2012, interview, 27 July; El Norte 2012, interview, 03 August). The data collected in *Bordering on Failure* suggests a lack of uniform procedure at the border and significant disparities in the practices of front-line officials. The assessments are largely subjective and vary between officers and ports of entry. As one US attorney explained: 'The Canadian officials do have a lot of discretion…they can decide at any point that they don't believe the person or there is something not quite right and just return them to the US' (Freedom House 2012, interview, 27 July). Another US attorney remarked:

> You've got some officers up there who are relatively sympathetic and understanding and humane and you've got others that think they're

protecting the border from Osama Bin Laden... You have the whole gambit. I tell refugees when I'm talking with them that to a certain extent it's a crapshoot... As far as I can tell, it's entirely subjective (Vive 2012, interview, 27 July).

These accounts are further supported by a 2010 study about the experiences of refugee claimants at port-of-entry interviews, conducted by the Canadian Council for Refugees and Sojourn House. That study found significant inconsistencies between border agents in evaluating the family member exception to the STCA, observed a pattern of 'unreasonable and inconsistent assessments of family relationships', and concluded that this pattern had 'in some cases undermined the fair application of the family member exception' (2010, pp. 3, 23–25). These findings suggest that despite assurances to the contrary, refugee claimants are at risk of being blocked at the Canadian border for arbitrary or unprincipled reasons.

Data collected along the border further suggests that despite recommendations to the contrary in the operations manual, Canadian officials often demand original documents to prove familial relationships. One US attorney noted, 'The Canadians are really big on documents. They like to see an original birth certificate and original photo ID, or passport preferably or a country ID from the individual coming into Canada' (Vive 2012, interview, 27 July). Another Canadian faith worker remarked that while Canadian border officials would sometimes accept photocopied documents in the past, 'now they're getting much more strict. They're insisting on original documents' (El Norte 2012, interview, 03 August). Due to the difficulties asylum seekers face in securing official documents, many may be unfairly prejudiced by this requirement. In some cases, even the presentation of several original documents, as well as testimony from family members, proved insufficient (El Norte 2012, interview, 03 August; VIAA 2012, interview, 10 August).

The tendency toward inflexibility in assessing family relationships is well illustrated by the case of *Cishahayo v. Canada* (2012 FC 1237). Mr. Cishahayo, applicant in this case, fled Burundi to seek asylum in Canada. He left Burundi in November 2011 by plane and landed in Washington, DC. He made a refugee claim at the Canadian border 12 days later and sought admission under the STCA's family member exception (*Cishahayo v. Canada,* paras. 1–3; VIAA 2012, interview, 10 August). Mr. Cishahayo had two sisters in Canada, one of whom was a Canadian citizen and the other a Convention refugee. He presented several original identity documents at the border, in apparent compliance with the STCA: his passport, national identification card, and health insurance card (VIAA 2012, interview, 10 August). The CBSA officer tasked with reviewing his file interviewed him in person and also interviewed his Canadian citizen sister over the telephone to confirm the relationship. The CBSA officer assessing Mr. Cishahayo's claim doubted the authenticity of his documents and returned him to the United States where he was detained in Clinton County Jail (VIAA, para. 62). When Mr. Cishahayo requested that the refusal be reconsidered, he provided six additional identity documents to supplement his claim: a birth certificate, proof of residence, marriage certificate, baptismal certificate, and copy of the biographic page of a previous Burundian passport. The CBSA officer assessing his claim again denied his application, on grounds that the new documents 'did not bring any new information to light' (*Cishahayo v. Canada*, para. 8). Eventually, with legal assistance on both sides of the border, Mr. Cishahayo appealed his negative eligibility decision before the Federal Court of Canada. The Court heard his case in October 2012, allowed his claim, and sent his case back for redetermination by a different CBSA officer (para. 26). Mr. Cishahayo's case points to the broad discretionary powers of front-line officials and highlights the inflexible application of the STCA's family member exception at certain border crossings.

In addition to inflexible and inconsistent standards for assessing the STCA's exceptions, the data collected for *Bordering on Failure* also points to a growing culture of hostility toward refugee claimants along the Canadian border. Advocates, attorneys, and NGO workers on both sides of the border described the current climate as one of disbelief, suspicion, and antagonism, wherein Canadian officials routinely dismiss and demean refugee claimants. As one US advocate described: 'I saw a huge shift...before it was an attitude of kindness and we're obligated as a country to accept refugees... After 9/11, people were being...some were called cockroaches. You know, just horrible' (VIAA 2012, interview, 10 August). A Canadian faith worker observed a similar pattern, noting that with some exceptions, Canadian officers have become 'much more strict' and tend to be 'very insensitive', such that increasingly, 'people are treated as if they're criminals before they're found guilty. Even people that just come in regularly' (El Norte 2012, interview, 03 August).

The inconsistent application of the STCA's exceptions, as well as the hostility of front-line officials, raise concerns about whether the STCA is being properly applied at the Canadian border. This pattern resonates with the questions posed by Nadya Pittendrigh's (this volume) treatment of US supermaxes, as to whether law enforcers interpret people as deserving or undeserving of protection based on criteria that have little to do with their legal status or need (see also Hannah-Moffat & Klassen and Reiter & Blair in this volume, discussing arbitrary decisions about whether the mentally ill are treated or punished for their acts). The pattern further suggests that the lines between protection and punishment are increasingly being blurred at the Canadian border, sometimes for arbitrary or unprincipled reasons. For many, seeking asylum at the Canadian border is not a matter of law so much as a matter of luck: 'a crapshoot' (Fort Erie 2012, interview, 25 July; Vive 2012, interview, 27 July).

Reproducing irregularity

These accounts tell only part of the story of the STCA. Insofar as the STCA only applies to refugee claimants at the land border (STCA, Art. 4), but does not bar claimants who cross the border clandestinely, it creates clear incentives for irregular entries.[10] Well before the STCA came into effect, critics cautioned that its implementation would prompt both irregular migration and human smuggling. In the course of parliamentary hearings before the Standing Committee on Citizenship and Immigration Canada in 2004, for example, UNHCR warned that '[a]sylum seekers who know they can no longer seek admission at the border...may very well engage the services of smugglers to take them across the border illegally in order to make a claim inland' (CIMM 2004, para. 1604). Amnesty International Canada similarly warned that a 'crude instrument' like the STCA 'is going to increase the likelihood that people are going to take dangerous, stupid chances...and cross borders illegally' (CIMM 2004, para. 1715). Writing of the STCA in 2005, Macklin warned that while the agreement 'may initially thwart asylum seekers arriving on the US side of the border... [e]ventually, smugglers will divert asylum seekers who would otherwise present themselves at the Canadian border into a clandestine flow of undocumented migrants crossing the border surreptitiously' (2005, p. 398). Even the Department of Homeland Security acknowledged that the STCA could prompt more unauthorized border crossings. The supplementary information accompanying the US regulations, for example, states clearly that the department is 'aware of the potential for increased smuggling and trafficking after the Agreement is implemented' (Department of Homeland Security, cited in Macklin 2005, p. 398).

And indeed, the data collected for *Bordering on Failure* suggests that since its implementation, the STCA triggered a rise in irregular border crossings and human smuggling into Canada (MOSAIC BC 2012, interview, 16 May; VIAA 2012, interview, 10 August; Vive 2012, interview, 27 July; El Norte 2012, interview, 03 August). Away from official ports of entry, the border is now more disorderly and dangerous, and more refugee claimants are resorting to perilous measures to seek asylum in Canada, sometimes risking their lives doing so (Arbel & Brenner 2013, p. 12). Before the STCA, it was estimated that 90 percent of migrants crossed into Canada at 20 of the 130 ports of entry along the 5,255-mile border (Coderre, cited in Harvard Law Student Advocates for Human Rights 2006). As one Canadian faith worker explained, '[T]here was no reason for irregular entry... It was not the dangerous situations we see now' (El Norte 2012, interview, 03 August). In contrast, after the STCA, practitioners saw a marked increase in unauthorized border crossing. 'It's really common' (MOSAIC BC 2012, interview, 16 May), said one Canadian advocate. Another explained:

> We see more now than ever... People are risking their lives because they don't have an anchor relative. It is their only way to get into Canada. For us, to see someone swim the Niagara river, or take the canoe across the river, they're obviously desperate (El Norte 2012, interview, 03 August).

Statements issued by Canadian and US government agencies support these anecdotal accounts. In 2007, for example, in a bilateral Integrated Border Enforcement Threat Assessment report, Canadian and US agencies concluded that '[m]ore migrants are attempting to find a way around the provisions for the Safe Third Country Agreement, arriving in Canada by air, ferry or illegally between the ports of entry in order to enter refugee claims in Canada inland' (Integrated Border Enforcement Team 2007). In a 2010 evaluation study, the CBSA identified a rise in 'irregular migrants entering Canada between [ports of entry]...to avoid being turned back at the border based on the Safe Third Country Agreement' (CBSA 2010). In a more recent report, Canadian and US agencies recorded a staggering 58 percent increase in Canada-bound human smuggling attempts between ports of entry between 2011 and 2012 (Integrated Border Enforcement Team 2012).

It is against this backdrop that the DFN regime was implemented, and by reference to which it must be understood. Facing this steady rise in irregular migration and human smuggling activities, the Canadian government decided it was high time to crack down on the 'dangerous and despicable crime' of human smuggling (Public Safety Canada 2012b). It did so without examining the links between the human smuggling activities it was steadfastly trying to curb and the restrictive border policies it was all the while enforcing. Examining the DFN regime by reference to the law and practice of Canadian border enforcement, as this chapter has done, helps illuminate the fact that irregular migration does not simply occur in violation of border laws but is, at least partially, produced by them. As Anna Triandafyllidou and Thanos Maroukis convincingly show, migration controls sometimes 'inadvertently foster the migrant smuggling phenomenon and the smuggling "business"' (2012, p. 1; see also Düvell 2011 and Macklin 2005). Indeed, just as exclusionary policies and restrictive border measures converge to 'make people illegal' (Dauvergne 2008), so too do they make people 'irregular'. The STCA serves as a clear example: by prompting a rise in irregular border crossings, it has played a key role in constructing the very problem the DFN regime was designed to address. In doing so, as Macklin rightly cautioned, the STCA has discursively disappeared countless refugee claimants (2005, p. 365). With the STCA, a growing number of claimants have entered Canada not as refugees but as 'irregulars' or smuggled persons. And with the DFN regime, a growing number of these claimants are now at risk of being designated as 'irregular arrivals', and produced not as legitimate entrants entitled to protection, but as transgressors deserving of punishment.

Conclusion

On 5 December 2012, then Canadian Minister of Citizenship and Immigration Jason Kenney announced the first application of the DFN regime at a press conference held at the Stanstead border crossing.[11] Standing by the snow-filled flowerpots, Minister Kenney announced that 85 Romanian nationals, 35 of whom were children, would be designated as 'irregular', arrested, and detained (Public Safety Canada 2012a).[12] According to the Canada Border Services Agency, only 14 of the 85 designated individuals had outstanding theft and fraud criminal charges against them (CBSA 2014b).[13] Since the designation was made, six of the 85 claimants have been declared Convention refugees, while 64 have made refugee claims that are still in process (CBSA 2014b). Notwithstanding that some of these claimants are indeed genuine refugees, all 85 individuals were cast as lawbreakers whose very arrival threatened the 'security and safety of Canadians' (Public Safety Canada 2012b). They were scripted in Canadian law not as refugee claimants who are lawfully entitled to protection, but as dangerous subjects to be captured, contained, and punished.[14]

That Minister Kenney chose to announce this designation in the cold chill of the Stanstead border crossing, some 200 miles away from the national capital, is telling. Quite apart from being the site at which the claimants were suspected of having entered Canada, the announcement gestured a decisive shift: it signaled the Canadian border's reconstitution from a site of hospitality and rights protection for refugee claimants, consistent with the principles outlined in *Singh v Canada*, to a site of restriction, exclusion, and punishment. Indeed, with the DFN regime, it is not just the role of punishment in the Canadian refugee system, but also its location, that has shifted. Punishment is no longer enacted in the confines of the jail or the detention center, but is increasingly being meted out on the Canadian border, reflecting a global pattern whereby state borders are becoming legal and symbolic sites of punishment (Aas & Bosworth 2013; Bowling 2013). Indeed, the DFN regime may be understood as marking the innermost borderline in the Multiple Borders Strategy. Except rather than 'push the border out' like the STCA and Canada's other border measures, the DFN regime pushes the border in: it builds a shifting, fictional border around designated persons and imagines that border as traveling with them into Canada to deem them as 'irregular' even after they cross the geographic boundary line. Their irregularity is both defined and maintained by reference to this imaginary border, in relation to which they are always defined as transgressors.

There are clear dangers in reconstituting the Canadian border as a site of punishment for refugee claimants in this way. These dangers lie not only in the erosion of legal protections available to refugee claimants, or the weakening of the legal instruments designed to guarantee them. They lie rather in providing tacit justification for the Canadian government to produce refugee claimants as 'irregulars' and cast them as criminal transgressors without requiring proof of wrongdoing. By punishing refugee claimants for their deemed 'irregularity'—an irregularity that is itself produced in and by Canadian border law—the DFN regime turns a core principle of Canadian refugee protection on its head. By the letter of the law, the Immigration and Refugee Protection Act (IRPA)—the federal statute governing immigration and refugee matters in Canada—proclaims that Canada's refugee system 'is in the first instance about saving lives and offering protection to the displaced and the persecuted' (IRPA, s.3(2)(a)). While the IRPA also delineates certain offences and penalties (ss.122–128), it prohibits Canada from enforcing these on refugee claimants pending a disposition of their claim (s.133). The logic behind this is simple: as a signatory to the United Nations *Refugee Convention*, Canada must first offer claimants protection, and can only dispense penalty where protection is unwarranted. The DFN regime inverts this logic, thus blurring the lines between protection and punishment in Canadian law. By allowing the government to arrest and detain refugee claimants prior to hearing their claims and absent concrete proof of wrongdoing, the DFN regime first dispenses punishment, and only allows for the possibility of protection as an afterthought. In doing so, the DFN regime effectively punishes refugee claimants for trying to avail themselves of the right to seek asylum in Canada. It does so based on their deemed irregularity, an irregularity that is itself scripted into Canadian law, in part, through the law and practice of Canadian border enforcement.

Notes

1 In *Singh v. Canada*, the Supreme Court of Canada held that refugee claimants present at or within Canada's borders can claim protection under s.7 of the *Charter of Rights and Freedoms*. This principle is grounded in the rationale that a refugee claimant's presence at or within the Canadian border makes him/her amenable to Canadian law and thus also entitles him/her to benefit from its protection. As Catherine Dauvergne illustrates, however, despite its early promise, *Singh* has failed to secure meaningful rights protection for non-citizens under the *Charter* (2013b).

2 In a Global News interview dated 9 December 2012, for example, then Minister of Citizenship and Immigration Jason Kenney drew direct links between the STCA and the DFN regime. While being interviewed about the first DFN designation, made on 5 December 2012, Minister Kenney explained: 'Well, the reason why these folks crashed across the border and didn't stop to register their refugee claim at the port of entry is because they would have been turned back at the port of entry because of this agreement where we say, look, if you were in the States, you come north to seek asylum, you should be seeking protection in the United States.... That's the principle of the law, but by crashing across the border getting inland, they're then exempt from that Safe Third Country Agreement.... So the agreement become [sic] a bit of a paper tiger unfortunately, and that's why we have to find other ways to deter people who are not bonafied [sic] refugees but are trying to abuse our generosity from doing so' (Global News 2012).

3 For an analysis of the unprecedented moral panic triggered by these boat arrivals, see, for example, Neve & Russell (2010).

4 More specifically, s.20.1(b) of the IRPA empowers the Minister of Public Safety to make this designation if he or she 'has reasonable grounds to suspect' that the group entered Canada in contravention of the IRPA through 'association with a criminal organization or terrorist group'.

5 As Jennifer Bond explains, while the regime does not specify what happens to designated persons under the age of 16, several government ministers have indicated that children would either be detained with their parents or taken into custody by the relevant welfare agency (2014, 17–18).

6   The IRPA empowers the Minister of Public Safety to release designated foreign nationals from detention on request by a designated foreign national, but only in exceptional circumstances (s. 58.1(1)), or on the minister's own initiative, where the minister is of the opinion that the reasons for the detention no longer exist (s. 58.1(2)).

7   Notably, since the STCA applies at official ports of entry, and does not prevent asylum seekers from crossing the border clandestinely to lodge asylum claims inland, it is not clear how it would address 'irregular' movements into Canada. This question is not asked or answered in the report.

8   In Canada, the public interest exception has been applied narrowly and extends primarily to refugee claimants facing the death penalty.

9   While Canada recognizes married couples as well as common-law spouses (same sex and opposite sex) for the purposes of the STCA's family member exception, the United States only recognizes opposite-sex married couples.

10 The STCA does not apply to asylum seekers entering Canada by air or water. It can apply at airports, but only if 'a person seeking refugee protection in Canada who has been determined not to be a refugee in the United States, has been ordered deported from the United States and is in transit through Canada for removal from the United States' (CBSA 2009).

11 The overlap between criminal and migration law powers that underpins the DFN regime is evident in the manner in which the 5 December 2012 designation was made: formally designated by the Minister of Public Safety in the exercise of law enforcement, corrections, crime prevention, and border control powers, but publicly announced by the Minister of Citizenship and Immigration in the exercise of immigration powers.

12 While Minister Kenney's announcement conveyed the impression that all 85 nationals would be designated 'irregular' under the DFN regime, materials provided by the CBSA responding to an Access to Information request indicate that of the 85 individuals designated on 5 December 2012, only 40 individuals (21 adults and 19 children) entered Canada after the DFN regime came into effect. The remaining 45 individuals (29 adults and 16 children) entered Canada at two different points before the DFN regime was implemented: on 2 February 2012 and 26 April 2012. They were not formally designated 'irregular' but nonetheless produced as such. Of these 45 individuals, it appears that only 29 were located, of whom at least 18 (including five children) were detained and 13 (including four children) were removed. The remaining individuals advanced refugee claims that are still in process.

13 Since the 5 December 2012 designation was made, two of the designated individuals were found not to be Convention refugees, and 13 individuals, including four children, were removed (CBSA 2014b). The CBSA does not specify whether the removed individuals were the same individuals that had outstanding theft and fraud charges against them.

14 The language of chase and capture was used by various news sources soon after the 5 December 2012 designation was made. That same day, for example, several news sources issued stories bearing the headline 'Hunt is on for Romanians believed to be part of human smuggling ring' (Levitz 2012).

References

Cases and Legislation

Agreement between the Government of Canada and the Government of the United States for Cooperation in the Examination of Refugee Status Claims from Nationals of Third Countries, 5 December 2002 (Safe Third Country Agreement) 29 December 2004.

Canada Gazette, Regulation Amending the Immigration and Refugee Protection Regulations, 143 (16) 5 August 2009.

Canadian Charter of Rights and Freedoms, s. 2, Part I of the *Constitution Act, 1982,* being Schedule B to the *Canada Act* 1982 (UK), 1982, c. 11

Cishahayo v. Canada, 2012 FC 1237.

Immigration and Refugee Protection Act, S.C. 2001, ch. 27.

Immigration and Refugee Protection Regulations, SOR/2002-227.

Protecting Canada's Immigration System Act, S.C. 2012, ch. 17.

Singh v. Canada, [1985] 1 SCR 177

United Nations Convention Relating to the Status of Refugees (Refugee Convention), 28 July 1981, 189 UNTS 137.

Secondary Sources

Aas, KF & Bosworth, M (eds) 2013, *The borders of punishment: citizenship, crime control, and social exclusion,* Oxford University Press, Oxford.

Aiken, S 1999, 'Racism and Canadian refugee policy: diverse perspectives on refugee issues', *Refuge,* vol. 18, no. 4, pp. 1–9.

Arbel, E 2013, 'Shifting borders and the boundaries of rights: examining the Safe Third Country Agreement between Canada and the United States', *International Journal of Refugee Law,* vol. 25, no. 1, pp. 65–86.

Arbel, E & Brenner, A 2013, *Bordering on failure: Canada-US border policy and the politics of refugee exclusion,* Harvard Immigration and Refugee Law Clinical Program, Cambridge, MA.

Austen, I 2007, 'Quebec and Vermont towns bond over a sleepy border', *The New York Times* 18 July. Available from: <http://www.nytimes.com/2007/07/18/world/americas/ 18border.html?_r=2&>. [5 December 2014].

Bond, J 2014, 'Failure to report: the manifestly unconstitutional nature of the Human Smugglers Act', *Osgoode Hall Law Journal,* vol. 51, no. 2, pp. 377–425.

Bosworth, M & Kaufman, E 2011, 'Foreigners in a carceral age: immigration and imprisonment in the United States', *Stanford Law & Policy Review,* vol. 22, pp. 429–54.

Bowling, B 2013, 'Epilogue. The borders of punishment: towards a criminology of mobility', in *The Borders of Punishment: Migration, Citizenship, and Social Exclusion,* eds KF Aas & M Bosworth, Oxford University Press, Oxford, pp. 77–89.

Brouwer A & Kumin, J 2003, 'Interception and asylum: when migration control and human rights collide', *Refuge,* vol. 21, no. 4, pp. 6–24.

Canadian Council for Refugees 2005, *Closing the front door on refugees: report on the first year of the Safe Third Country Agreement,* Canadian Council for Refugees. Available from: <http://ccrweb.ca/closingdoordec05.pdf>. [5 December 2014].

Canadian Council for Refugees & Sojourn House 2010, *Welcome to Canada: the experience of refugee claimants at port-of-entry interviews*, Canadian Council for Refugees. Available from: <http://ccrweb.ca/files/poereport.pdf>. [5 December 2014].

Canadian Red Cross Society 2012–2013, *Annual Report on Detention Monitoring Activities in Canada*. Released under the *Access to Information Act*, R.S.C. 1985, c. A-1. On file with author.

CBSA 2009, *Admissibility screening and supporting intelligence activities — Evaluation study, final report*, Canada Border Services Agency. Available from: <http://www.cbsa-asfc.gc.ca/agency-agence/reports-rapports/ae-ve/2009/assia-aeasr-eng.html>. [5 December 2014].

CBSA 2012, *Data Re: Refugee Claims Received by Canada between 2001–2012*, Citizenship and Immigration Canada (CIC) Data Warehouse. [8 May 2012].

CBSA 2014a, *Data Re: Refugee Claims Received by Canada between 2012–2014*. Released under the *Access to Information Act*, R.S.C. 1985, c. A-1. Request #A-2014-04409/YM. [25 July 2014].

CBSA 2014b. *Data Re: Designated Foreign Nationals*. Released under the *Access to Information Act*, R.S.C. 1985, c. A-1. Request #A-2014-04412/LL. [14 July 2014].

CBSA 2015, *Data Re: Designated Foreign Nationals*. Released under the *Access to Information Act*, R.S.C. 1985, c. A-1. Request #A-2014-13848/MC [16 January 2015].

CIC 2002, *Procedural issues associated with implementing the agreement for cooperation in the examination of refugee status claims from nationals of third countries: statement of principles*, Citizenship and Immigration Canada. Available from: <http://www.cic.gc.ca/ english/department/laws-policy/safe-third.asp>. [5 December 2014].

CIC 2003a, *Report of the Auditor General of Canada to the House of Commons, chapter 5: Citizenship and Immigration Canada—Control and enforcement*, Citizenship and Immigration Canada. Available from: http://www.oag-bvg.gc.ca/internet/docs /20030405ce.pdf>. [5 December 2014].

CIC 2003b, *Statement of Mutual Understanding on Information Sharing*, Citizenship and Immigration Canada. Available from: <http://www.cic.gc.ca/english/department/laws-policy/smu/smu-ins-dos.asp>. [5 December 2014].

CIC 2012, *Backgrounder: protecting our streets and communities from criminal and national security threats*, Citizenship and Immigration Canada. Available from: <http://www.cic.gc.ca/english/department/media/backgrounders/2012/2012-06-29k.asp>. [5 December 2014].

CIMM 2002, Citizenship and Immigration Committee of the Parliament of Canada, 37th Parl, 2nd Session, 19 November, Parliament of Canada. Available from: <http://www.parl.gc.ca/HousePublications/Publication.aspx?DocId=575306&Language=E&Mode=1&Parl=37&Ses=2!>. [5 December 2014].

Cohen, T 2012, 'Human-smuggling operation result of unmanned border crossing, opposition charges', *O Canada News* 5 December. Available from: <http://o.canada.com/news/national/human-smuggling-bust-rounds-up-85-people>. [5 December 2014].

Crépeau, F & Nakache D 2006, 'Controlling irregular migration in Canada: reconciling security concerns with human rights protection', *Immigration And Refugee Policy Choices*, vol. 12, no. 1, pp. 1–32.

Dauvergne, C 2004, 'Sovereignty, migration and the rule of law in global times', *Modern Law Review*, vol. 67, no. 4, pp. 588–615.

Dauvergne, C 2008, *Making people illegal: what globalisation means for migration and law,* Cambridge University Press, Cambridge.

Dauvergne, C 2013a, 'The troublesome intersection of refugee law and criminal law', in *The borders of punishment: citizenship, crime control, and social exclusion,* eds KF Aas & M Bosworth, Oxford University Press, Oxford, pp. 77–89.

Dauvergne, C 2013b, 'How the *Charter* has failed non-citizens in Canada: reviewing thirty years of Supreme Court of Canada jurisprudence', *McGill Law Journal,* vol. 58, no. 2, pp. 663–728.

Düvell, F 2011, Paths into irregularity: the legal and social construction of irregular migration, *European Journal for Migration and Law,* vol. 13, no. 3, pp. 275–95.

Global News 2012, 'The words: episode 14, season 2 (full transcript)', *Global News* 9 December. Available from: <http://globalnews.ca/news/317414/the-words-full-transcript-from-episode-14-season-2/>. [5 December 2014].

Harvard Law Student Advocates for Human Rights et al. 2006, *Bordering on failure: the US-Canada Safe Third Country Agreement fifteen months after implementation,* Human Rights @Harvard Law. Available from: <http://www.law.harvard.edu/programs/hrp/clinic/documents/Harvard_STCA_Report.pdf>. [5 December 2014].

Hathaway, JC 2005, *The rights of refugees under international law,* Cambridge University Press, Cambridge.

House of Commons, Parliament of Canada 2012, *Debates,* 41st Parliament, 1st Session, vol. 146 no. 97 15 March, pp. 1025–1399.

Integrated Border Enforcement Team 2007, *Canada-United States IBET Threat Assessment 2007,* Royal Canadian Mountain Police. Available from: <http://www.rcmp-grc.gc.ca/ibet-eipf/reports-rapports/threat-menace-ass-eva-eng.htm#ii>. [5 December 2014].

Integrated Border Enforcement Team 2012. *Canada-United States IBET Threat Assessment for 2012.* Obtained under the *Access to Information Act,* R.S.C. 1985, c. A-1. On file with author.

Kenney, J 2011, 'Our plan to combat human smuggling', *The National Post* 27 September. Available from: <http://fullcomment.nationalpost.com/2011/09/27/jason-kenney-our-plan-to-combat-human-smuggling/>. [5 December 2014].

Levitz, S 2012, 'Hunt is on for Romanians believed to be part of human smuggling ring', *Global News* 5 December. Available from: <http://globalnews.ca/news/316025/hunt-is-on-for-romanians-believed-to-be-part-of-human-smuggling-ring-4/>. [5 December 2014].

Maclin, A 2005, 'Disappearing refugees: reflections on the Canada-US Safe Third Country Agreement', *Columbia Human Rights Law Review,* vol. 26, pp. 365–426.

Morrison, J & Crossland, B 2001, *The trafficking and smuggling of refugees: the end game in European asylum policy?* (Working Paper No. 39), The UN Refugee Agency. Available from: <http://www.unhcr.org/3af66c9b4.pdf>. [5 December 2014].

Mountz, A 2010, *Seeking asylum: human smuggling and bureaucracy at the border,* University of Minnesota Press, Minneapolis.

Neve, A & Russell, T 2011, 'Hysteria and discrimination: Canada's harsh response to refugees and migrants who arrive by sea', *University of New Brunswick Law Journal,* vol. 62, pp. 37.

Pratt, A 2005, *Securing borders: detention and deportation in Canada,* UBC Press, Vancouver.

Public Safety Canada 2012a, *Minister of Public Safety makes first designation of irregular arrival under protecting Canada's Immigration System Act*, Public Safety Canada. Available from: <http://www.publicsafety.gc.ca/cnt/nws/nws -rlss/2012/20121205-eng.aspx>. [5 December 2014].

Public Safety Canada 2012b, *News release: Harper government takes action against human smuggling*, Public Safety Canada. Available from: <http://www.public safety.gc.ca/ cnt/nws/nws-rlss/2012/20121205-1-eng.aspx>. [5 December 2014].

Shachar, A 2009, 'The shifting border of immigration regulation', *Michigan Journal of International Law*, vol. 30, pp. 809–840.

Story, B 2005, *Politics as usual: the criminalization of asylum seekers in the United States* (Working Paper No. 26), Oxford University Refugee Studies Centre. Available from: <http://www.rsc.ox.ac.uk/files/publications/working-paper-series/wp26 -politics-as-usual-2005.pdf>. [5 December 2014].

Stumpf, J 2006, 'The crimmigration crisis: immigrants, crime, and sovereign power', *American University Law Review*, vol. 56, pp. 367–419.

Triandafyllidou, A & Maroukis, T 2012, *Migrant smuggling: irregular migration from Asia and Africa to Europe*, Palgrave Macmillan, London.

US Customs and Border Patrol, Canada Border Services Agency, & Royal Canadian Mountain Police 2010, *US-Canada: joint border threat and risk assessment*, Public Safety Canada. Available from: <http: http://www.publicsafety.gc.ca/cnt/rsrcs/ pblctns/archive-us-cnd-jnt-thrt-rsk/index-eng.aspx>. [5 December 2014].

Weber, L 2006, 'The shifting frontiers of migration control', in *Borders, mobility and technologies of control*, eds S Pickering & L Weber, Dordrecht, Springer, pp. 21–44.

11
From Man to Beast: Social Death at Guantánamo

Alexa Koenig, University of California, Berkeley

> Man is by nature a social animal.... Anyone who either cannot
> lead the common life or is so self-sufficient as not to need to, and
> therefore does not partake of society, is either a beast or a god. —
> Aristotle (Politics)

This chapter explores how indefinite detention in military prisons can
be experienced as particularly egregious because it threatens a social—
not just physical—death. Based on an analysis of 78 interviews with
men formerly detained at Guantánamo, the research presented here illu-
minates the mechanisms through which social death occurred, and the
ways in which it could extend beyond confinement into release.

The semi-structured interviews that underlie this chapter were collected under the auspices of two studies: one at the University of California, Berkeley (62 interviews) and one at the University of San Francisco
(an additional 16).[1] Questions were designed to elicit former detainees'
stories about the institutional practices they considered most difficult to
endure and their post-detention experiences. Interviewees came from
13 countries but identified with one of three geographic regions and/or
cultural groups, broadly defined: 1) Afghanistan and the Middle East (34
interviews), 2) Western Europe (18 interviews), and 3) men who identify
as Uighur, most of whom hail from East Turkestan in Western China (16
interviews). Almost all are or were married (72 percent) and are fathers
(70 percent). All identified as Muslim.

The focus of this chapter is on social death instead of civil death (the
criminal law term that indicates a loss of legal rights and responsibilities) or a lack of legal personality (the human rights equivalent) because
the latter terms refer to the *legal* limitations imposed on individuals as a
result of conviction. Here, interviewees spoke of a broader social stigma.

In addition, none of the interviewees were convicted of a crime, and thus the phenomenon of legal or civil death triggered by conviction is irrelevant.

Ultimately, this study builds on the work of scholars who make an explicit connection between social death, loss of identity, and the relationship between identity and meaning (Card 2003), to suggest that indefinite detention in military facilities is especially difficult to endure because of the extreme threat it poses to one's social and self-identities. To provide a basis for this argument, this chapter proceeds in four parts. First, I review the literature on social death to demonstrate the ways in which this concept has been applied to diverse contexts. Second, I describe Guantánamo to illustrate the context in which detainees were held and to lay a foundation for suggesting the ways in which architecture and geographic space potentially impact detainee experiences. Third, I provide an overview of the various mechanisms through which many detainees entered a state of social death at Guantánamo, one that frequently extended beyond captivity. I close by noting the constitutive aspects of detainee experiences, concluding that a large part of what makes such spaces feel so punitive is the negative impact of detention on one's self and social identities. This negative impact is especially extreme when detainees find themselves trapped in a liminal space of indefinite duration, which disconnects them from both their pasts and their futures.

What is social death?

The literature on social death is sparse. Erving Goffman (1986) has been credited with coining the phrase, although it does not appear in any of his published works: it first emerges in one of his students' dissertations (that of David Sudnow) in the 1960s (Norwood 2009, p. 6). However, Orlando Patterson's book *Slavery and Social Death* (1985) provides the seminal sociological treatment. While Patterson primarily talks about the phenomenon in relation to slaves, not prisoners, he does mention its relevance to captivity more generally (Patterson 1985, pp. 39–40). Later scholars have extended the concept to a variety of social experiences, including aging (Norwood 2009), alcoholism among the Navajo (Schwarz 2001), and the marginalized status of women in Kenyan society (Kabira et al. 1997).

Avery Gordon provides one of the clearest definitions of what is meant by social death: the term 'refers to the process by which a person is socially negated or made a human non-person as the terms of their incorporation into a society: living, they nonetheless appear as if and are treated as if they were dead' (Gordon 2011, p. 19). As Frances Norwood has further explained in the context of aging and illness, social death 'is probably best described as a series of losses—loss of identity and loss of the ability to participate in social activities and relationships that eventually culminates in a perceived disconnection from social life' (Norwood 2009, p. 7).

Ultimately, both Patterson and Gordon are clear that social death is, at its core, a 'relational idiom of power' (Gordon 2011, p. 35) and thus not solely a construct of the individual, but of the larger society in which he or she is embedded. Maureen Trudelle Schwarz, in a section of her book titled 'The Making and Unmaking of Persons'—which perhaps not coincidentally echoes Elaine Scarry's description of torture as 'the making and unmaking of the world' (1985)—discusses Navajo conceptions of personhood and their relationship to social death, describing how within the Navajo culture, one can lose one's social vitality a little at a time, pointing out that 'in many cultural contexts "social life/death and physical life/death may not coincide"' (Schwarz 2001, p. 157). And as Beth Conklin and Lynn Morgan have relatedly theorized,

> personhood is more of an interactive process than a fixed location on a social grid. Rather than being bestowed automatically at a single point in time, personhood is acquired gradually during the lifecycle; it can exist in variant degrees. The accrual of personhood is not necessarily a one-way process; under certain conditions, personhood may be lost, attenuated, withdrawn, or denied (Conklin & Morgan 1996, pp. 157–58).

Thus, not only is social death relational, it is also 'dynamic, fluid and contested' (Conklin & Morgan 1996, p. 667).

Patterson has identified what he calls 'two conceptions' of social death: the intrusive and extrusive. In the intrusive mode, slaves are the 'defeated enemy' symbolically representative of the 'power of the local gods, and the superior honor of the community' (Patterson 1985, p. 39).[2] According to the 'extrusive' conception, 'the dominant image of the slave [is] that of an insider who [has] fallen, one who ceased to belong and had been expelled from normal participation in the community because of a failure to meet certain minimal legal or socioeconomic norms of behavior' (p. 41). The extrusive mode predominated in imperial China and in Russia, for example, where 'slavery was very closely tied to the penal system.... In the eyes of the law [criminals] were nonpersons; their property was distributed to their heirs; [and] their wives could remarry' (Patterson 1985, p. 43). Patterson further explains that 'in the intrusive mode the slave was conceived of as someone who did not belong because he was an outsider, while in the extrusive mode the slave became an outsider because he did not (or no longer) belonged.... The one fell because he was the enemy, the other became the enemy because he had fallen' (Patterson 1985, p. 44).

As this chapter demonstrates, many former detainees appear to have experienced *both* the intrusive and extrusive forms of social death as a result of their detention. They generally experienced the intrusive mode while detained and the extrusive after their release. While Guantánamo detainees have certainly been framed as external threats—their imprisonment justified by their war-time capture and their presumed status as 'the enemy'—many interviews suggest that once returned to their homes or released to a third country, several have experienced life as 'the [internal] enemy because [they have] fallen' (Patterson 1985, p. 44). This has led to Guantánamo feeling like a particularly punitive experience in their lives—despite the fact that their detention was technically not punishment, since they were never found guilty of any crime. The experience of indefinite detention, accompanied by a social stigma so negative and so powerful that it continued to follow them even after their release, made their punitive experiences even more extreme.

Guantánamo: The place and the people

Guantánamo Bay is the largest harbor on the southeast side of Cuba. Twelve miles long and six miles across, the bay is surrounded by steep, green hills to the east and south and mountains to the north. Hot, humid weather is punctuated by rain in summer, which disappears in winter (Mahaney 2010). The island is home to the United States' oldest existing military base outside of the mainland US, and the only one located in a communist country (Mahaney 2010).

Comprised of 45 square miles, the base has been described as a '1950s style enclave where US soldiers live, and which offers drive-in movies, cheap restaurants, and the blessed relief of air conditioning' (Horrck & Iqbal 2005). In 1996, then-President Clinton signed a law that modified the United States' treaty with Cuba to offer an end to the naval base's contested existence on the island when 'Cuba has a government that Washington approves of' (Horrck & Iqbal 2005). Until that happens, the United States continues to pay its lease each year with checks that the Cuban government refuses to cash (Horrck & Iqbal 2005).

On 11 January 2002, the first 20 war-on-terror detainees arrived at the Guantánamo Bay naval camp. The detainees were initially housed in Camp X-Ray, a series of open-air cages topped with corrugated metal roofs (Fletcher & Stover 2009, p. 47). Exposed to the elements, detainees suffered from cold and heat, rain that would flood the corner cells, and the companionship of rats and other creatures that scurried into their cells. The number of detainees quickly swelled, straining X-Ray's capacity. In the meantime, construction began on Camp Delta, a more permanent facility that could house nearly 2,000 people and was based on architectural plans for supermaximum prisons in the United States. Characterized by barren concrete cells, the newer facility promised protection from the elements, but also significant isolation from other living beings. Delta opened on 28 April 2002.

Operating under the somewhat-ironic motto 'honor bound to defend freedom', Delta is comprised of seven camps, which are designed to hold inmates at different security levels. Camp 7—the final camp—is believed to have housed a small collection of detainees in extreme isolation. A 'secret' camp or 'dark site', its precise location has never been disclosed (Fletcher et al. 2008, pp. 33–34).

Guantánamo has held a total of 779 men in conjunction with the war on terror. Many have been subjected to harsh interrogation, including physical and psychological abuse, such as short shackling, environmental manipulation, and sexual humiliation (Fletcher & Stover 2009). By 2012, the ten-year anniversary of the first detainees' arrival, 171 were left, 89 of whom had been cleared for release but not let go (Jacobson 2012). By January 2015, 122 remained (Pearce 2015).

While Guantánamo detainees originated from 46 different countries, the vast majority were captured in Afghanistan or Pakistan. Those let go were released due to the United States' inability to link them to the terrorism of which they were initially suspected. Early into the war on terror, US officials acknowledged that as many as 94 percent of the men at Guantánamo should never have been there (Mayer 2008, p. 187).

Most of the men who ended up in Guantánamo appear to have come to the United States' attention because of bounties (Fletcher & Stover 2009). By May 2012, the United States had paid more than $100 million to approximately 70 people for information related to 'alleged terrorists' (Rewards for Justice Program, accessed 2012). While fruitful for motivating leads, such bounties also resulted in what has been called an 'unscrupulous dragnet', which resulted in the detention 'of thousands of people, many of whom it appears had no connection to Al Qaeda or the Taliban'—or at best had questionable links to those organizations (Fletcher & Stover 2009, p. 118). The US failed to narrow or refine this broad sweep during subsequent screening (Fletcher & Stover 2009, p. 118).

Many of the men captured by non-Americans were strangers traveling through Afghanistan or Pakistan who were easy targets for quick payouts. Several of those captured locally suspect they were 'sold' by rivals, who thereby eliminated longstanding enemies or profited by stealing coveted land or cattle. Finally, for those captured by Americans, the most common explanation has been mistaken identity. While a small handful of former detainees appears to have worked for the Taliban, they often did so because of an inability to pay the bribes the then-powerful Taliban demanded for recusal from military service. Any ideological affinity has typically been disavowed.

Social death at Guantánamo

> The very first time it was like dying... Capture, imprisonment is the closest thing to being dead that one is likely to experience in his life (Former prisoner George Jackson).

The arrival of detainees into American custody was riddled with rumors and symbols of a literal death, fitting preludes to the social death that followed. For example, one interviewee's description of his arrival leaves the sense that he has been bagged and tagged and left for dead: when first handed over to American Special Forces by the Northern Alliance in December 2001, he was strip searched, plastic ties were tightened around his wrists and ankles, and a sandbag placed over his head. He reports that the bag was then duct taped and a number written on the tape to identify him before he was set aside with other faceless detainees. Notably, in many cultures, people's faces are covered and their bodies labeled only after their demise.

Detainees' capture and arrival echoes an entry into social death discussed by Patterson in the slavery context. Patterson, in his book, notes Claude Meillassoux's earlier, highly structural perspective on the phenomenon: that social death through slavery 'must be seen as a process involving several transitional phases' that culminate in social negation (1985, p. 38). In the first phase, the slave is 'violently uprooted' from his native context, and then 'desocialized and depersonalized'. In the second, the slave is introduced to his master's community, but is, paradoxically, introduced as a 'nonbeing', a process that culminates in 'a kind of social death' (Patterson 1985, p. 38).

Suggesting that the process of social death may operate similarly for prisoners and slaves, most former detainees experienced a parallel to the structural 'phases' identified by Meillassoux. The majority were abducted by American or Pakistani forces and/or sold to the United States in exchange for a bounty (typically $5,000, but more for those who spoke English), much as slaves were once sold at auction. At least one former detainee made the relationship between slavery and his capture explicit. When asked whether any US government authority had ever told him why he was being held in Guantánamo, he explained:

> They haven't told us, but we usually [asked] them...why were we brought to Guantánamo?... Once an American soldier or officer told us in Kandahar that we were sold to them by money. Like slaves. And I told the officer that you claim that you know the rights of human[s], and how you buy the people or human being through the trade, and the business of human beings is prohibited all over the world. How you do it? And he told me, 'Don't say these words to me. It will affect you severely'.

Interviews with former detainees ultimately suggest there were six ways in which detainees entered into the process of social death: 1) dehumanization, 2) isolation, 3) sensory deprivation, 4) insanity brought on by psychological abuse and medical intervention, 5) a lack of acknowledgment or other support from their home governments, and 6) an indefinite or permanent period of separation from their families and home communities. Most detainees experienced the cumulative impact of more than one of these phenomena—an impact that several scholars have suggested is not just additive, but may be exponential (Koenig et al. 2009). Each of these phenomena is touched on briefly below.

The first mechanism consisted of treating detainees as something other than human—as a number, object, or animal. Many former detainees described such treatment as among the worst to which they were subjected. Such practices facilitated the process of social death by 'erasing' their sense of being human. Even among those detainees who experienced severe beatings, witnessed murders or suicide attempts, or endured other extreme violence, having their humanity disregarded threatened their identities and thus was experienced as particularly severe. As one former detainee explained, 'The beatings, after a while you don't even feel them, you no longer feel the pain because there's so much. They step on your hand if they—you don't feel that. But on the other hand, if they put you naked in front of other people, if they put things up your ass, what they want to do is to destroy your dignity and to tell you you're just animals. We are human beings, *but you're just animals'*.

Such stories mirror the dehumanization experienced by individuals in other prison settings, as reported in other chapters in this anthology—such as those by Liebling, Reiter & Blair, and Murray & Holmes—and in other detention contexts, as described by Bosworth and Turnbull, and Kaufman and Weiss. The consistency of these findings hints at the critical role that dehumanization plays in exacerbating the sense of punitiveness relevant to captivity—especially in contexts where captivity seems to depend less on an official finding of individualized, legal wrongdoing, than on an administrative conclusion that the detainee represents a category of people generally deemed undesirable (such as the mentally ill, immigrants, or suspected terrorists).

The second mechanism contributing to an experience of social death was separating detainees from other humans, and thereby eliminating most aspects of their social life. This happened in two ways: 1) physical isolation and 2) social isolation triggered by linguistic and cultural differences.

Placement in solitary confinement is the paradigmatic example of forced isolation (see Gawande 2009). While many interviewees decried the infamously harsh conditions of Camp X-Ray, where they were kept in cages, being moved to the more modern Camp Delta was often even more psychologically challenging. As noted by Jewkes (this volume), architecture can have a profound effect on prisoner experiences, an observation borne out by detainees at Guantánamo. Camps 5 and 6 were 'brick to brick' replicas of American supermax prisons in Indiana and Michigan: solid-walled facilities devoid of interaction with the outside world. While exposure to the elements was significantly less than in X-Ray, in the modern Camp Delta detainees found themselves plunged into an opposite extreme, one where it was impossible to tell night from day, and especially difficult to communicate with others. One former detainee from France explains that between the two prison camps,

> Delta was worse. X-Ray in fact was better because we were outside... we could see out...[W]e had hope when we were in X-Ray, we knew that there were journalists...we knew they could not keep us there indefinitely.... I remember the day I was transferred to Delta, it was absolutely horrible, because Delta was, you were in an enclosed place, it was dark...and we had kind of lost hope.

When asked how he survived his 30 months in Delta, he answered 'I don't know how I survived, I think it's just, I thought I was going crazy. There was a guy next to me in X-Ray, when I arrived he was fine, and then he became crazy, he went nuts. And I was looking at him and I was thinking I'm going to do the same, the same'.

One interviewee endured three years in such extreme isolation that few of the other prisoners knew he was there. Another languished in isolation for more than a year before the International Committee of the Red Cross learned of his presence; two years passed before he had contact with other prisoners. He credits the limited contact he had with guards, writing poetry, and memorizing the Koran as making a significant difference in his ability to mentally endure.

The interviews also suggest a much less explored but just as powerful form of isolation that occurred simply by separating detainees from others who spoke their language. This cultural and linguistic isolation created 'social islands' within the prison facility, which effectively operated as physical isolation to eliminate social vitality.

Prisoners' responses—including their stories of resistance to such social isolation—reveal the extremity of the experience. Indeed, lingual isolation was so difficult to endure that some prisoners created disturbances within the prison—even though they were individuals who prided themselves on being rule followers, and even though it meant they would likely be beaten—just to motivate guards to move them to a different block, with the hope that they would be placed near another detainee who spoke their language. Many had noticed that after detainees were punished and sent to isolation, they were never sent back to the same cell block as before.

Learning languages from and teaching them to fellow detainees became a key coping mechanism, facilitating human interaction and serving as a bridge between social islands. One detainee described the critical role the acts of teaching and learning languages played in his ability to maintain his sanity, even during a period when he had otherwise lost hope:

> *Interviewer:*   Did you become friends with other prisoners or other prison personnel?
> *Former Detainee*: Yeah, with a lot of prisoners. Because…that's all you need is communication really. And just to keep yourself sane, you start talk[ing] to them. If you're sitting in your cell and thinking all the time, you will go crazy. So what we used to do was teach people English…. And we starting learning Arabic as well, so we could…translate for the guys next to us. That was like to keep ourselves sane really.

Staying sane ultimately became a critical goal designed to avoid crossing over into a living death.

The third mechanism that facilitated a sense of social death was, in some ways, a hybrid of the other two (dehumanization and isolation). It involved separating detainees not just from other people but also from themselves, negating the five senses that are almost definitional to human life. As a nursery rhyme so aptly states:

> Let's count up our senses,
> One, two, three, four, five,
> Hearing, sight, smell, taste and touch,
> They make us feel alive.

Military personnel subjected all of the interviewees to 'sensory deprivation', placing goggles over detainees' eyes, gloves over their hands, headsets over their ears, and hoods over their heads. This cut prisoners off from almost all sensory experience, destroying their ability to perceive and communicate with the world around them. It also damaged their ability to perceive *themselves*: this technique was known to produce auditory, visual, and tactile hallucinations in as few as six hours (see Mason & Brady 2009). Such practices and the resulting hallucinations challenged guards' and interrogators' protestations that they had not engaged in torture (which, per the US definition, includes the administration or application of procedures 'designed to disrupt profoundly the senses or personality' (18 US Code section 2340(2)(D)). Detainees' bodies—and those bodies' involuntary responses to institutional treatment—became one of the strongest advocates for institutional change, recalling Pittendrigh's findings on the power of bodily rhetorics in this volume.

In addition to the temporary hallucinations created by sensory deprivation, many prisoners reported feeling as though they were going mad, or witnessed other prisoners who had apparently gone insane. This insanity, a phenomenon that frequently results in extreme detention contexts, as noted by Reiter and Blair, and Murray and Holmes (this volume), was the fourth mechanism facilitating a sense of social death in Guantánamo. These prisoners became like the living dead in that their bodies continued on, but their minds were gone. As one former detainee noted, such erasure, like death, threatened permanence. He explained that with abuse, 'the psychological part is much worse than the physical: you can always recover from physical pain, bruises, broken arms, but once…your mind is pushed to its limit, you can't come back'.

Insanity could occur in several ways. Some former detainees were kept in a medically induced stupor. One former detainee told of an 'Arab guy' who would lapse in and out of mental illness. One day, the Arab detainee started to pray but then began to cry, sobbing, 'I don't remember how to pray, I don't know where Mecca is, I don't even remember my son's name'. The interviewee explained that after being prescribed 800 mg of a particular medication, the Arab detainee had begun to lose his mind. The interviewee used this example to illustrate his ultimate conclusion that 'the biggest criminals in Guantánamo are the doctors'.

For others, insanity resulted from the pressures of prison life, including psychological abuse and the cumulative nature of the detention experience. One former detainee spoke of the need for human interaction and its role in survival. When asked by researchers if he had made any friends at Guantánamo, he explained, 'because of the situation... you have contact with the people next to you and you empathize with the people immediately around you—and if not, you would go crazy immediately. It's unavoidable, just to survive'.

The link between death and insanity was even more explicit in another interview. When asked if he saw other detainees being abused at Guantánamo, he answered that he had heard 'one guy died' but wasn't dead. When asked what he meant, he explained that the detainee had hung himself but didn't die; the soldiers were able to bring him 'back', but he had lost his mind.

Detainees faced a fifth mechanism of social death when their home governments failed to acknowledge or support them. The detainee described above, who taught fellow prisoners English, and learned Arabic from them in return, described when his greatest loss of hope occurred: when he realized his own government had failed to intervene on his behalf, rendering him (like a ghost) institutionally invisible— yet another manifestation of social death. The Holocaust literature has established how such periods of lost hope can be—quite literally—fatal (Bettelheim 1979; Frankl 1997).

Another former detainee, who identifies as Uighur, explained that the worst aspect of his detention came *after* he was declared a non-enemy combatant. While he was initially overjoyed to hear that the United States had no evidence against him, his joy faded when he was informed that no country would take him. It was then that he began to realize that his fate had less to do with his status as an individual, than as a pawn in a political struggle. While he initially thought it would take just a few weeks to find a willing country, those weeks stretched into a year, at which point he and a fellow detainee were released to Albania.

The latter detainee, who was also interviewed, blasted the United States for sending them to the impoverished nation. Noting that the United States is the greatest power in the world, he argued that they could have sent him to a different country, but that the choice to send Uighurs to Albania was the result of a 'game' between the US and China, with the Uighurs functioning as mere bargaining chips, and not as human beings with lives, families, and interests.

A sixth mechanism contributing to social death became evident when former detainees talked about their families. Many families lived for quite some time with the uncertainty of whether their loved one remained alive and/or when they would return home, creating a purgatory of sorts. One former detainee explained:

> I know that my parents' life stopped when I was away, and they don't want to talk to me about it.... The problem is that I was not there, but I was not dead, they knew I was not dead, so they could not just decide that I wasn't going to be there anymore. And what my brother told them, 'well, what you should do is act as if he were dead, because otherwise you will never be able to survive. Just consider that he's dead'. That's what my brother told them.

Bruno Bettelheim, a psychologist who once struggled for survival in a Nazi concentration camp, has noted the ambivalence some concentration camp inmates experienced toward their families and former lives during the process of their old life dying (Bettelheim 1979, p. 69), especially when family members sold off their property or otherwise undertook changes at home. Bettelheim suggests that inmates' anger over these acts lay in 'some sort of magical thinking running along the following lines: "If nothing changes in the world in which I used to live, then I shall not change, either"' (Bettelheim 1979, p. 69).

However, their distress may reflect something deeper: not a fear of change (which is characteristic of life), but a fear of death. While Bettelheim attributes the anger prisoners feel to 'not only the fact of change, but also the change in standing within the family which it implied'— the switch from being the individual upon which one's family depends, to one who is dependent—there may also be something more: a sense that one is staying the same, unable to progress in one's life—or even worse, decaying—while they are allowed to grow, move, and change.[3]

At its most extreme, detainees' decay and 'erasure' could become quite literal. Many interviewees spoke of fellow detainees disappearing entirely. One former detainee, when asked to describe some of the tortures he witnessed at Kandahar said, 'When we talked about it amongst ourselves I would hear that there were other people who were tortured differently. [T]here were a lot of people that just disappeared.... If you were British or you were French then that was a problem for the Americans, but there were a lot of Afghans that went missing'. To actually *disappear* from all of social life, even the social life of the prison, could be considered the ultimate social death. Importantly, the likelihood of disappearing was linked to the relative power of nations, not individuals, further underscoring these men's relative invisibility and the irrelevance of their particular identities to their fates.

So what, then, allows one to surpass this sense of being stuck, socially dead, while detained? Gordon has argued that 'to achieve a measure of agency and possibility...it is necessary... "to redeem time" or "master the present." This redemption involves refusing...to be treated as if one was never born, fated to a life of abandonment and spectrality' (Gordon 2011, p. 15).

As she explains, '[s]ocial death is not a singular biographical condition but a relational idiom of power. And so regardless of the social death sentence, prisoners must make a life as best they can while in prison' (Gordon 2011, p. 13), enacting their agency to the greatest extent that they can (see Pittendrigh in this volume for an overview of the types of agency available to prisoners). 'There the question of the past, the present and the future—indeed time itself—looms large in many complicated ways', much as it does in death. 'Perhaps the most obvious or seemingly definitive is the way in which the law renders punishment in units of life-time, giving present time and taking away life, where life is conceived as the right to futurity' (Gordon 2011, p. 13).

Thus, to ward off social death, detainees had to find a way to grow and change. At Guantánamo, those who seem to have survived most intact learned new languages or studied the Koran. In this way, they could fight the never-ending sameness of prison, the purgatory of a cyclical existence.

Others found it critical to accept their fates. As relayed by one former detainee when asked how he endured his detention, 'at first it was incredibly difficult, but humans learn to adapt and so I just learned to accept what was happening—not agree with it, but accept it. There were others who went crazy'.

This need to make a life in detention was exacerbated—even beyond the 'typical' prison experience—by the fact that none knew how long he would be there. No sentence had been given, and thus no future could be conceived. Many were told they would live the rest of their lives at Guantánamo. As noted by University of California, Berkeley, researchers, the worst experience for many detainees was 'not knowing, you know, why you're there, or when you can go home' (Fletcher et al. 2009, p. 81), and thus existing in a liminal space in which one struggled to endure as a person 'without future' (Gordon 2011, p. 26). Thus, a strange relief for many detainees—one they could not, however, always trust—was learning that they were heading home, that a future outside of Guantánamo might actually be possible.

Social death after Guantánamo

> So I was living in hell before Guantánamo, and I was living in hell in Guantánamo, and when I returned home, it was another hell (Former detainee).

While an expanded discussion of post-detention experiences is beyond the scope of this anthology, it is important for purposes of this chapter to note that former detainees' experiences of social death persisted *after* their release from Guantánamo. For some men, release resembled heaven; for others, it created a limbo; still others descended into hell. Regardless, they all found that detention had irrevocably altered their pre-Guantánamo lives.

In many interviews, former detainees expressed distress at finding that post-Guantánamo, they were unable to integrate back into the land of the 'living'. Upon release, many were imprisoned in their home countries for anywhere from a few hours to a few years. Others returned to find that they were unable to obtain jobs and resume social connections (Fletcher & Stover 2009).

With the rise of mass incarceration in the United States over the last few decades, research has emerged about the social lives of former prisoners and their inability to reintegrate into society. For example, Devah Pager (2003) has demonstrated the negative impact of a prison record on the ability of former convicts to secure jobs. More generally, Patterson, in *Slavery and Social Death*, notes an inability to return to social viability following captivity as having been typical of release from slavery. He cites the experience of the Kongo Community of Zaire during the 19th century as illustrative: 'Once a person became a slave, there was no way ever of releasing him from this condition, even though he might have been released from a particular master or even from his master's community' (Patterson 1985, p. 215). Similarly, while hundreds of detainees were released from Guantánamo, many of them found it extraordinarily difficult to 'recover first-class citizenship' (Patterson 1985, p. 215). At the time of their interviews, almost none of the interviewees had been able to secure a job or otherwise integrate into society, regardless of educational or professional backgrounds.

The experience of social death post-release is particularly evident in the following:

> So when we were in Guantánamo people have such nature that they are very [adapting].... You start having the real torture, the real discomfort, once [you] are out [of] Guantánamo. For instance...old friends, old circles, they are even afraid of greeting because they think then they may also be taken under custody or interrogated or the like.... Guantánamo is of short duration, it was only two years [for me]. I left Guantánamo at age 23. And it felt, [it] put me...in distress until the end of my life.

Many former detainees returned home to discover that family members had died or disappeared; that their homes had been bartered to facilitate their return; and that government and non-government organizations would ignore their pleas for help when the private sector refused to employ them. This dealt serious blows to their identities, in terms of their profession, their status as husband or father or child, their status as a landowner, and in some cases, as a citizen of a particular country, when they found that even their citizenship had been stripped away.

Several found themselves released thousands of miles from family members with no means of securing a visa to return home. Or, when they returned home, they were greeted by children who didn't remember them. This latter phenomenon was particularly devastating: for the individuals whom these men had helped bring into the world, it was as if they had never existed.

The sense of social negation is particularly poignant in the following passage shared by a man who was released to Albania instead of his native China. He can never return home because of the likelihood that he would face imprisonment and execution:

> Emotionally...another difficulty I have...is when I talk to my children on the phone. They talk to me like a stranger. Just talk for a couple words, hi how are you, fine. Bye...I don't have that father and children bond between them, because I am a stranger for them. They didn't hear my voice for five years, and in five years this children's life is a long time. And, when I asked my wife why don't they talk to me, and when my wife asked them, they say we don't really know

him. He says he's our father, you know this guy...but we don't have any memory of this father.

I don't like going to store, I mean, going to outside or walk around and go to places. Even on the weekends we don't go anywhere because when I see couples holding hands, loving and caring and having their children, and going out, and visit, having good time, it really affects us in a very negative way because we have had a life like that, we had had a normal life, falling in love with a woman, and being married, and having children. Now I'm, what am I basically? I am not a normal person. I have three kids who I don't have the actual bond with them. I have a wife over there. I cannot even talk to her in a loving and passionate manner on the phone because I don't even remember how to do that. I don't look at myself [as] a normal human being. I'm more like the animal in the zoo, or something, and just— it's not real human feeling.

Gordon extends Patterson's conception of social death to all 'captives', pointing out the enormous sacrifice that is expected both during *and* following imprisonment: 'In exchange for avoiding immediate death, what's taken from the captive is his past, his family, his culture, his honor, his future, his very being. In exchange for his life, he must give his life' (Gordon 2011, p. 11). For this particular man, his wife, children, former employment, nationality—all those key aspects of his identity are beyond his reach.

Another, younger individual, who has also been released to a third country, has a similarly fatalistic sense of his future, despite having enrolled in college classes and taken other concrete steps to move forward. When asked whether he thinks the world's negative reaction to him will ever change, he responds, 'I believe it will always be like this'. He is unable to openly communicate with his family in East Turkistan; he explains that the Chinese police have been threatening his family, 'in front of neighbors', creating 'pressure for their lives'. He says that they are scared, and because of that, they say they don't know where he is, and he tries to minimize communication, thereby relegating himself to a social island even within his own family.

Patterson has noted that when a slave was released from his master's household, there was a ceremony that claimed to be one of redemption; however, the ceremony ultimately functioned as a 'gift exchange' between the master and the slave's former clan members. In many cases, release in the Guantánamo context has not been true freedom, but an exchange between the United States and the detainee's native government—or a third party government—to which the detainee has been entrusted.

Once transferred, many detainees have found themselves—like slaves—financially destitute and dependent on neighbors, family, or the state. They have usually been released without compensation or even the money they had in their pockets when captured. For most interviewees, that destitution continues, in large part because of their inability to secure jobs. The reasons have been multiple. But perhaps most commonly, they have continued to experience social isolation brought on by the 'mark of Guantánamo' (Fletcher & Stover 2009), a stigma similar to the 'mark of a criminal record' that Devah Pager has noted in the domestic US context (2003). As Patterson has famously explained, 'The captive always appears...as marked by an...indelible defect which weighs endlessly upon his destiny' (Patterson 1985, p. 20).

In the following passage, a former detainee explains how this mark continues to stain his future prospects:

> Something should happen to the people who are responsible for arresting all these people and then releasing them back, and not really clearing their names... It's just that we still have this black mark on us... If they're going to charge [detainees], they should charge them. It didn't take five and [a] half years to convict someone of a crime. And either close the camp down, or something should happen. But to just leave them there and say to the world, oh these people are terrorist[s] based on what, we don't know, is just ridiculous.

A former detainee from the West, when asked what he would want in terms of compensation for his imprisonment, replies:

> Clear my name to the world. Officially come on the stage...and say 'These guys were innocent and what happened to them was our fault.'...I would want my name to be cleared and people to give me a chance in life. That's what I would want.

In discussing the Margi of Nigeria, Patterson has explained that the enslaved criminal 'remained in the society: a part of it, yet apart from it. He was not physically expelled, for that would be less humiliating.... Rather, it was the loss of identity and normality that was so objectionable' (Patterson 1985, p. 46). For many released detainees, it is as if they exist in a similar state, one divorced from their previous, 'normal' lives. Patterson has pointed out that in this 'institutionalized marginality, the liminal state of social death was…one of the most difficult aspects of his or her condition for the slave to bear' (p. 46). Importantly, this implicates the role of government—both the United States and detainees' home governments, and—when released to another country—third-party governments. As Patterson has explained, the power to 'mediate' between those who are socially dead and those who are socially alive imbues the slave master with a godlike power, a power in which the master's authority ultimately rests. The refusal of the United States and other governments to declare these men 'innocent', and thereby help them begin the process of rebuilding their identities, and thus their lives, represents a similar power to mediate—or to refuse to mediate—between the socially dead and alive.

In addition to the structural difficulties former detainees have encountered, many also appear to suffer from psychological trauma, which negatively impacts their ability to make social connections and resume a baseline of normal social functioning. One man, a Uighur released to the tiny island of Palau, retains hope that someday he will be reunited with his family in East Turkistan. For this man, the sense of social death—of living on a social island, although physically surrounded by others—is manifested in his release to an island that is not only metaphorical, but literal. For him, hope hinges on the possibility that the United States will fulfill the promise it made that his time on the remote island will be temporary. He dreams of getting off the island and resettling in a larger country. In Palau he is permanently a refugee; as a non-citizen, he cannot get a passport to visit his wife and children, suggesting his identity as a spouse and father has also been buried.

Conclusion

From a macro perspective, recognizing social death has important implications for our understanding of the ways in which the United States uses punishment, symbols of punishment, and the threat of crime as means of governance (see Simon 2007). The *threat* of terrorism (which has largely been framed as an external threat)[4]—as opposed to *proof* of terrorism—has been used by the United States since 11 September 2001 to justify the spread of US-run military prisons overseas, just as the hyper-active building of prisons within the United States has been rationalized by a perceived threat of *internal* crime. Terrorism has been invoked to motivate domestic and international allies and to justify the international spread of prisons to incarcerate shockingly high numbers of mostly Muslim men—who have arguably become as ideologically linked to terrorism as African American males have been to domestic crime. (As one former detainee begged during his interview, 'What was my crime? Was being Muslim my crime?') These ideological frames demonstrate the diffusion of US penal practices, rhetoric, and technologies to a much larger geographic space.

One of the dangers of this criminological shift, in which policy has moved away from individualized retribution and toward a more general concern with prevention and harm reduction, is that the individual who is criminalized becomes increasingly inconsequential. As Garland has noted, 'instead of concentrating upon individual offenders, [this] preventative sector targets criminogenic situations' (2002, p. 171). The 'situation' that Guantánamo symbolizes demonstrates the extent to which individuals can be made to 'disappear'.

Importantly, physical, psychological, and social control of detainees is not just exerted within the detention context but frequently extends post-release. In the context of domestic crime-control, offenders are now less likely to be dealt with by probation and parole and more likely to be depicted as 'culpable, undeserving and somewhat dangerous individuals who must be carefully controlled for the protection of the public and the prevention of further offending. Rather than clients in need of support they are...risks who must be managed' (Garland 2002, p. 175). There is a very real danger that, in this new paradigm, the imprisoned will disappear from geographic, temporal, political, and social space, locked away in a far and undisclosed location, for an undisclosed and indeterminate length of time.

Much like domestic supermax prisons in the United States, military prisons are operating as 'a kind of reservation, a quarantine zone in which purportedly dangerous individuals are segregated in the name of public safety...function[ing] as a form of exile, its use shaped less by a rehabilitative ideal and more by...an "eliminative" one' (Garland 2002, p. 178). Those individuals who are incarcerated in our political-military prisons are similarly no longer perceived as men, but as 'terrorists'. The dehumanization of detainees, which results in their reduction from human beings to mere objects or symbols, is also evident in their 'sentence', namely indefinite detention: as Garland has noted in the domestic context of revised sentencing laws, 'the offender is rendered more and more abstract, more and more stereotypical, more and more a projected image rather than an individuated person' (2002, p. 179). Subjecting individuals to indefinite detention for the remote possibility that they *might* be a terrorist takes this reliance on stereotypes and de-individuation to the extreme.

As suggested by the literatures and findings above, the experience of social death seems to operate most through a devolution of identity. The potential blows to identity are myriad: they can manifest through physical damage; damage to one's position within his familial or professional unit; and damage to one's overall social standing. The relationship between detention and death is an intimate one.

One former detainee, when asked to reflect back on Guantánamo, references social death quite eloquently, stating simply, 'When I remember Guantánamo, I feel that I woke up from [a] grave or a tomb'. Post release, former detainees have labored to negotiate new identities and regain hope for the future, in a struggle for social life. As Card has reasoned regarding social death, '[l]oss of social vitality is loss of identity and thereby of meaning for one's existence' (2003, p. 63). It is only by recovering meaning that the cycle of life, to death, to rebirth can occur. In the meantime, interviews, speaking engagements, and writings by former detainees offer the greatest promise for forcing some degree of social acknowledgment—whether through the words they say, or the bodily rhetorics they share (Pittendrigh this volume)—thereby helping them to reclaim some small piece of social space.

Notes

1 The UC Berkeley study was led by Laurel E. Fletcher and Eric Stover, professors at the University of California, Berkeley School of Law. The University of San Francisco study was led by law professor Peter Jan Honigsberg. The author served the former study as a graduate student researcher and the latter as program manager.

2 Especially interesting in light of the Muslim faith of most of the Guantánamo detainees, 'it is in Islamic religious and social thought that we find the purest expression of the intrusive conception of social death. The outsider was foreigner, enemy, and infidel, fit only for enslavement after the jihad, to be incorporated as the enemy within. ... The slave is primarily a person taken captive in war, or carried off by force from a foreign hostile country' (Patterson 1985, p. 41).

3 Dan McAdams and Philip Bowman (2001) have noted an apparent correlation between redemption stories, which often reference personal change, and psychosocial adaptation and overall mental wellbeing.

4 Exceptions include the rounding up of Muslim-Americans in the immediate aftermath of 9/11, and the post-9/11 interweaving of immigration and anti-terrorism policies.

References

Başoğlu, M & Salcioglu, E 2011, *A mental health care model for mass trauma survivors: control-focused behavioral treatment for earthquake, war, and torture trauma*, Cambridge, Cambridge University Press.

Bettelheim, B 1979, *Surviving and other essays*, Alfred A. Knopf, New York.

Card, C 2003, 'Genocide and social death', *Hypatia*, vol. 18, no. 1, pp. 63–79.

Conklin, B & Morgan, LM 1996, 'Babies, bodies and the production of personhood in North America and a native Amazonian society', *Ethos*, vol. 24, no. 4, pp. 657–694.

Fletcher, LE & Stover, E 2009, *The Guantánamo effect: exposing the consequences of US detention and interrogation practices*, University of California Press, Berkeley.

Frankl, VE 1997, *Man's search for meaning*, Pocket Publishers, New York.

Garland, D 2002, *The culture of control: crime and social order in contemporary society*, University of Chicago Press, Chicago.

Gawande, A 2009, 'Hellhole', *New Yorker* 30 March. Available from: <http://www.newyorker.com/>.

Goffmann, E 1986, *Stigma: notes on the management of spoiled identity*, Simon & Schuster, New York.

Gordon, AF 2011, 'Some thoughts on haunting and futurity', *borderlands*, vol. 10, no. 2. Available from: <http://www.borderlands.net.au/vol10no2_2011/gordon_thoughts.htm>.

Horrock, NM & Iqbal, A 2005, 'Waiting for Gitmo', *Mother Jones* January/February. Available from: <http://www.motherjones.com/politics/2004/01/waiting-gitmo>.

Jackson, G 1970, *Soledad brother: the prison letters of George Jackson*, Bantam Books, New York.

Jacobson, B 2012, 'Guantánamo ten years later: "It's a Disgrace", Says Expert Andy Worthington', *Truthout* 12 February. Available from: <http://www.truth-out.org/news/item/6424:guantanamo-ten-years-later-its-a-disgrace-says-expert-andy-worthington>.

Kabira, WM, Masinjila, M & Obote, M 1997, *Contesting social death: essays on gender and culture*, Kenya Oral Literature Association, Nairobi.

Koenig, KA, Stover, E & Fletcher, L 2009, 'The cumulative effect: a medico-legal approach to United States torture law and policy', *Essex Human Rights Review*, vol. 6, no. 1, pp. 145–68.

Mahaney, E 2010, 'Guantánamo Bay: historic naval base meets suburban America', About.com. Available from: <http://geography.about.com/od/croatiamaps/a/Guantanamo-Bay.htm>.

Mason, OJ & Brady, F 2009, 'The psychotomimetic effects of short-term sensory deprivation', *Journal of Nervous and Mental Disease*, vol. 197, no. 10, pp. 783–85.

Mayer, J 2008, *The dark side: the inside story of how the war on terror turned into a war on American ideals*, Doubleday, New York.

McAdams, DP & Bowman, PJ 2001, 'Narrating life's turning points: redemption and contamination', in *Turns in the Road: Narrative Studies of Lives in Transition*, eds DP McAdams, R Josselson & A Lieblich, American Psychological Association.

Norwood, F 2009, *The maintenance of life: preventing social death through euthenasia talk and end-of-life care—lessons from the Netherlands*, Carolina Academic Press, Durham, NC.

Pager, D 2003, 'The mark of a criminal record', *American Journal of Sociology*, vol. 108, no. 5, pp. 937–975.

Patterson, O 1985, *Slavery and social death: a comparative study*, Harvard University Press, Cambridge, MA.

Pearce, M 2015, '5 Yemeni detainees released from Guantanamo Bay despite GOP resistance', *LA Times* 15 January. Available from: <http://www.latimes.com/nation/nationnow/la-na-nn-gitmo-releases-20150115-story.html>.

Rewards for Justice [2012], *Rewards Paid*, Rewards for Justice. Available from: http://www.rewardsforjustice.net/index.cfm?page=success_stories&language=English

Scarry, E 1985, *The body in pain: the making and unmaking of the world*, Oxford University Press, New York.

Schwarz, MT 2001, *Navajo Lifeways: Contemporary Issues, Ancient Knowledge*, University of Oklahoma Press, Norman, OK.

Simon, J 2007, *Governing through crime: how the War on Crime transformed American democracy and created a culture off fear*, Oxford University Press, New York.

Afterword

Hadar Aviram, University of California, Hastings College of Law

In the 1960s television series *The Prisoner* (1967–68), a British agent, kidnapped and knocked unconscious, finds himself in a mysterious seaside enclosure called The Village. The Village's inhabitants use numbers in lieu of names, and the series hero is repeatedly referred to as Number Six. Suppressed, surveilled, and supervised by numerous tools—physical barriers, security monitoring systems, and mind-control operations, Number Six is at the mercy of his nameless, faceless captors, first among whom is Number One. Our hero, however, refuses to submit; he is relentless in his efforts to escape The Village and defy his captors. 'I am not a number,' he bravely cries out, 'I am a free man'.

The series' popularity can, in part, be attributed to the thickening mystery surrounding The Village in general, and Number Six's incarceration in particular. What has he done to be confined there? Who controls his fate? When Number Six finally outsmarts his captors at the end, arriving at the command center and coming face to face with Number One, he tears the mask off his captor's face and discovers, horrifyingly, inconceivably, his own face looking back at him.

The scene could be simplistically construed to suggest that the entire incarceration experience was Number Six's dream, or stemmed from a nervous breakdown. But I suspect it hints at a more profound truth, one that all chapters of this anthology share: that there are no 'others'; that captors and captives alike, regardless of the situational factors that cast them in these antagonistic roles, share an ember of humanity; and that anyone, regardless of such situational factors, is worthy of dignity, love, and belonging. The daring social psychology experiments of the 1960s—Stanley Milgram's *Obedience to Authority* (1963, 1965, 1974) and Philip Zimbardo's famous *Stanford Prison Experiment* (1971)—provided the grim, frightening realization that the extremes to which captors and captives will go in cruelty and oppression, defiance and rebellion, conformity and breakdown, are highly contingent upon situational variables and arbitrary role assignments.

But the strength of the chapters in this anthology is that each of them reinforces this disturbing conclusion without needing to recur to an artificial experimental setting. In the real stories told here, the roles of captor and captive are created by structures that encourage alienation, separation, and fear, support xenophobia, and reinforce myths of evil and inhumanity. What is 'extreme' about these structures is the extent to which they mold the people who are subjected to them, transforming them from immigrant to criminal, from somebody to nobody, from healthy to sick, and from sick to sicker. These structures can be physical; Yvonne Jewkes' critical analysis of prison architecture shows how physical structures instill fear and persecution, and Keramet Reiter and Thomas Blair's chicken-and-egg account of long-term isolation and mental illness shows how conditions of confinement themselves shape those confined within them. Isolation plays an important role in Alexa Koenig's account of Guantánamo inmates, which shows the profound erasure of social and personal identity brought about by confinement. But some of these structures are legal and no less powerful: As Mary Bosworth, Sarah Turnbull, Emma Kaufman, Sam Weiss, and Efrat Arbel show in the different settings they illuminate, xenophobic laws can transform immigrants, asylum seekers, and workers into criminals. And other structures come from overarching perceptions and understandings of evil, disease, and protection—whether those are definitions of evil, monstrosity, and undeservedness, as Alison Liebling points out in her development of Craig Haney's 'ecology of cruelty', or definitions of sickness, as Stuart J. Murray, Dave Holmes, Kelly Hannah-Moffat, and Amy Klassen powerfully demonstrate in their analyses of the interface between extreme punishment and extreme treatment. These transformations are profound, testing the limits of the human and nonhuman, denying people their basic dignity (as Mona Lynch's analysis of Joe Arpaio's festival of extreme incarceration shows), and even denying them agency over their own suffering, making their statements about their own experiences circumspect (as Nadya Pittendrigh demonstrates in her analysis of Tamms prison).

But extreme punishment extends beyond merely establishing the structures that instigate these transformations; each setting presented in the book is rife with painful examples of gratuitous cruelty and degradation. The techniques employed by the incarcerating authority, ranging from isolation and deprivation, through the equivalent of social death, to the infliction of gendered humiliation and poetic punishments (of which the techniques employed by Joe Arpaio, the 'penal cartoon', are classic examples) target the dignity of inmates in the most basic ways, reinforcing their liminal place between the human and nonhuman.

And it is not only the quality, or content, of this punishment that matters—it is its endlessness. In some of these cases, particularly in supermax facilities and in settings that evoke the psychiatric treatments of yesteryear, confinement itself causes those subjected to it irreparable damage, which will haunt their lives on the outside long after such confinement ends. In other cases, the shame and stigma associated with these degradation practices is so fierce that they create not only external limitations on rehabilitation and reentry, but also internal psychological and physical scars that will be difficult to overcome. And some punishments do not even have an end date in sight, pushing away the one glimmer of hope that would sustain inmates in their suffering. Ironically, as pointed out in the introduction, what is 'extreme' about these examples of 'extreme punishment' is precisely that they often lie outside the traditional definition of 'punishment', their endlessness justified by the very mechanisms that place them outside the realm of legal protections. This distinction is a reminder to critical criminologists that criminalization is not the only, and not necessarily the most oppressive, form of social control, and that medicalization and immigration control, which define the enemy and its threat differently, can sometimes have a far more pervasive reach.

At the close of this collection's grim journey in the realm of extreme punishment, two important questions must be asked: what are the forces that allow such methods of confinement to persist, and what are the necessary conditions to fight them? Both of these questions can, and should, be answered with regard to individuals as well as in the aggregate; there are essential connections between the ways in which each of us, personally, deals with oppression and cruelty, and the overarching social structures that tolerate them.

In the foreword to this volume, Marc Mauer insightfully maps out the big societal changes that stretch beyond national contexts and have led to a proliferation of extreme punishment structures. One of these developments is the emergence of neoliberalism as a global regime, manifesting itself in the retreat of governments from welfare obligations toward their subjects. Indeed, many commentators on neoliberalism and punitivism have pointed out that this development, often accompanied by an increase in privatization, manifests a relinquishment of responsibility for the lower rungs in the socioeconomic ladder, leaving those mired in poverty and need without a solution or a safety net. As Rusche and Kirchheimer predicted in their seminal work *Punishment and Social Structure* (1939), a surplus of labor supply is bound to lead to oppressive regimes of social control. The logic of their analysis has been since examined through historical quantitative methods, finding that increases in unemployment and in socioeconomic gaps lead to an increase in punishment, irrespective of crime rates (Inverarity & McCarthy 1988; Chiricos & Delone 1992; Barlow, Barlow & Chiricos 1993; Freeman 2000; Michalowski & Carlson 2006).

But something else happens on the individual level in neoliberal regimes, which I find more interesting and disturbing than the big economic forces at work. In *The Age of Fracture* (2012), Daniel Rodgers argues that the last quarter of the 20th century, in which an aggressive form of market economy came to be the dominant hegemony, was characterized by the demise of solidarity and collectivity and the emergence of individualism, power, and individual search for identity. These fragmented battles, special interests, and self-oriented policies have not only torn the intellectual social fabric, but also eroded our social commitment to community-building and empathy.

This phenomenon has particularly important implications for the emergence of extreme forms of oppression and social control. Loic Wacquant (2009) shows how American society has given up on its poor, essentially shifting the paradigm for addressing poverty from economic reform to crime control. Joe Soss, Richard Fording, and Sanford Schram (2011) see this process as a destructive combination of indifference to the plight of others and severe paternalism brought about by fear. Alessandro de Giorgi (2006) argues that this lack of empathy and fear of crime is particularly conducive to oppression of the most disenfranchised of subjects, such as undocumented immigrants.

Changes and transformations in the market are heavily complicit in this loss of empathy. Indeed, studies of public punitivism have found that white men of low income and education are the most likely to harbor punitive perspectives toward others, and these feelings strongly correlate with their sense of economic insecurity (Hogan, Chiricos & Gertz 2005; Costelloe, Chiricos & Gertz 2009). As old traditions and power structures fall apart, those who felt part of the hegemony resent those whom they perceive to be the instruments of their downfall, which also explains why—both in real policy and in jury deliberation simulations—this punitivism is heavily racialized. It is therefore not only that individual feelings of rage and frustration evoked by economic insecurity and job instability are attached to convenient scapegoats, but that the resulting punitivism is a manifestation of the threat posed by large numbers of minorities to the economic and political wellbeing of the majority (Greenberg 1993, 1999; Garland 2001).

These processes partially explain, for example, Sheriff Arpaio's alarming political success among immigrant-fearing Anglos, the support for the controlling mechanisms in the various immigrant detention facilities surveyed in this volume, and the ability to justify terrifying degrees of isolation and abuse through fear and control.

But what about the rest of us? How is compliance with these approaches brokered and maintained? In *States of Denial* (2001), Stanley Cohen examines public indifference to mass atrocities, concluding that indifference to the suffering of others is the normal state of affairs. By contrast, perspectives that require outside observers to take action against atrocities—which he refers to as the 'Oxfam/Amnesty view'—are outliers, and their proponents face an uphill battle in shaking the public out of indifference. Physical distance, obstructive architecture, and mysterious funding can all hide the realities of extreme punishment from view, but they are underscored by the power of inertia and by our tendencies to 'otherize' suffering and continue with our lives unperturbed. There is plenty of scientific evidence for this inertia, starting with Solomon Asch's conformity experiments (1955) and ending with the human tendency to resent those whom we have treated badly, otherwise known as the 'Benjamin Franklin' effect, tested by John Schopler and John Compere (1971). In the face of strong disincentives to act on behalf of the victims of extreme punishment, resistance is unlikely.

It is not, however, impossible. Cohen's examination of helpers in mass atrocity contexts led him to conclude that these people had an inclusive worldview, perceiving themselves as sharing a common humanity with those they supported and helped. Maybe one way to create the 'deep shame of passivity' that will lead us to value others' dignity and wellbeing as a moral imperative is to pay close attention to the people in vulnerable situations. This collection features people who strongly resist their categorization as criminals, deviants, animals, and who struggle against the degradation involved in their confinement. The spiritual growth of Guantánamo inmates, the nonviolent struggle of inmates in solitary confinement, and the strong resistance to stigmatizing categorization among detained immigrants is impressive and inspiring. More than merely a reminder of their plight, it is a reminder of their humanity, a call to overcome inertia and indifference and create an alliance of people on both sides of the walls of confinement. The writings in this collection are certainly an important contribution to the understanding that there really are no 'others', that everyone, no matter their transgression and status in life, is worthy of minimal dignity and belonging.

'But when the dawn will come, of our emancipation, from the fear of bondage and the bondage of fear, why, that is a secret' (Paton 1948).

References

Asch, SE 1955, *Social psychology*, Prentice Hall, New York.
Barlow, DE, Barlow, MH & Chiricos, TG 1995, 'Long economic cycles and the criminal justice system in the U.S.', *Crime, Law and Social Change*, vol. 19, pp. 143–69.
Chiricos, TG & Delone, M 1992, 'Labor surplus and punishment: a review and assessment of theory and evidence', *Social Problems*, vol. 39, pp. 421–46.
Rodgers, DT 2012, *The age of fracture*, Belknap Press, New York.
Cohen, S 2001, *States of denial: knowing about atrocities and suffering*, Polity Press, New York.
Costelloe, MT, Chiricos, TG & Gertz, M 2009, 'Punitive attitudes toward criminals: exploring the relevance of crime salience and economic insecurity', *Punishment & Society*, vol. 11, no. 1, pp. 25–49.
de Giorgi, A 2006, *Rethinking the political economy of punishment*, Aldershot Ashgate, Surrey, UK.
Freeman, A 2000, 'Crime and the labour market', in *The Economic Dimensions of Crime*, eds N Fielding, NA Clark & R Witt, St. Martin's Press, New York.
Garland, D 2001, *The culture of control: crime and social order in contemporary society*, University of Chicago Press, Chicago.
Greenberg, DF 1993, *Crime and capitalism: readings in Marxist criminology*, Temple University Press, Philadelphia.
Greenberg, DF 1999, 'Punishment, division of labor, and social solidarity', in *The criminology of criminal law: advances in criminological theory*, vol. 8, eds WS Laufer & F Adler, Transaction Press, New Brunswick, pp. 283–362, 334.
Hogan, MJ, Chiricos, TG & Gertz, M 2005, 'Economic insecurity, blame, and punitive attitudes', *Justice Quarterly*, vol. 2, no. 3, pp. 392–412.
Inverarity, J. & McCarthy, D 1988, 'Punishment and social structure revisited: unemployment and imprisonment in the United States, 1948–1984', *Sociological Quarterly*, vol. 9, pp. 263–79.
Michalowski R & Carlson, S 2006, 'Unemployment, imprisonment, and social structures of accumulation: historical contingency in the Rusche-Kirchheimer hypothesis', *Criminology*, vol. 37, pp. 217–50.
Milgram, S 1974, *Obedience to authority: an experimental view*, HarperCollins, New York.
Milgram, S 1965, 'Some conditions of obedience and disobedience to authority', *Human Relations*, vol. 18, no. 1, pp. 57–76.
Milgram, S 1963, 'Behavioral study of obedience', *Journal of Abnormal and Social Psychology*, vol. 67, no. 4, pp. 371–378.
Paton, A 1948, *Cry, the beloved country*, Charles Scribner's Sons, New York.
The Prisoner 2008 [1967–1968] (DVD), A&E (CBS).
Rusche, G & Kirchheimer, O 1939, *Punishment and Social Structure*, Columbia University Press, New York.
Schopler, J & Compere, JS 1971, 'Effects of being kind or harsh to another on liking', *Journal of Personality and Social Psychology*, vol. 20, no. 2, pp. 155–159.

Soss, J, Fording, RC, & Schram, SF 2011, *Disciplining the poor: neoliberal paternalism and the persistent power of race*, University of Chicago Press, Chicago.

Wacquant, L 2009, *Punishing the poor: the neoliberal government of social insecurity*, Duke University Press, Durham.

Zimbardo, P, Haney, C, Banks, WC, & Jaffe, D 1971, *The Stanford Prison Experiment: a simulation study of the psychology of imprisonment*, Stanford University. Available from: <http://web.stanford.edu/dept/spec_coll/uarch/exhibits/Narration.pdf>. [18 January 2015].

Index

Printed and bound by CPI Group (UK) Ltd, Croydon, CR0 4YY